First
Man
West

Berkeley and Los Angeles, 1962

First Man West

Alexander Mackenzie's Journal
of His Voyage
to the Pacific Coast
of Canada in 1793

EDITED BY
WALTER SHEPPE

University of California Press

University of California Press

Berkeley and Los Angeles, California

Cambridge University Press

London, England

© 1962 by The Regents of the University of California

Library of Congress Catalog Card Number 62–15084

Designed by Theo Jung

Printed in the United States of America

For Michael

ALEXANDER MACKENZIE

Preface

On JULY 20, 1793, Alexander Mackenzie completed the first crossing of the North American continent, more than a decade before Lewis and Clark. The journal he kept during his trip is lost, but a book based on it—and probably prepared by a professional editor as discussed in detail in Appendix 3—appeared first in 1801. It included the account of an earlier trip by Mackenzie to the Arctic Ocean and bore the title *Voyages from Montreal, on the River St. Laurence, through the Continent of North America, to the Frozen and Pacific Oceans; in the years 1789 and 1793.*

Numerous other editions of the *Voyages* appeared later, but none was annotated. This is especially surprising because the *Voyages* is the first item listed in Wagner-Camp's important bibliography, *The Plains and the Rockies,* and therefore of unusual interest to collectors and students of Western history.

Alexander Mackenzie was one of the most important North American explorers, but he is surprisingly little known. Although I had lived in British Columbia for some time and traveled through much of western Canada, I first became aware of Mackenzie in the U. S. Army library in Frankfurt, Germany.

He interested me for his daring and initiative as well as for what he achieved. I thought he deserved more attention than he had been given, and I thought it would be interesting to retrace his route, so far as possible. Several years later, in 1959, I had the chance to do this. I spent most of June and July driving across Canada, touching Mackenzie's route in as many places as I could. The course he took is fairly well known, but most of it is still as difficult to travel as it was in his time, and in fact much of it is visited less now than it was during the great days of the fur trade.

The notes from my trip, printed in part in Appendix 2 of this book, may shed a little light on some of the questions concerning the route and the places mentioned by Mackenzie, and may give some idea of the nature of the country through which he traveled.

When I was studying Mackenzie's account in preparation for my own trip, I found it difficult to follow in places. I decided to prepare this edition of the 1792–93 journal, hoping that others would find it useful. My own comments are indicated by square brackets or, when longer, by indentation. Long passages by Mackenzie describing compass courses have been set in reduced type.

Acknowledgments

I could have done much less on my trip if I had not had the help of many people along the way. Some of them are mentioned in my notes, but I am grateful to them all. Of those not mentioned I am especially indebted to Mr. F. W. Broderick, president of the Northern Transportation Company, who permitted me to travel on his company's boats over the first part of Mackenzie's route.

In identifying places, Indian tribes, plants, and animals, Wade's biography of Mackenzie has been especially helpful. I have used the best available government maps, the *Gazetteer of British Columbia Place Names,* and gathered information on place names along Mackenzie's route. Mr. Wilson Duff provided information on British Columbia Indians, Mr. Donald Tannas on Alberta geography, Colonel G. S. Andrews on British Columbia geography, Dr. E. H. Moss on Alberta plants, Mr. J. W. Eastham on British Columbia plants, Dr. C. C. Lindsey on fish, Dr. I. McT. Cowan on birds and mammals. Further, I found useful: Bishop on Mackenzie's route on salt water, Jenness and McIlwraith on the Indians, and also Burpee, Dawson, Haworth, Morice, Morton 1939, Sage 1950, Smith, Swanton, and Woollacott as listed in the bibliography.

Bard College provided secretarial help.

W. S.

Contents

Prologue

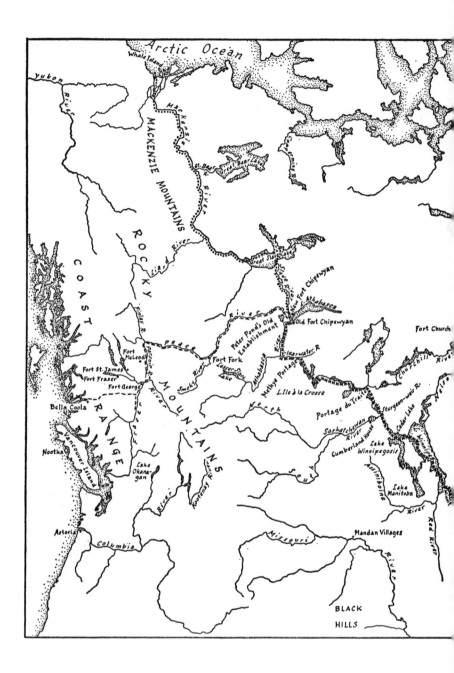

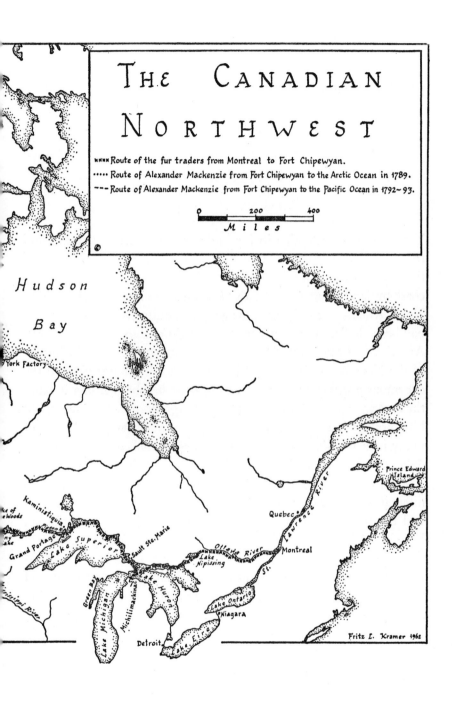

THE CANADIAN NORTHWEST

ⱮⱮⱮ Route of the fur traders from Montreal to Fort Chipewyan.
⋯⋯ Route of Alexander Mackenzie from Fort Chipewyan to the Arctic Ocean in 1789.
--- Route of Alexander Mackenzie from Fort Chipewyan to the Pacific Ocean in 1792~93.

0   200   400
Miles

Hudson

Bay

York Factory

Kaministiquia

ke of
e Woods

Grand Portage

Lake Superior

Sault Ste. Marie

Green Bay

Lake Michigan

Michilimackinac

Lake Huron

Lake Ontario

Niagara

Detroit

Lake Erie

Quebec

St. Lawrence River

Montreal

Ottawa River

Lake Nipissing

St.

Prince Edward Island

ippi River

Fritz L. Kramer 1962

PROLOGUE

THE HILLS were hidden in fog and there was a strong head wind that morning when they came out of the swift river into an arm of the sea. The fur trader Alexander Mackenzie had reached the Pacific coast by land from Canada, the first man ever to cross the entire North American continent. This was the fulfillment of a dream that had been challenging men since the first Europeans arrived in North America, and Mackenzie had earned a prominent place in the history of the New World. In so doing he had added a major piece to the enormous geographic puzzle that explorers had been filling in since the first voyage of Columbus. It was a magnificent achievement, but like most such achievements it was the culmination of the work of many men who had gone before. Mackenzie took the last long step on a trail that men had been blazing for almost three centuries.

We are so familiar with the geography of the continent that it is difficult to conceive of the total ignorance in which the first-comers had to grope their way.[1] When Columbus landed on a Caribbean island he thought that he had reached Asia, but we know that he had come less than half way. We know that the continent is thousands of miles wide, but in 1524 Verrazano sailed along the east coast and thought he saw the Pacific on the other side (he probably was seeing Pamlico Sound). We know that the continent is continuous from Panama to the Arctic Ocean, but the unshakable faith in a Northwest Passage drew explorers into futile voyages for centuries. It required many generations of effort after the first settlements before men had put together the major pieces of this puzzle and had a reasonably reliable picture of their new continent.

4

Prologue

Balboa crossed the narrow isthmus of Panama only twenty-one years after Columbus's first voyage, and became the discoverer of the Pacific Ocean. In later years the Spanish made many crossings of their Central American possessions, and in the 1530's Cabeza de Vaca and his comrades crossed most of the southernmost United States. They were lost wanderers, but their travels were of the greatest importance because they led directly to the Coronado expedition. By Mackenzie's time the Spanish were well established in New Mexico and California, but these were northern outposts of Mexico. There was no transcontinental enterprise and by then hardly even a transcontinental dream.

Settlement and exploration of the continent north of Mexico lagged far behind that of the south. Spain did not think that the northern regions were worth the trouble or expense, and Britain, France, and Holland came into the picture late. Even after these countries had settlements along the Atlantic coast the main body of the continent remained a challenge.

It was not lack of interest that kept the French and English colonists from reaching the Pacific. From the very beginning they tried, but it was a task far beyond their abilities and their imaginations. Men simply could not conceive that Asia could be far away, or that the continent which was so narrow in the south could be so wide in the north.

In the same year that Captain John Smith founded the Jamestown colony, he sailed up the little Chickahominy River in Virginia to reach the Pacific. He did not make it, but he tried again the next year and sailed up the Potomac. Eventually every inlet, every river on the coast were explored as possible routes to the riches of Asia. North America was not an opportunity, but a barrier on the route to Cathay. In the meantime settlements were made and men's energies began to be taken up with destroying the hostile wilderness and killing or driving out its original inhabitants. As colonization became more important exploration came to be of secondary interest.

Perhaps it was inevitable that most of the westward advances 5 would be made first in the north, by the French and later by the British who displaced them. In the American colonies the short coastal rivers ended in a continuous chain of mountains, but in Canada the St. Lawrence River and the Great Lakes offered a relatively easy route into the very heart of the continent. To the north and west, the innumerable glacial lakes and rivers provided access to every part of the country. In the south, climate and soil permitted a prosperous agriculture, but in Canada the climate was harsh and the amount of tillable land was limited. In compensation the cold climate and vast forests of the north provided great numbers of high-quality furs. As a result the American colonists became primarily sedentary farmers, whereas many of the Canadian colonists became roving fur traders.

There were also human reasons for this exploration from Canada. Foremost was the character of the French colonists. The Spanish enslaved the Indians, the English drove them out, but the French married them. Much later the British were to earn the loyalty and respect of the Indians, but always it was the superior Briton stooping to deal with savages. The French were different—the fur traders lived intimately with the Indians, adopted many of their ways, and took Indian wives. In so doing they became the greatest masters of the wilderness that the continent has ever seen. Their friendship with the Indians permitted them to travel unharmed through regions where other men would not have dared to go. Their knowledge of Indian ways permitted them to live off the country, and the Indian birchbark canoe furnished the only practical means of travel in a country of thick forests and many streams. In addition to all this, the paternalism of French colonial policy was a great incentive for men to escape its restrictions by going out beyond the reach of the king's representatives.

The first step on the journey that was later to be completed by Mackenzie was made in 1535 by Jacques Cartier. He sailed up the St. Lawrence River as far as the site of Montreal, looking for the Pacific. He soon realized that he was on a river, not a strait, but he heard from the Indians of the existence of fresh-water seas to the west and he thought that these might lead to the ocean that he sought. He was a mariner, though, and could go no farther in this unfamiliar environment.

Almost a century elapsed before the next step was taken. Samuel de Champlain founded the city of Quebec in 1608, and in the following years he sent men west with the Indians to learn their country and language. In 1615 he followed their route up the St. Lawrence as far as Cartier had gone, and from there west up the Ottawa River and via Lake Nipissing to Lake Huron. This route later became the main highway of the fur traders. Eight years later he sent Etienne Brulé farther inland. Brulé reached Sault Ste. Marie and probably Lake Superior. In 1659 two remarkable men—Médard Chouart, Sieur des Grosseilliers, and Pierre Radisson—explored the south shore of Lake Superior and the country north and west of the lake.

The *coureurs de bois,* as the fur traders were called, followed on the heels of the explorers or even pushed on ahead of them. A sizable trade developed in what was then the Far West, and in 1684 Daniel Greysolon (Duluth to us) built a trading post at Kaministiquia, on the northwest shore of Lake Superior. Duluth wanted to reach the Western Sea, but official interference and the press of other duties kept him from setting out to find it.

In 1688 another officer, Jacques de Noyon, learned that the Kaministiquia River was the Indian route west from Lake Superior. He traveled up this river, portaged across the height of land, and finally reached Rainy Lake. He built a post and wintered there, and the next year probably continued west to Lake of the Woods. This was the first major effort to extend the fur trade into the Northwest, where it would later have its greatest success.

The Kaministiquia post had been abandoned soon after it was built by Duluth, but it was reoccupied in 1717, and in 1728 it was put under the command of Pierre Gaultier de Varennes, Sieur de la Vérendrye. La Vérendrye was one of the greatest French explorers, and he made major contributions to opening up the West and holding it for France. Like Duluth he dreamed of reaching the Western Sea, like Duluth he thought that it could not be far away, and eventually, like Duluth, he was to be defeated by official incompetence and greed and by the vastness of the continent.

When La Vérendrye arrived in the West, the route via Kaministiquia to Lake Winnipeg was known. In 1731 he pioneered the easier Grand Portage route, which was used thereafter.[2] The next year he followed this route to Lake of the Woods, where he built his headquarters. Two years later he sent one of his sons down the Winnipeg River to Lake Winnipeg, where he built a post on the Red River near its mouth.

The French had now developed the best canoe route into the interior, and they had a chain of posts as far as Lake Winnipeg. The canoes from Montreal left Lachine, above the Montreal rapids, and went up the Ottawa River via Lake Nipissing to Lake Huron. On Lake Huron they went to Michilimackinac, near the entrance to Lake Michigan. This was the most important center of the fur trade west of Montreal. Here trading was done with the local Indians, here the canoes were supplied with food from Detroit and other points on the Great Lakes, and from here the traders set out for the more distant fur fields. Those heading south went via Lake Michigan and Green Bay to Wisconsin and the Mississippi. Those heading west went via Sault Ste. Marie to Lake Superior and along its north shore to Grand Portage. Grand Portage was the beginning of the Northwest, as the British traders were later to call it. It was the dividing point between the familiar St. Lawrence basin and the strange wild country of long winters and lonely forests that stretched out to the north and west.

At Grand Portage the goods were carried overland for nine miles to avoid the rapids of the lower Pigeon River. From here the route led through a maze of lakes and streams which now form the northern border of Minnesota to Rainy Lake, down the Rainy River to Lake of the Woods, and down the Winnipeg River to the great Lake 8 Winnipeg. This lake was to be the hub of the fur trade for as long as that trade depended on water transport, because of the streams leading into or out of it in all directions. To the southeast the Winnipeg River led toward Lake Superior, to the south was the Red River, to the northeast the Nelson River flowed into Hudson Bay, and to the west the Saskatchewan River formed a broad highway leading as far as the Rocky Mountains.[3]

One of the main reasons for the determined French push northwest was to intercept the profitable trade of the Hudson's Bay Company. For a century this English company had been trading for furs with the Indians at its posts on Hudson Bay, and both patriotism and profit led the French to try to capture this trade for themselves. There had been open warfare on the Bay, with both sides capturing and destroying the other's ships and forts. La Vérendrye was now leading an attack on the Company from another direction. The Company had never ventured to trade inland, insisting that the Indians bring their furs to its forts on the Bay. The French took their goods to the Indians, and by intercepting them on their way to the Bay the French were able to capture much of the Company's trade. It was to further this plan that La Vérendrye built posts on Lake Winnipeg and later even farther west.

The first penetration of the Saskatchewan River was made in 1739 by La Vérendrye's son Louis-Joseph. He went up the river as far as the point where the north and south forks join. Two years later La Vérendrye's son Pierre built the first fort on the Saskatchewan—Fort Bourbon, at Cedar Lake.[4] Later other forts were built as far up as the joining of the forks.

La Vérendrye's personal interests seem to have been in exploration more than in trade, and in search for a route to the elusive Western Sea he next turned south. He had heard of the Mandan Indians who lived in what is now North Dakota, and he had heard that the River of the Mandans (the Missouri, but not recognized as such) flowed west. In 1738 he and his sons traveled overland to the Mandan villages, but he was prevented by illness from going farther. Four years later two of his sons returned to the Missouri and traveled west with various tribes to within sight of mountains which probably were either the Black Hills of South Dakota or the Medicine Bow Range of Wyoming.[5] They had to turn back when their Indian hosts did, without reaching the mountains or the sea which they were sure was just beyond, and the last and greatest attempt by the French to cross the continent was ended.

La Vérendrye was recalled from the West before he could make another attempt, and he was replaced by lesser men who accomplished little. One of La Vérendrye's sons had been up the Saskatchewan to its fork and had heard there the first rumor of the Rocky Mountains. In 1751 Boucher de Niverville went far up the Saskatchewan and built a temporary post. He claimed to have seen the Rockies, and he may have gone as far as Calgary, but his efforts were not followed up. The political difficulties that had plagued New France from the beginning were becoming overpowering, and the colony was struggling to survive. The struggle ended in 1759 when Quebec fell to the invading British army. Thereafter all exploration would be in British hands, not French.

The French and Indian War halted the fur trade for only a few years, but completely destroyed its organization. After the war, goods had to come from Britain rather than France. Only British traders had the necessary contacts in London, but only the French had the necessary skills and experience to trade with the Indians. At first British and French traders formed partnerships, but as the British learned the trade they displaced the French from the higher ranks. There was one job the British never learned—they never acquired the mastery of the canoe on which the entire trade was dependent, and the French *voyageur* remained an essential member of the organization as long as canoes were used.

Even before the treaty of peace in 1763 traders were pushing into the West again. Pontiac's Rebellion and the destruction of Michilimackinac in 1763 interrupted this revival of trade, but not for long. Before the arrival of Europeans the Indians had been entirely self-reliant, but under the French regime they had learned to use European goods and had become dependent on them. The war had stopped the flow of goods, and the furs accumulated. By the time the trade was resumed the demand for goods was great, and though some of the first traders to venture into the country were robbed by the Indians, others made large profits. One of the first traders to reach the Saskatchewan was able to retire after a single season.[6]

The details of the reopening of the trade are not clear, but British traders reached as far as the last French post before the end of the decade. Within a few years the desire to escape from the competition of other traders was pushing the more enterprising of them still farther afield, into previously untouched areas. Some went west, up the Saskatchewan, but in 1774 Joseph Frobisher pioneered the route that was to lead to the richest fur fields of them all and that later would lead Alexander Mackenzie to the Pacific.[7] He left the Saskatchewan at Cumberland Lake, in what is now eastern Saskatchewan, and headed his canoes north up the Sturgeon-weir River. After threading a complex maze of waterways he reached the divide between the Saskatchewan and Churchill drainages. Crossing what was thereafter called Portage du Traite he reached the Churchill River, which flows east to Hudson Bay. Here he met a group of Chipewyan Indians on their way to trade at the Hudson's Bay Company post Fort Churchill, at the mouth of the river. Their furs belonged to the Hudson's Bay Company in payment for goods received on credit the year before, but Frobisher persuaded the Indians to sell them to him, and he got as many furs as his canoes could carry.

In 1775 Joseph Frobisher, his brother Thomas, and the American trader Alexander Henry pooled their goods and agreed to act together to avoid the evils of competition. The next year they returned to Portage du Traite and continued west up the Churchill as far as Lake Ile à la Crosse. There they met Chipewyan Indians from Lake Athabasca and learned for the first time something of the geography of that far country.[8] They heard of the Peace River flowing from the Rocky Mountains, beyond which lay a big salt lake, and they heard 11 of the Slave River, which flowed north from Lake Athabasca and emptied into another lake. The Chipewyans did not know whether this was the sea or whether it emptied into the sea. Here was a major piece of the continental puzzle being described for them, but their concern was trade and it remained for others to exploit this information. While Joseph Frobisher and Henry returned to Grand Portage, Thomas Frobisher tried to reach Lake Athabasca. He did not make it and had to turn back.

The next step in the westward advance was taken two years later, when four Saskatchewan traders pooled their surplus goods and sent the American trader Peter Pond north with them. Pond followed the Frobishers' route to Lake Ile à la Crosse and continued through a series of lakes and rivers to Methye Lake, beyond which lay one of the major divides in the fur country, that between the Hudson Bay drainage on the south and the Arctic drainage on the north. Pond crossed the thirteen-mile Methye Portage to the Clearwater River, went west down the Clearwater to the Athabasca River, and north down the Athabasca to within fifty miles of Lake Athabasca. He built a post and wintered here. The trade with the Cree and Chipewyan Indians of this region was so good that when he left the next spring Pond had twice as many furs as his canoes could carry. Within a few years other traders were following Pond's route to Athabasca.[9]

The arrival of traders from Canada at Athabasca was another serious blow to the Hudson's Bay Company. When the French trade was stopped by the French and Indian War the Company had been freed of their troublesome competition, but the British traders who took their place proved to be even worse. The Company's charter gave it title to all the lands draining into Hudson Bay, which included almost the entire Northwest. A short distance west of Grand Portage the Montreal traders became trespassers on Company land, and legally Rainy Lake, Lake of the Woods, Lake Winnipeg, the Saskatchewan, and the Churchill were the exclusive domain of the Company. After the fall of New France the British government had tried to regulate the trade from Canada to protect the Indians from exploitation and the Hudson's Bay Company from competition. Canadian traders were forbidden to trade in Company territory, but it was impossible to enforce this rule and it was ignored from the first. Finally the government abandoned its attempt at regulation and the Company was left to defend its privileges as well as it could.

In its competition with the French the Company had had two great advantages—its transportation costs were much lower because it could bring its goods by ship into the heart of the country, and its British goods were both better and cheaper than the French goods. In spite of this the French had been able to capture much of the Company's trade, partly because of their good relations with the Indians and partly because the Indians had been willing to pay much higher prices to avoid the long and dangerous trip to the Bay. The Company attempted to combat this competition by sending men into the interior to persuade the Indians to bring their furs down to the Bay. In 1754 Anthony Henday traveled to within sight of the Rocky Mountains and in later years other Company men made many trips to the upper Saskatchewan and Churchill.

Now the Canadian traders were equipped with the same cheap British goods that the Company used, and they had extended the trade farther than the French had gone. New tactics were called for to meet this crippling competition, and the Company decided to abandon its policy of trading only at its posts on the Bay. In 1774 the explorer Samuel Hearne was sent to build a post on the Saskatchewan. He built on Cumberland Lake, the strategic point where the trade from the west and that from the north converged. He named the post Cumberland House, and it long remained an important trading center. The Canadian traders had had temporary posts in the area for several years, and they soon built a Cumberland House of their own near Hearne's post.[10] The competition had now entered a new phase, in which the establishment of a post by one group led to the establishment of a rival post nearby by the other group. Eventually this competition was to lead to much violence.

Meanwhile important changes were being made in the organization of the fur trade from Montreal. Throughout the history of the trade there was a strong trend toward unification. In the early days independent *coureurs de bois* had traded with the local Indians in Quebec, but as the trade moved farther and farther west more capital and a larger organization were needed. The *coureur de bois* came to be an employee rather than an independent trader. After the failure of the British government's attempt to regulate the trade it became open to anyone with enough capital. Many traders, with French clerks and boatmen, went into the Northwest, and the resulting competition threatened to destroy both traders and Indians. The fur trade was a rough business at best, but now it became completely lawless and unprincipled. Traders used violence against each other and against the Indians. To get the Indians' business prices were slashed and the Indians were bribed with liquor.[11]

Another problem faced by the traders was the increasing expense of the trade. As the trade moved deeper into the Northwest the transportation lines became longer and the cost of getting the goods to the Indians and the furs back to Montreal mounted. For example, a canoe-load worth £500 at Montreal was worth £660 at Michilimackinac and £750 at Grand Portage, and the costs increased even faster west of there.[12] Several years' credit was required, as it took that long before goods shipped from London could be paid for by the arrival of furs there. This required large amounts of capital. The traders also had to be supplied with food along the way, because their canoes could not carry enough for the long journey, and they had no time to hunt or fish. A large organization was required to procure quantities of food in the West and carry it to depots along the traders' routes.

Unification of the trade became essential to prevent competition and to make possible the large organization necessary for efficient operation. Some of the earliest attempts at coöperation have been mentioned. A North West Company is mentioned in letters as early as 1776, and temporary organizations were formed in the following

14

years.[13] In 1783-84 the principal traders of the region formed an expanded North West Company, which was to dominate the trade from Canada for many years.[14] The Frobishers and later Peter Pond were among the partners. At one time the North West Company was the largest commercial enterprise in North America. It was really a combination of independent concerns which retained their own identity. Initially sixteen shares were held, some by partners in Montreal who conducted the business of the Company there, providing the necessary trade goods and selling the furs. The remaining shares were held by the wintering partners, that is, the traders who went into the Northwest and wintered there, trading with the Indians.

A conspicuous feature of the organization was that shares could not be sold outside the Company. Any shares that were to be disposed of had to be offered to an employee who had proved his worth in the trade. In this way the young men were attached to the Company by the hope of becoming partners if they did their work well. This proved to be one of the Company's strongest points. One of its weakest was that it was loosely held together by temporary agreements.

The North West Company developed a complex and efficient organization for getting the trade goods to the outlying posts and getting the furs to Montreal. The point of contact between Montreal and and the Northwest was Grand Portage. Here the Montreal partners and the wintering partners met each summer to report on their activities and make plans for the future. This was a time of feasting and drinking and carousing with the Indian women. It was the high point of the year for the men who had spent the long winter in the wilderness far from civilized comforts, with only Indians and the rough voyageurs for companions.

Some of the bulkier goods reached Grand Portage by ship via the Great Lakes. This was less expensive than bringing them in by canoe, but canoes were faster and surer, and they were used for most goods.[15] A special group of men took the goods from Montreal to Grand Portage in the summer and carried them across the portage to the point of departure for the canoes from the Northwest. These 15 men then returned to Montreal for the winter, carrying the season's fur returns.

The traders at the posts in the Northwest spent the winter trading with the Indians and left for Grand Portage in the spring. There they turned the furs over to the Montreal partners and received trade goods from them. They left in time to reach their posts before the rivers froze. Athabasca was so remote that it was not possible for the big freight canoes to get from there to Grand Portage and back in a single season, so a special depot was set up at Rainy Lake to supply this district.[16]

A wide variety of goods was sold to the Indians—cloth, blankets, clothing, guns and ammunition, knives, axes, kettles, tobacco, paint, and many others. Liquor was an important item in the trade, but it usually was given rather than sold. In return the trader received furs —muskrat, otter, marten, mink, bear, fox, wolf, lynx, buffalo, and above all beaver. Beaver was the great staple of the trade and accounted for perhaps two-thirds of its total value. Because of its aquatic habits the beaver thrived in the fantastic maze of lakes and rivers left by glaciers in the northern forest belt. In response to the bitter northern winters its fur grew thicker than in the south, and the farther north the traders reached the more valuable were the furs they found.

It was the good fortune of the North West Company that it was organized in a time of rising beaver prices. The price doubled or even tripled during the second half of the eighteenth century.[17] This was because of a new demand in Britain for hats made of beaver felt. The expulsion of the Huguenots from France in 1685 by Louis XIV drove many of France's best artisans to Britain and some of them brought with them the closely guarded secret of making felt. Changing fashion later adopted the beaver hat, and though such hats were expensive the British were enjoying a period of prosperity and could afford to buy them. The Continental trade also was important during the periods when Britain was not at war with France.

16 An important influence in the history of the trade was the decline

of the beaver fields. When the Indians had hunted only for their own use they had no effect on the beaver population, but now high prices and the desire for rum stimulated them to hunt intensively. The attachment of beaver to the water and their habit of building conspicuous lodges made them too easy a prey, even for the relatively primitive Indian methods of hunting and trapping. Originally only winter pelts had been taken, because these were thicker and more desirable than those of animals killed in summer. This had had the effect of protecting the beaver during the season in which they raised their young. Now summer pelts were taken, too, and reproduction was hindered. All this resulted in the rapid decline of beaver populations. The beaver in the area of a new fort might be exhausted after four or five years. This made it necessary for the Company to expand into untouched regions, and the newest district usually was the most profitable.

One of the most troubling problems faced by the North West Company was feeding its men. The cost of transportation made it impossible to bring food for them from Montreal. It had to be procured in the West, and Detroit was the principal source of supply. The staple food item in this region was hominy, boiled with fat. This was all that the canoemen were given, but the higher ranks had additional delicacies.[18] Often not even hominy was available, when a party would run out of food before reaching its destination, and hunger was a common experience in the Northwest.

West of Grand Portage wild rice was important, but beyond Lake Winnipeg another food supply was needed. This problem was solved by adopting the Indian food pemmican, which consisted of dried powdered meat mixed with an equal amount of melted fat. Sometimes berries and marrow were added for improved flavor. This was an excellent concentrated food. It kept indefinitely and could satisfy both body and soul for long periods of time. West of Lake Winnipeg it was the staple food of the traders when they were traveling. It was made by various Indian tribes, but especially by those on the prairies south of the forest belt, where the buffalo provided an abundant supply of meat and fat. This country was poor in furs, but posts were established there to trade with the Indians for pemmican, and special brigades carried it north to the main trade routes. Later the Company itself manufactured large quantities of pemmican on the Red River.

Even this supply would not do during the long winters at the posts. Not only did large numbers of men have to be fed, but many of them had Indian wives and children who were supported by the Company. Game was hunted or bought from Indians, but the northern forests were poor in game and the main reliance was on fish. Posts had to be placed where there was a plentiful supply of fish, and the men spent much of their time during the winter fishing through the ice with nets. For months at a time they had nothing to eat but unsalted fish, and if this supply failed they went hungry.[19]

A typical trading party might consist of a partner or *bourgeois,* a clerk, an interpreter, a guide, and several dozen canoemen, the voyageurs. The partners and clerks usually were British, with a high proportion of Scots. This was a time of economic hardship in Scotland and many of her young men left to seek better fortune in the colonies. The lower ranks were filled mostly by the French or *métis* —men of mixed European and Indian blood. In the 1790's the Company employed altogether several dozen each of clerks, interpreters, and guides, and more than a thousand voyageurs.[20]

Though the voyageurs were the backbone of the trade they were paid only a pittance, and this was often in goods on which the Company made a large profit. They were rough and simple men, and though used to doing hard work they preferred doing nothing at all and would not even hunt or fish for themselves unless told to do so by their employers. The work that they did while traveling was amazing. On the river at first light and going until dark, their usual respite from the hard work of paddling was the even harder work of portaging. The portages were many and difficult, and everything had to be carried over them. Shouldering two or more ninety-pound bales of goods or furs, the voyageur set off at a trot across the portage, and later returned for more. At certain seasons the worst enemy was not the work but the flies—mosquitoes, black flies, and various other kinds, in thick swarms that sometimes drove animals wild and made life miserable for men. During the winters at the posts these troubles were exchanged for others—temperatures far below zero, food scarce and terribly monotonous, and the boredom of long nights and cramped quarters.

The hardships of the voyageur's life were made bearable by resignation, by singing in rhythm with the paddles, by a drink of rum at the end of the day, and by the ready availability of Indian women. They took their toll, though. Work and cold and hunger, rum, and venereal disease aged men quickly and the voyageur who was not drowned in the rapids or killed by a drunken Indian was wise to retire early to Quebec. In spite of all this, many of them loved their life and stayed with it as long as they were able to swing a paddle and lift a bale.

The voyageur's great achievement was his skill with the canoe. He may have been born in one and he certainly grew up in one and he knew all its ways. His skill was most needed in the white water, where the river broke over rocks, and in the treacherous black stretches where strong currents could send a canoe crashing against a submerged rock or snag. If a rapids was not too bad he ran it in the canoe; if it was impassable he portaged. The canoe and the voyageur were inseparable, a functional unit. They had evolved together and both had helped make the other what he was. This relationship had made the man smaller and the canoe larger. A big man took up too much room in the canoe, so the voyageur had to be small.

The canoe was still basically the canoe of the Indian, but it had been enlarged and modified to meet the needs of the trade. Made of a cedar frame covered with the thin bark of the paper birch and held together by roots and rosin, it was strong and capacious but light enough to be carried by two men. Between Lachine and Grand Portage big canoes up to six feet wide and forty feet long were used. Such canoes could carry four tons of goods and required a crew of eight to fourteen men. West of Grand Portage smaller canoes were needed. These were perhaps twenty-five feet long, carried a ton and a half, and had a crew of five to eight. In addition, the partner had a smaller personal canoe in which he could travel independently of his party, lagging behind or going on ahead.

The North West Company's men were the sole representatives of civilization in a vast region. Unlike the Hudson's Bay Company, the North West Company did not have legal authority to govern the area in which it did business, but there was no military post west of Lake Huron and it was difficult or impossible for the courts of Quebec to deal with offenses in the Northwest. During periods of relative peace in the fur trade there was little need for formal law enforcement. A wronged person either retaliated or had to overlook the wrong and carry on as well as he could. It was during the period of vicious competition between rival trading interests that lawlessness became rampant and threatened to destroy both traders and trade. Later prominent traders were made justices of the peace, but they tended to use these commissions to further their own interests rather than the interests of justice.

This, then, was the North West Company and the trade it carried on. The fur traders opened up the Northwest, brought that great region into the British Empire, and reluctantly paved the way for settlers, missionaries, and the law. They have been praised as men of great achievements should be, but it should be remembered that they were seeking profits, not adventure, glory, or lands for the king. The trade was a rough one, and during times of competition between two companies it became merciless. The men were underpaid, the Indians were overcharged, and both were kept submissive by liberal quantities of rum. Rival traders were killed or driven out; their goods were stolen and their canoes sunk. It was standard practice to buy from the Indians furs that they already owed to your competitor. In spite of all this, some of the traders were well read and took an intelligent interest in the affairs of the world and even

20 in literature. They made the long winters bearable by reading (as

well as by taking an Indian wife), and they made great efforts to exchange letters and books with the traders at other posts. Roderick McKenzie accumulated an impressive library at Fort Chipewyan, which was sometimes called "the Athens of the North."

After his pioneering venture to Athabasca, Peter Pond returned there at least once before he joined the North West Company.[21] When he joined the Company he was sent to organize the Athabasca district in 1785, and it soon became one of the most important in the Northwest. The post on the lower Athabasca River remained his headquarters, but he had outlying posts built on Great Slave Lake and on the Peace River. He had an excellent vegetable garden at Athabasca to supplement the food supply—perhaps the most northern agriculture in the New World at the time.

Pond was tied down with the practical business of trading, but he was a born explorer and his mind roamed far afield. He wanted to know what lay beyond Athabasca and how to get from there to the Pacific. The need to reach the Pacific was apparent to everyone interested in either geography or the fur trade at that time. Samuel Hearne of the Hudson's Bay Company had discovered the Coppermine River and descended it to the Arctic Ocean in 1771. This was proof that there was no Northwest Passage far enough south to be of any value, but men of strong faith ignored Hearne or refused to believe him, and even the British Admiralty continued its efforts to find the passage which had to exist because everyone said it did. The search was now shifted to the northwest coast of the continent.

Captain James Cook of the Royal Navy had explored this coast in 1778. He had not found the passage he was sent to find but he had found a fur trade and what he thought was a great river. When his *Voyages*[22] was published in 1784, Europeans became aware for the first time of the fantastically rich Russian trade in marine furs in the North Pacific. The Russian traders had first arrived there in the 1740's and had soon discovered the fur seal and the sea otter. The sea otter has the finest of all furs, and in China it could be sold for many times its original cost. The methods used by the Russian traders were far more vicious than even those of the beaver trade. Eventually they brought both the otter and the natives almost to extinction, but in the meantime there were profits to be had, and soon after the publication of Cook's account traders from all maritime nations were operating in the North Pacific. This trade provided a great incentive for the Canadian traders to reach the Pacific.

Another incentive was political—British North America needed an outlet to the Pacific. Britain's principal rival on the Northwest coast at this time was Spain, but farther north were the Russians and to the south there was the threat of American expansion. The American states were still confined east of the Mississippi, but the Americans were a restless breed and no one expected them to stay confined for long. Britain had some slight claims along the coast, but exploration and permanent occupation of the mainland were needed to establish possession.

The main reason for wanting to reach the Pacific was the same problem that had been plaguing the Canadian traders since they first entered the Northwest—the high cost of transportation. The farther west they went the more these costs mounted and the more their profits were reduced. The north country was especially bad. It was more difficult to travel through than anything the traders had encountered before, and its bleak forests sheltered little game to feed them. In winter the cold was so intense that it cracked the logs of the cabins and split the bark on the canoes unless they were buried. All this made it imperative to find a short water route to the Pacific, where ships could provide cheap transport.

Pond was well aware of these things, but he also seems to have had an inquiring mind, interested in knowing things for their own sake. He was one of the most colorful and important men in the history of the fur trade. Rough, almost illiterate, morose, and apparently violent, he nevertheless excites admiration for his achievements and even more for the things he planned but was not able to do.

22   He was born in Milford, Connecticut, in 1740.[28] He joined the

army when he was sixteen and served in the war against the French. Later he went into the fur trade and pioneered the trade with the Sioux. He went to the Northwest in 1775 and three years later became the first trader into the Athabasca district. At Athabasca he closely questioned the Indians who came to trade with him about their home country and he got a good idea of the lay of the land to the west and the north. At least it was as good as could be gotten in this way. No Indian knew more than a small part of this great country. He may have told Pond what he knew well, pieced out with what he vaguely remembered and what he had heard tales of and what he thought he was expected to say, or he may simply have lied out of hostility or indifference. Pond had to collect all the accounts that he could, translating them as well as he could, sort the scattered fragments, and put them all together into a consistent whole that fitted what he knew of the country from his own travel. He made mistakes, but they were understandable mistakes, and he knew more about the country than any of his contemporaries.

We have no written account of his knowledge, but we can trace the development of his ideas in a series of maps that he laboriously prepared under the trying conditions of the fur posts.[24] Ironically, he was closer to the truth at first than he was when he left. He had visited Great Slave Lake and the Peace River himself, and from the Indians he knew that the Peace came from the Rocky Mountains and that a great river flowed west out of Great Slave Lake and eventually turned north to the sea. This was the river we now call the Mackenzie, flowing to the Arctic Ocean, and at first Pond had it right, but then he read Cook's report.

On his 1778 voyage Captain Cook had discovered the long inlet in the Alaska coast that is now named for him. No one then knew how large Alaska was or whether it was part of the mainland, and Cook sailed up this inlet to be sure that there was no passage there. It ended in small local rivers, but Cook misread the signs and thought that a large river must empty there. So his reports showed, and "Cook's River" was to beguile North West Company men for years. 23

Pond was one of the first to be misled. Cook's River was in about the same latitude as Great Slave Lake; the river out of Great Slave Lake flowed west, toward Cook's River; and there was no other known outlet for one or source for the other. Also, Cook had reported that there were quantities of driftwood that had been brought down by his river. The Athabasca, Peace, and Liard rivers carried much wood when they flooded, and there was not enough wood farther north to account for the quantities that Cook saw. Such circumstantial evidence led Pond to disregard the Indian report that the river from Great Slave Lake flowed north. He became convinced that this was Cook's River, and to get the river across the Rockies he decided that they must end south of it. This was good news. A river flowing north to the Arctic was of little use to the traders, but a river flowing straight to the center of the Russian fur trade would give them access both to this trade and to cheap marine transport. The wish may have been at least one parent to the thought.

Pond arrived at this concept of the country near the end of his stay in the Northwest. In the meantime he and others had proposed to the British government various plans for solving the mystery of what lay between Athabasca and the Pacific.[25] Some of the planners wanted knowledge, others wanted commercial advantage. In 1781 Alexander Henry sent to Sir Joseph Banks of the Royal Society a plan for reaching the Pacific via Athabasca. He described the canoe route as far west as he knew it, but he had no clear picture of the Athabasca country and no conception of what lay beyond. Four years later Pond and the Frobishers proposed to the government that the North West Company explore to the Pacific at its own expense, in return for a monopoly of the trade in the areas explored. This request was not granted, probably because of Hudson's Bay Company opposition. As late as 1790, after Mackenzie's first exploration but before news of it reached England, some men in London were planning another voyage to find the Northwest Passage and others were planning to do what Mackenzie had already done the year before.

Pond had great plans, but he was not to carry them out. Soon after he took charge of the Athabasca department for the North West Company he was disturbed by the arrival of a competitor. When the Company was organized, a prominent Northwest trader named Peter Pangman was excluded. Disgruntled, he joined forces with the Montreal firm of Gregory and Macleod to enter the Northwest fur trade in competition with the North West Company.[26] This new organization, known as the XY Company, sent representatives to the principal fur districts of the Northwest. Though it suffered heavy losses from the North West Company's ruthless opposition, it continued in the trade. Its representative at Athabasca, opposing Pond, was John Ross.

Before coming to the Northwest Pond had killed a man in a duel at Michilimackinac, and in 1782 he had been involved in the death of a trader named Waden. According to Mackenzie, Pond and one of his clerks "were tried for this murder at Montreal, and acquitted: nevertheless, their innocence was not so apparent as to extinguish the original suspicion." [27] Now Ross suffered a similar fate. During the winter of 1786–87 he was killed in a scuffle with Pond's men.

This killing shocked the partners of both companies and led to the merger of the competitors in 1787 into an enlarged North West Company. Pond's company wanted the merger to prevent Ross's company from pressing charges against it, while Ross's company wanted it because it was losing money.[28] Both companies were to send representatives to work together in the various districts. The Gregory-Macleod interests sent a young man named Alexander Mackenzie to Athabasca to work with Pond.

When Mackenzie arrived at Athabasca he was at the most active outpost of a trading empire that extended from Montreal to the Rocky Mountains, north to Great Slave Lake, and south to the Missouri River. Beyond lay an enormous stretch of the Pacific coast that was visited by trading ships but had never been colonized. To the north the Russians had posts on Kodiak Island and Cook Inlet, and in California the Spanish were established as far north as San Francisco, but for two thousand miles in between the coast was open to the first men who took it. By virtue of Balboa's discovery of the Pacific, Spain claimed title to all the shores of that ocean, but other nations ignored this modest claim and Spain was in no position to defend it. The Russians had defied the Spanish claim and now the fur traders of Canada were prepared to do so too.

From the point of view of exploration, Mackenzie's arrival at Athabasca in 1787 was a case of the right man in the right place at the right time. He was the right man because he combined the vision and ambition to think on a large scale and plan great things with the strength and leadership ability to carry out these plans. It was the right place because this was the natural starting point for an attempt to get beyond the mountains and reach the Pacific. It was the right time because Peter Pond was there to teach Mackenzie all that he knew about the country and fill him with the desire for exploration, and the next year he conveniently left the country forever, giving Mackenzie a free hand to do as he pleased.

Mackenzie was to become one of the great figures in North American exploration, but we are not even sure when he was born and we know little about his early life.[29] He was born at Stornoway on the Island of Lewis, in Scotland, probably in 1764. His parents were Kenneth Mackenzie and Isabella Maciver. He had an older brother and two sisters. After his mother died his father took him and two aunts to New York, where his mother's brother John Maciver was a well-to-do merchant. They arrived in 1774, but they found the colonies in revolutionary turmoil. The next year young Alexander's father and uncle joined the British army, and his aunts took him to old Johnstown, New York (probably the present village of Scotch Bush). By 1778 the war was getting too close, and Alexander was sent to Montreal for safety. He attended school there briefly, but the next year, when sixteen, he entered the firm of Gregory and Macleod as a clerk in their Montreal warehouse.

After five years with Gregory and Macleod in Montreal, Mackenzie was sent to Detroit to trade. This was in 1784, when he was twenty.[30] It was his first independent venture, his first experience in dealing with Indians, his first trip west. It was the beginning of the long road that would lead him to wealth and fame and power, and perhaps to the illness that eventually killed him.

Apparently he did well at Detroit. At any rate, later that year Gregory sent Macleod to offer Mackenzie a partnership in the firm, if he would agree to go to the Saskatchewan the next year. He gladly accepted the offer, and early the next summer he and the other partners of the so-called XY Company came together at Grand Portage. They camped on the north side of the Pigeon River, several miles from the North West Company's fort. One of the XY Company clerks present was Mackenzie's cousin Roderick McKenzie, who had arrived from Scotland the year before.[31]

This was the first attempt by the XY Company to enter the Northwest fur trade. At Grand Portage the partners decided to challenge the North West Company in all its principal departments. Duncan Pollock was sent to the Red River, Peter Pangman to the Saskatchewan, John Ross to Athabasca, and Mackenzie to the Churchill River. Roderick McKenzie remained at Grand Portage to help build the Company's fort there. The next year Mackenzie returned to the Churchill, and this time took Roderick with him and put him in charge of a sub-post. In the spring of 1787 Roderick was sent to Lake Ile à la Crosse, and while there he learned of the death of John Ross at Athabasca. He immediately set off for Grand Portage to take the news to the XY Company partners. After the merger of the two companies Mackenzie was sent to replace Ross at Athabasca and Roderick returned to the Churchill.[32]

On his way to Athabasca that fall Mackenzie wrote Roderick that "I put all your books but the History of England into you *Cassette*. I have no necessaries to send you—you must pass the winter in the best manner you can—we must hope for better times." [33]

He was delayed by accidents, and the rivers froze over while he was still far from Athabasca. The party had to proceed on foot, leaving the goods behind. They reached Athabasca on October 21. There 27 they found that although another canoe brigade had arrived with supplies two weeks earlier the early freeze had prevented sending the supplies on to the posts on Great Slave Lake and the Peace River.

Now Mackenzie and Peter Pond were together for the winter. The two men were of very different character and they did not become friends, but they seem to have gotten along together. Early in December Mackenzie wrote to Roderick, "Thus far my neighbour and I have agreed very well and I believe we shall continue on the same good footing for the season." [34]

Mackenzie hated Athabasca and seriously considered leaving the Northwest, but in the end he stayed on. In January he traveled by snowshoe to Lake Ile à la Crosse to visit his cousin Roderick and the partner there, Patrick Small. Roderick was not satisfied with his wages and was planning to leave the Company the next summer, although Mackenzie tried to change his mind. Mackenzie later returned to Athabasca.

It was during this winter that he conceived of his plan to try to reach the Pacific by going down the river that flowed out of Great Slave Lake. Just what part Pond had in forming this plan is not known. Some think that he had to leave Athabasca because of the shooting of Ross, and that he deserves no credit at all for Mackenzie's work. At the other extreme, one authority holds that Pond planned to make the trip down the river himself, but that when he went out to Grand Portage in 1788 to get final instructions for the trip it was decided that he would be of more value in Montreal, getting the support of the government, and that Mackenzie should make the trip. [35]

Mackenzie himself gives no credit to Pond, [36] but a letter that he wrote several years later makes clear the source of his ideas: "I followed the course of the Waters which had been reported by Mr. Pond to fall into Cook's River, they led me to the Northern Ocean. Tho' this Expedition did not answer the intended purpose, It proved that Mr. Pond's assertion was nothing but conjecture, and that a North West Passage is impracticable." [37]

28   That Pond at least knew of Mackenzie's plans is shown by a puz-

zling document, the Ogden letter. In 1789 Pond talked with Isaac Ogden at Quebec, told him his theories about the country beyond Athabasca, and showed him his latest map. Ogden wrote all this to a relative in London, and added, "Another man by the name of McKenzie was left by Pond at Slave Lake with orders to go down the River, and from thence to Unalaska, and so to Kamskatcha and thence to England through Russia, etc." [38] We know that in 1787 Pond was preparing to do just this himself, and that he had prepared a map to lay before the empress of Russia. When he left Athabasca in 1788 he probably was planning to return, but we do not know whether he still hoped to make this exploration. [39] At any rate, he did not return and Mackenzie took over his plan, except that Mackenzie had no intention of going to Russia. It seems unlikely that he was under orders from Pond. A reasonable estimate of Pond's role seems to be that he gave Mackenzie the plan but that Mackenzie needed no orders—he had abundant initiative of his own.

It is equally uncertain how much credit the North West Company deserves for this trip. The authorities are divided, some pointing to the large amount of exploration that was done under orders from the Company, others claiming that the Montreal partners were interested only in the practical business of trading furs and would not have encouraged anyone to waste time in such a way. Certainly it is true that Mackenzie had written to his cousin Roderick McKenzie in early 1788: "I already mentioned to you some of my distant intentions—I beg you will not reveal them to any person—as it might be prejudicial to me—though I may never have it in my power to put them in execution." [40] This is thought to refer to his plans for exploration, and suggests that he expected opposition from his partners. In the preface to his *Voyages* he gives a different impression: "The general utility of such a discovery, has been universally acknowledged; while the wishes of my particular friends and commercial associates, that I should proceed in the pursuit of it, contributed to quicken the execution of this favourite project of my own ambition." [41]

In May Pond left the region that had been his personal kingdom. The next year he sold his interest in the Company and went home to Milford. When he left he carried with him a letter from Mackenzie to Roderick:

You say—you were informed that I was displeased with you. . . . Your refusing what I offered by no means displeased me. Circumstanced as I was, I might have offered you less—but I believe I never advised you to accept of less or worse terms than the best clerk the Company had—As for notion of slavery I cannot approve of It shows you never were acquainted with that abject condition. If you had for five or six years been subject to caprice of a master and tyranny of a mistress, and that for no pecuniary consideration, your ideas of it would be quite different. . . . I will not forget your Books.[42]

With Pond out of the way, Mackenzie had a free hand. Although Pond had found abundant furs when he first came into the country ten years before, a disastrous smallpox epidemic a few years later had killed many of the Indians and almost destroyed the trade.[43] It had not fully recovered since, and Mackenzie's first job was to make the department productive enough to offset the high cost of transportation. The previous winter he and Pond had ordered their trader on Great Slave Lake to abandon the post there and return to Athabasca. This post had not been paying its way, and most of the furs were coming from the Peace River. This was because the Beaver Indians on the Peace were glad to trade with the North West Company, but the Chipewyans from Great Slave Lake preferred taking their furs to Hudson Bay, where they got much better prices for them.[44] To encourage the Peace River trade Mackenzie sent Charles Boyer to build a post farther upstream.

The business was demanding of Mackenzie's time and efforts, but his mind was already on exploration. Apparently he had mentioned his plans to Roderick on his visit in January. In May he had not known whether he would ever make the trip, but by the time he went out to Rainy Lake in July he had decided to do so the next year.

He needed someone to take charge of the district while he was exploring, and chose Roderick. They met at Rainy Lake and Mackenzie informed his cousin

in confidence—that he had determined on undertaking a Voyage of Discovery the ensuing spring by the Water Communications reported to lead from Slave Lake to the Northern Ocean [the Pacific?]—adding in a tone of regret that if I could not return & take charge of the Department in his absence he must from that moment abandon his intentions. considering his regret at my refusal and the great importance of the object he had in view I without hesitation yielded to his wishes—& immediately set to work and accompanied him into Athabasca.[45]

They made the trip in fifty-two days, a new record for loaded canoes, but two men were drowned when a canoe sank. Mackenzie sent most of his men with Roderick on to Lake Athabasca to build a fort there. He was still using Pond's Old Establishment on the Athabasca River, but a post on the lake would be more convenient for the trade and would offer a better supply of fish. Roderick chose a site on the south side of the lake, and there built the first Fort Chipewyan. It was to be the headquarters of the Athabasca department until about 1800,[46] it was to become "the Athens of the North," and it was the starting point for both of Mackenzie's voyages of exploration. It was famous for its comfort, and unlike most posts it was painted inside. By December, the fort was ready for use, and Mackenzie came down to spend some time with his cousin. He returned to the Old Establishment in February.

In May Roderick set out for Grand Portage, to represent Mackenzie at the annual meeting of the partners. Mackenzie was now busy with the thousand details necessary to get ready for his voyage and to leave the business of the department in order. Supplies had to be assembled and checked—food, tents, guns and ammunition, and all the other things necessary for living in the wilderness, as well as trading goods for dealing with the natives. The men who would stay behind had to be given final instructions, and the local Indians had to be admonished again to be industrious and loyal to the Company.

At last everything was ready, and at nine in the morning on June 3, 1789, Mackenzie set out on the voyage that he hoped would lead him to the Pacific.[47] In his pocket were rubles for trading with the Russians. His canoe carried four French Canadians, two of them accompanied by their Indian wives, and a German. An important Indian, called the English Chief, followed in another canoe with his two wives, and two of his followers were in a third canoe. The Indians were to act as interpreters and hunters. At first the group was accompanied by a trading party under Laurent Leroux. Leroux was an old Athabasca hand, and had built the first post on Great Slave Lake. During the preceding winter he had gone to the north shore of that lake and there encountered great numbers of Yellowknife and Slave Indians. They had traded with him and agreed to meet him again during the summer. Now he was on his way to meet them and establish a trading post in their country.

That day the party crossed Lake Athabasca and entered the Slave River. The next day they passed the mouth of the Peace, flowing in strong from the west. They continued down the Slave for several days, hindered by difficult portages and ice and rain. One of the Indian canoes was smashed in the rapids, but the woman who was in it escaped unharmed. On the ninth they embarked at half past two in the morning (a bit earlier than usual, but not much) and at nine reached Great Slave Lake. The weather was much colder here and the lake almost covered with ice. They made camp and prepared to stay until the lake was open. The nets were set for fish, the hunters were sent out, and the women gathered berries.

They were not able to get away until the fifteenth. During the next week, in spite of cold weather, torrential rains, high winds, grinding ice on the lake, and hordes of mosquitoes, they crossed to the north side of the lake and searched among its deep bays for the river that flowed from it. They met the Yellowknife Indians whom Leroux had found a few months earlier, and he stayed here to trade with them. One of the Yellowknives offered to guide them to the outlet, but it turned out that he did not remember the way himself, and the English Chief threatened to kill him. On the twenty-ninth, almost three weeks after they had reached the lake, they found the entrance to the river which was later to be called the Mackenzie in honor of its discoverer. It is one of the great rivers of the continent and they probably were the first members of our culture to see it.[48]

Now they began the long journey down the river, not knowing which way it would take them or how far, not knowing whether they could get back to Athabasca before winter made traveling impossible. They were short on both time and food, and Mackenzie pushed them to the limit. On most days they were in the canoes by three or four in the morning and did not camp until late afternoon. The cold and the rain and the flies were still with them, and ice was piled high on the banks of the river. The Indians were not accustomed to such sustained effort and complained bitterly. On July 1 they passed the mouth of the Liard River from the south, and farther on they buried two bags of pemmican for use on the way back.

At first the river flowed west toward the coast, as Pond had said it would, though its twistings and turnings made it difficult to know what the general direction was. Later the trend was northwest, and on July 2 they came within sight of a great chain of mountains which formed a continuous barrier to westward travel. These were the Mackenzie Mountains, a northern continuation of the Rockies, and Pond was wrong about one thing, at least—the mountains did not end in the latitude of Great Slave Lake. The river now flowed almost north and Mackenzie's disillusionment began. The farther he traveled the clearer it became that he was not on Cook's River and that this river did not flow into the Pacific. As he realized that he would not reach his goal, the trip took on a quality of desperation. He climbed a mountain to observe the lay of the land, but could not see very far. On the river they traveled cautiously, in fear of a great waterfall that the Indians had reported.

On July 5 they found a small camp of Slave and Dogrib Indians, 33 so primitive that they still used stone axes. At first they ran off terrified, but later were persuaded to come back. Mackenzie questioned them about the course of the river, but their replies were mixtures of wild rumor and superstition. They attempted "to persuade us that it would require several winters to get to the sea, and that old age would come upon us before the period of our return; we were also to encounter monsters of such horrid shapes and destructive powers as could only exist in their wild imaginations." [49] There were also two impassable falls in the river.

Mackenzie understandably did not put much faith in these tales, but his Indians did, or at least pretended to. They had long since lost their enthusiasm for the trip, and these new perils which they thought lay ahead made them very reluctant to go on. The new Indians had said that there was little game in the country ahead, and the English Chief predicted that they would starve if they continued. This was the first major test of Mackenzie's leadership, but he was equal to it and finally persuaded his own Indians to go on and also hired one of the new Indians to come with them. When they embarked they had to force the new guide into the canoe, and that night they kept watch to prevent his escaping. That afternoon they had passed Great Bear River on the east.

On July 7 they came to the first of the great falls, which proved to be only a minor rapids which could be shot easily in the canoe. Later in the day they encountered a small group of Indians, all of whom ran away except an old man and woman. The old man approached and "represented himself as too far advanced in life, and too indifferent about the short time he had to remain in the world, to be very anxious about escaping from any danger that threatened him; at the same time he pulled his grey hairs from his head by handfuls to distribute among us, and implored our favour for himself and his relations." [50] The other Indians returned, were given a few trinkets, and in turn gave Mackenzie's party some boiled fish. They said that there was another rapids nearby, and some of them went along to guide them through it, but no rapids appeared.

Now the party passed the Ramparts of the Mackenzie, where the river narrows and flows between vertical limestone cliffs as much as two hundred fifty feet high. Below they found other groups of Indians, who provided them with more food but who had no more knowledge of the river than the groups encountered earlier. Their guide continued to give trouble, for fear of meeting Eskimos who would kill them all. The next day they sent him back after getting a new guide, but the new one was as reluctant as the old.

For the next few days more Indians, more guides, but still there was no reliable information. The Indians had Eskimo objects that they had obtained in trade, and there were repeated tales of Indians killed by Eskimos. On the ninth, Indians told them that the sea was only a short journey overland to the east or west, and the next day they reached the head of the delta of the Mackenzie—a great maze of channels and marsh. Mackenzie took an observation for latitude and found that he was farther north than he had expected. Now "it was evident that these waters emptied themselves into the Hyperborean Sea; and though it was probable that, from the want of provision, we could not return to Athabasca in the course of the season, I nevertheless, determined to penetrate to the discharge of them." [51]

His Indians were less determined, and he had to promise that he would turn back if they had not reached the sea in seven days. It is a measure of his character that, tired and discouraged as he was, he sat up all that night to observe the midnight sun. "At half past twelve I called up one of the men to view a spectacle which he had never before seen; when, on seeing the sun so high, he thought it was a signal to embark, and began to call the rest of his companions, who would scarcely be persuaded by me, that the sun had not descended nearer to the horizon, and that it was now but a short time past midnight." [52]

The next day the English Chief and the guide had to be bribed to go on. On the twelfth Mackenzie reached the sea, but his account is ambiguous here and has caused much speculation by his readers. The Indians said that this was a lake and at first Mackenzie calls it such. 35

It is only later that he realizes that this is indeed the sea, but nowhere in his journal does he clearly say so. He makes no mention of tasting the water to see whether it was salty, but at the mouth of such a large river it would have little salt anyway. The "lake" was covered with ice and they landed and made camp on an island. "My people could not, at this time, refrain from expressions of real concern, that they were obliged to return without reaching the sea: indeed, the hope of attaining this object encouraged them to bear, without repining, the hardships of our unremitting voyage." [53]

That night they had their first clue as to where they were, when they had to move their baggage away from the rising water. This was the incoming tide, but they were familiar with fluctuations in the water level of lakes, caused by the wind, and now they attributed this to the same cause. The next day the men fished and Mackenzie took observations for latitude and compass variation, and climbed a hill to get a view of the area. On the fourteenth, white whales were sighted and the men rashly went in pursuit. Fortunately they did not get close, and Mackenzie realized then how easily the canoes could have been destroyed by the big beasts. He named the island where he was camped "Whale Island." Later they went out again to observe the ice, but fog and rough seas almost kept them from getting back. The next morning they found the water under the baggage again, and since the wind had not changed they decided at last that this was the tide.

Mackenzie wanted to contact the Eskimos of the area and spent several fruitless days looking among the islands for them. On July 16 they went back to the river and headed upstream, toward Athabasca. The weather was warmer here, but there were clouds of mosquitoes. Still no natives, though there were many signs of them. There was little game and few fish, and a few inches below the surface the ground was permanently frozen. On the twenty-first they reached the head of the delta and entered the river proper. Here the current was so strong that they had to tow the canoe with a line from the bank. The return trip, fighting the current instead of going with it, would be much slower and harder than the trip down. Fortunately the water was three feet lower than before. That night they stopped at their camp of the ninth.

More Indians, more long interrogations, but still there was no answer to the question that interested Mackenzie most of all—how to get to the Pacific? And still there was the problem of feeding ten men and four women. "I have always observed, that the north men possessed very hearty appetites, but they were very much exceeded by those with me, since we entered this river. I should really have thought it absolute gluttony in my people, if my own appetite had not increased in a similar proportion." [54]

More days of travel, by line or paddle or sail, and at last there was news about the country west of the mountains. None of these Indians had been there, but they had talked with others who had, and knew that the natives of that country were giants, that they had wings but did not fly, and that they could kill with their eyes. Mackenzie discounted this, but was much interested in the account of a river larger than the one he was on, which ran into a great lake where there was a white man's fort. He thought that the river was Cook's River, that the fort was the Russian one at Unalaska, and that the Mackenzie River communicated with Norton Sound. He was way off, but then he did not have much to go on. The river, if not pure fiction, must have been the Yukon or one of its branches.

But how stubborn the man was! It was late in the season, he was running out of food, and his Indians were ready to desert, but still he tried to get one of the local Indians to guide him across the mountains to this other river. It is just as well that the man refused, because such a trip could only have ended in disaster. Mackenzie could get no more information from other Indians, and he suspected that his interpreter was keeping it from him, afraid that it would prolong the trip. When he threatened to force some Indians to accompany him across the mountains they all grew sick at the same moment.

They kept on up the river, paddling most of the time now, and 37 living largely on wild geese. The night of August 1 was dark enough for them to see stars, the first they had seen since leaving Athabasca. The next day they passed the Great Bear River. There was cold weather, then rain, then fine weather. On the tenth they came to the last mountains near the river on the west, and Mackenzie set out to climb one. After much difficulty he finally had to give up and turn back. He had trouble with the English Chief and learned that he and his people were planning to desert the party before reaching Great Slave Lake.

On the thirteenth they recovered the pemmican that they had cached on the way down. There was more trouble with the English Chief and at last Mackenzie told him off. The chief replied that he would go no farther, and he and his people began loud lamentations for their dead friends. After two hours Mackenzie put a stop to this and persuaded them to continue on with him. That night they camped at the mouth of the Liard. Mackenzie invited the English Chief to have supper with him, and found that a drink of rum restored him to good spirits. "He informed me that it was a custom with the Chepewyan chiefs to go to war after they had shed tears, in order to wipe away the disgrace attached to such a feminine weakness, and that in the ensuing spring he should not fail to execute his design; at the same time he declared his intention to continue with us as long as I should want him." [55]

Now they were headed east. On August 21 the weather was so bad that they could not travel, but the next day they reached Great Slave Lake. On the twenty-fourth they met Leroux, as arranged. They spent several days on the lake, battered by strong winds. On August 30 they reached Leroux's new post on the north side of the lake, and Mackenzie paid the English Chief and bid him good-by. On September 3 they entered the Slave River, and here too the going was slow. They wrecked the canoe and had to repair it; it frequently required regumming, and the paddles broke and new ones had to be made. On the eleventh they passed the mouth of the Peace. The next day they crossed Lake Athabasca and at three o'clock in the afternoon arrived at Fort Chipewyan, where they found the men busy building a new house. In one hundred and two days they had traveled almost three thousand miles, discovered a major river, reached the Arctic Ocean, and seen much country never seen before by men of their kind. But they had not discovered a route to the Pacific.

Most men would have been satisfied with a good long rest after such a trip, but not Mackenzie. He must have been eager for civilized company, for someone to tell his adventures to, and for news of the outside world. His cousin Roderick was on the way back from Grand Portage, and shortly after Mackenzie reached Fort Chipewyan he set out up the Athabasca River to meet him. They met at the mouth of the Clearwater and returned to Chipewyan together. They had much to tell each other during the long winter. Mackenzie could tell about the new world he had discovered and Roderick could report on the partners' meeting at Grand Portage, on the latest news from Europe (six months old), and on his unsuccessful attempt to find a way to bypass the long and difficult Methye Portage. Presumably he brought a new supply of books with him from Grand Portage.

The next spring it was Mackenzie's turn to go to Grand Portage while Roderick stayed behind to manage the affairs of the district. At Cumberland Lake Mackenzie met the surveyor Philip Turnor, an employee of the Hudson's Bay Company. Turnor recorded in his journal that "Mr McKenzie says he has been at the Sea, but thinks it the Hyperborean Sea but he does not seem acquainted with Observations which makes me think he is not well convinced where he has been." [56]

A few days later Mackenzie received a letter from Simon McTavish, a Montreal agent of the Company and its most powerful member. The letter was a severe reprimand for the condition of the fur packs from Athabasca the previous year. Mackenzie had put exploration before business and gone off to the Arctic, sending out the furs in the care of a minor employee. They were received in poor condition and McTavish wanted to make sure that there would be no repetition of this mistake.[57]

In July Mackenzie wrote Roderick from Grand Portage that "My *Expedition* was hardly spoken of—but this is what I expected." [58] The small number and poor quality of the furs from Athabasca probably were spoken of at some length, though. Apparently the partners had little interest in Mackenzie's discoveries, but also they were busy with other things. At this meeting the Company underwent one of its periodic reorganizations, making the firm of McTavish and Frobisher its sole Montreal agents and thereby giving Simon McTavish even greater power—power that was to cause much trouble in later years.

Back at Chipewyan, Mackenzie sent Roderick and most of the men to build a post at the outlet of Great Slave Lake and to winter there, trading with whatever Indians they could contact. This was the beginning of a rapid extension of the trade into the lower Mackenzie Basin.[59] In March, 1791, Mackenzie wrote to Roderick, "It will be proper to appoint a Chief among the Red Knives [Yellowknives]. I think the English Chief may answer as none of their own men have sufficient authority." Ah, the White Man's burden—this is the spirit of the true empire builder. The Company will control the Indians by bribing their chief; if they do not have one the Company will supply one. Without proper control the Indians would not exert themselves as much as they could in trapping, and they might even sell their furs to a rival trader.

He went on to say that whether Roderick's fort was to be continued depended on how many furs it got, and that a fort would have to be established at the entrance of the Slave River into Great Slave Lake.

To accomodate the new discovered or Beaver Indians on the Grand River visited by me, a Summer Expedition to Trading Rendevous might for the present answer our purpose. This plan you may propose to them.

40   I hope you will make all possible enquiry regarding the Country of the

Beaver Indians as well as about the Country of the Slaves—and more particularly about the large River which falls into the Sea to the westward of the Grand River in which I *voyaged.*[60]

His first exploration was a failure and was largely ignored by his partners, but he was not ready to give up. The Indians on the Mackenzie had told him about a great river west of the mountains and he could not get it out of his mind. He did not know how to fit it into the little that was known of the coast, but he wanted to find out.

In the meantime events in other areas had been building up pressure on the British traders to take decisive action. The interests of Britain, Russia, Spain, and the United States were in conflict on the northwest coast, and in the center of the continent Britain and Spain were in active competition, with the United States threatening to enter the area as well.

In the Northwest this rivalry came to a head in the Nootka Sound controversy. Nootka, on the west coast of Vancouver Island, had been discovered by Cook in 1778, and it soon became a major center of the marine fur trade. No real settlement was made until 1789, when Spain planted a small colony there. Later that year the Spanish seized four British ships that came to do the same thing. The British government reacted strongly, and war threatened between Britain and Spain. It was averted by the Nootka Sound Convention of 1790, by which Spain gave up her claim of exclusive rights to the northwest coast.[61]

Spain had long since passed the height of her power in the New World, but in the last quarter of the eighteenth century she was faced with the problem of trying to assimilate a vast new territory into New Spain.[62] As a result of the Seven Years' War, France had given all the region west of the Mississippi (at least to the Rockies) to Spain, and now Spain had to defend this area against intruders.

The main intruders were British traders from Canada, coming down the Mississippi from the Great Lakes or coming overland from the Assiniboine to trade with the Mandans. The Spanish needed to defend their sovereignty, they wanted to secure this trade for their own merchants, and above all they wanted to keep intruders out of New Mexico. To defend New Spain they had to defend a buffer zone around it.

If they could establish a line of defense from St. Louis, their Mississippi headquarters, to the Pacific coast both New Mexico and California would be strengthened. Somehow there were never enough men, never enough money, to do the job, but in the 1790's an attempt was made to explore the upper Missouri, and if possible reach the coast.

Part of the over-all plan for securing the Missouri for Spain was to encourage Spanish traders to extend their activities farther up the river. After a brief attempt at free trade, a syndicate of Missouri traders was formed in 1793, called the Company of Explorers of the Upper Missouri. The next year they sent a party upriver to establish contact with the Mandans and obtain information about the country farther west. This party and others that followed accomplished little, and Spain was soon to be deprived of this whole territory by events elsewhere.

There was interest in western exploration in the United States too at this time. Most Americans were too busy organizing and settling the territory then held by the new republic to be much concerned about the region beyond the Mississippi, but Thomas Jefferson, then Washington's secretary of state, was an exception. He was already thinking in terms of a transcontinental nation. It was probably for this reason that in 1793 he sent the French botanist André Michaux on a poorly planned attempt to cross the continent by way of the Missouri. Michaux got involved in a comedy of international intrigue and did not get west of the Mississippi.[63]

These were some of the conflicting forces that would eventually determine the future of the western half of the continent. Mackenzie probably was well aware of the principal ones when he set out for Grand Portage in the spring of 1791, leaving Athabasca in Roderick's care.

On the way he met Philip Turnor again. Turnor was on his way to Athabasca to make surveys for the Hudson's Bay Company, and especially to determine the longitude of Fort Chipewyan.[64] The longitudes of Hudson Bay and of the coast had been determined and thus the distance between them was known. No one who had been to Athabasca had known the method of determining longitude, and the distance from the Bay to Athabasca had been greatly overestimated, so Athabasca was thought to be much nearer the coast than it really was.

Mackenzie wrote to Roderick, "I met Mr. Turner here this morning. I find the intention [of the] Expedition is only discoveries. [That is, Turnor is not trying to cut in on the North West Company's monopoly of the trade.] I also find the party is very ill prepared for their undertaking."[65] Neither Turnor nor the Hudson's Bay Company had had much experience in that far country, and he was not adequately supplied. Mackenzie told Roderick to make him at home at Fort Chipewyan. Turnor got to Chipewyan and spent several months surveying in the Lake Athabasca-Great Slave Lake region. When he had determined the longitude he realized that Athabasca was much farther from the Pacific than had been thought, and Mackenzie now had important new information about the difficulties that would face him on his next exploration.

But Mackenzie was not entirely eager to return to the field. He had spent six consecutive winters in the Northwest and during that time he had not been farther east than Grand Portage. He had never liked the hard crude life of the trading posts, and now he seems to have decided that he had to get out for a while. At any rate, in August he was on his way to Montreal, and wrote to Roderick, "I have some idea of Crossing the Sea—But this I cannot determine at present—However it is my fixed resolution if I live & in health—to meet you at Lac La Pluie next Spring."[66]

He did cross the ocean, to London, where he spent the following winter. This was his first visit to Britain since he left Stornoway seventeen years earlier, and probably his first visit to London. We 43 have no record of what sort of life he led there, but judging from his later career he must have enjoyed the pleasures of the city to the full.

His main reason for going to London seems to have been to learn enough astronomy to be able to determine longtiude, and to buy suitable instruments for making observations. On his Mackenzie River trip he had determined latitude with fair accuracy but he had not known how to determine longitude. Now he had crossed the ocean and enrolled in a school in order to be able to fix his position more closely. Clearly he was intending to make another try at reaching the Pacific, and clearly his interests were not limited to the fur trade.

Navigators had long known how to find their latitude from the position of the sun, but only recently had they learned how to determine longitude. One method was to carry an accurate clock or chronometer set at Greenwich time. Local time could be determined by the sun, and the difference between local and Greenwich time gave the longitude. But since chronometers were not entirely reliable, astronomical methods also were used. The most accurate of these was to measure the angle between the moon and the sun or a fixed star, but this required difficult calculations. Another astronomical method was to determine the time of eclipse of Jupiter's satellites. Both of these methods required the use of astronomical tables. Mackenzie seems to have learned his lessons well, because his subsequent observations of longitude were as good as could be expected for the time and place. He also bought the necessary equipment—compass, sextant, chronometer, and telescope—but these were not very good, even for that time.[67]

With his new skills and equipment and perhaps with pleasant memories of London life to warm his thoughts during the northern winters he sailed from England on May 9, 1792, for Canada.[68] From Montreal he went on to Grand Portage and Athabasca. There was no time to lose, because he had decided to make an effort to reach the coast the next summer, and he wanted to get a head start before winter. He had written Roderick to send men up the Peace far beyond the last fort to build a new fort where he could spend the winter. Did he hope that the Peace would lead him to the great river west of the mountains that he had heard of on the Mackenzie, or had he given up his idea of finding that river? We do not know. At any rate, he did not try to reach it from the Mackenzie. His second attempt was to be farther south. The Peace was an obvious route, because it led west and it flowed through the mountains, making a difficult mountain crossing unnecessary. It flowed east, though, which meant that it could not lead directly to the Pacific.

At Fort Chipewyan he exchanged news with Roderick, gave him instructions for the coming year, and gathered the supplies for his trip. He knew by now that the coast was much farther away than he had thought, and that he must be prepared for a long journey. At last he was ready, and on October 10 he started out. Now the story is his.

Alexander Mackenzie's Journal

ALEXANDER MACKENZIE'S JOURNAL

Mackenzie published his journals in London in 1801. The journal of the 1792–93 voyage is reprinted here. In his preface he says:

THESE VOYAGES will not, I fear, afford the variety that may be expected from them; and that which they offered to the eye, is not of a nature to be effectually transferred to the page. Mountains and vallies, the dreary wastes, and the wide-spreading forests, the lakes and rivers succeed each other in general description; and, except on the coasts of the Pacific Ocean, where the villages were permanent, and the inhabitants in a great measure stationary, small bands of wandering Indians are the only people whom I shall introduce to the acquaintance of my readers. . . .

I do not possess the science of the naturalist; and even if the qualifications of that character had been attained by me, its curious spirit would not have been gratified. I could not stop to dig into the earth, over whose surface I was compelled to pass with rapid steps; nor could I turn aside to collect the plants which nature might have scattered on the way, when my thoughts were anxiously employed in making provision for the day that was passing over me. I had to encounter perils by land and perils by water; to watch the savage who was our guide, or to guard against those of his tribe who might meditate our destruction. I had, also, the passions and fears of others to control and subdue. Today I had to assuage the rising discontents, and on the morrow to cheer the fainting spirits, of the people who accompanied me. The toil of our navigation was incessant, and oftentimes extreme; and in our progress over land we had no protection from the severity of the elements, and possessed no accommodations or conveniences but such as could be contained in the burden on our shoulders, which aggravated the toils of our march, and added to the wearisomeness of our way.

Though the events which compose my journals may have little in themselves to strike the imagination of those who love to be astonished, or to gratify the curiosity of such as are enamoured of romantic adventures; nevertheless, when it is considered that I explored those waters which had never before borne any other vessel than the canoe of the savage; and traversed those deserts where an European had never before presented himself to the eye of its swarthy natives; when to these considerations are added the important objects which were pursued, with the dangers that were encountered, and the difficulties that were surmounted to attain them, this work will, I flatter myself, be found to excite an interest, and conciliate regard, in the minds of those who peruse it. . . .

Before I conclude, I must beg leave to inform my readers, that they are not to expect the charms of embellished narrative, or animated description; the approbation due to simplicity and to truth is all I presume to claim; and I am not without the hope that this claim will be allowed me. I have described whatever I saw with the impressions of the moment which presented it to me. The successive circumstances of my progress are related without exaggeration or display. I have seldom allowed myself to wander into conjecture; and whenever conjecture has been indulged, it will be found, I trust, to be accompanied with the temper of a man who is not disposed to think too highly of himself: and if at any time I have delivered myself with confidence, it will appear, I hope, to be on those subjects which, from the habits and experience of my life, will justify an unreserved communication of my opinions. I am not a candidate for literary fame; at the same time, I cannot but indulge the hope that this volume, with all its imperfections, will not be thought unworthy the attention of the scientific geographer; and that, by unfolding countries

hitherto unexplored, and which, I presume, may now be considered as a part of the British dominions, it will be received as a faithful tribute to the prosperity of my country.[1]

Mackenzie's account is almost impossible to follow in places. Even men who know the country well have difficulty in deciding where he was at certain times, and many of his camps can be located only very roughly. He did not know the names by which the rivers and mountains that he saw are now called, of course, but also he fails to mention prominent geographic features. This may be because he was asleep in the canoe when they were passed, because they were hidden by fog or the high banks of the river, or because he was too busy with more pressing matters to note them. Some critical sections of his account are carelessly written, so that it is not possible to determine just what he is trying to say. Finally, he usually underestimated distances, and his compass bearings seem to be uncorrected for variation, which was about 23° east. His route has been traced by government surveyors and others, and the physical features that he mentions are identified in the text as far as possible. The editor's notes are in brackets or indented.[2]

[October 10, 1792] Having made every necessary preparation, I left Fort Chepewyan, to proceed up the Peace River. I had resolved to go as far as our most distant settlement, which would occupy the remaining part of the season, it being the route by which I proposed to attempt my next discovery, across the mountains from the source of that river; for whatever distance I could reach this fall, would be a proportionate advancement of my voyage.

In consequence of this design, I left the establishment of Fort Chepewyan, in charge of Mr. Roderic Mackenzie, accompanied by two canoes laden with the necessary articles for trade: we accordingly steered West for one of the branches that communicates with the Peace River, called the Pine River [Quatre Fourches River]; at the entrance of which we waited for the other canoes, in order to take some supplies from them, as I had reason to apprehend they would not to be able to keep up with us. We entered the Peace River at seven in the morning of the 12th, taking a Westerly course. It is evident, that all the land between it and the Lake of the Hills [Lake Athabasca], as far as the Elk River [Athabasca River], is formed by the quantity of earth and mud, which is carried down by the streams of those two great rivers. In this space there are several lakes. The lake Clear Water, which is the deepest, Lake Vassieu, and the Athabasca Lake, which is the largest of the three, and whose denomination in the Knistineaux [Cree] language, implies, a flat, low, swampy country, subject to inundations.[3] The two last lakes are now so shallow, that, from the cause just mentioned, there is every reason to expect, that in a few years, they will have exchanged their character and become extensive forests.

This country is so level, that, at some seasons, it is entirely overflowed, which accounts for the periodical influx and reflux of the waters between the Lake of the Hills and the Peace River.

> Mackenzie had a good concept of the geology of the area. The rocky Canadian Shield extends west almost to the western end of Lake Athabasca. The western end of the lake is bordered by the combined deltas of the Athabasca River and the Peace River. This extensive delta region is low and marshy, with many small lakes and channels. It is filling in as Mackenzie thought, but not nearly as rapidly. Most of it is still covered only by willow thickets. At high water it is flooded, and when the Peace is in flood the current in the Rocher River and the Quatre Fourches River is reversed and flows south into Lake Athabasca. The Quatre Fourches River is a side channel connecting the Peace River directly with Lake Athabasca. This was an easier route than going down the Rocher (Slave) River to the mouth of the Peace.

On the 13th at noon we came to the Peace Point; from which, according to the report of my interpreter, the river derives its name;

it was the spot where the Knisteneaux and Beaver Indians settled their dispute; the real name of the river and point being that of the land which was the object of contention.

When this country was formerly invaded by the Knisteneaux, they found the Beaver Indians inhabiting the land about Portage la Loche [Methye Portage, Saskatchewan]; and the adjoining tribe were those whom they called slaves [Slave Indians]. They drove both these tribes before them; when the latter proceeded down the river from the Lake of the Hills, in consequence of which that part of it obtained the name of the Slave River. The former proceeded up the river; and when the Knisteneaux made peace with them, this place was settled to be the boundary.

We continued our voyage, and I did not find the current so strong in this river as I had been induced to believe, though this, perhaps, was not the period to form a correct notion of that circumstance, as well as of the breadth, the water being very low; so that the stream has not appeared to me to be in any part that I have seen, more than a quarter of a mile wide.

The weather was cold and raw, so as to render our progress unpleasant; at the same time we did not relax in our expedition, and, at three in the afternoon of the 17th we arrived at the falls [Vermilion Falls]. The river at this place is about four hundred yards broad, and the fall about twenty feet high: the first carrying place is eight hundred paces in length, and the last, which is about a mile onwards, is something more than two thirds of that distance. Here we found several fires, from which circumstance we concluded, that the canoes destined for this quarter, which left the fort some days before us, could not be far a-head. The weather continued to be very cold, and the snow that fell during the night was several inches deep.

On the morning of the 18th, as soon as we got out of the draught of the fall, the wind being at North-East, and strong in our favour, we hoisted sail, which carried us on at a considerable rate against the current, and passed the Loon River [Wabiskaw River] before twelve

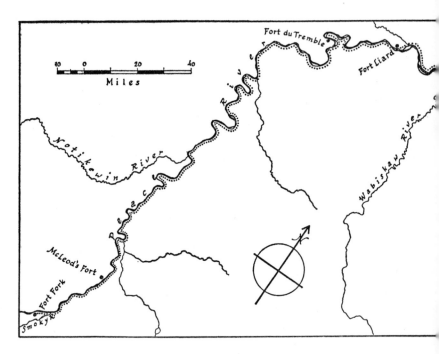

o'clock; from thence we soon came along the Grande Isle, at the upper end of which we encamped for the night. It now froze very hard: indeed, it had so much the appearance of winter, that I began to entertain some alarm lest we might be stopped by the ice: we therefore set off at three o'clock in the morning of the 19th, and about eight we landed at the Old Establishment. [Fort Liard. Mackenzie was about half way to his winter quarters.[4]]

The passage to this place from Athabasca having been surveyed by M. Vandrieu [Vaudrieu], formerly in the Company's service, I did not think it necessary to give any particular attention to it; I shall, however, just observe, that the course in general from the Lake of the Hills to the falls, is Westerly, and as much to the North as the South of it, from thence it is about West-South-West to this fort.

The country in general is low from our entrance of the river to the falls, and with the exception of a few open parts covered with grass, 54 it is clothed with wood. Where the banks are very low the soil is

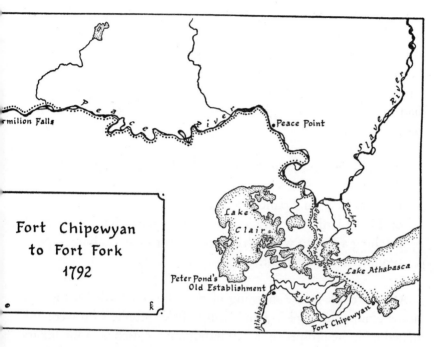

Fort Chipewyan
to Fort Fork
1792

good, being composed of the sediment of the river and putrefied leaves and vegetables. Where they are more elevated, they display a face of yellowish clay, mixed with small stones. On a line with the falls, and on either side of the river, there are said to be very extensive plains, which afford pasture to numerous herds of buffaloes. Our people a-head slept here last night, and, from their carelessness, the fire was communicated to, and burned down, the large house, and was proceeding fast to the smaller buildings when we arrived to extinguish it.

We continued our voyage, the course of the river being South-West by West one mile and a quarter, South by East one mile, South-West by South three miles, West by South one mile, South-South-West two miles, South four miles, South-West seven miles and an half, South by West one mile, North-North-West two miles and an half, South five miles and a quarter, South-West one mile and an half, North-East by East three miles and an half, and South-East by East one mile.

55

We overtook Mr. Finlay, with his canoes, who was encamped near the fort of which he was going to take the charge, during the ensuing winter, and made every necessary preparative for a becoming appearance on our arrival the following morning. Although I had been since the year 1787 in the Athabasca country, I had never yet seen a single native of that part of it which we had now reached.

> Mr. Finlay was James Finlay, a North West Company clerk and son of the Saskatchewan pioneer of the same name. The fort was Fort du Tremble, about twenty-five miles southwest of Fort Liard.[5] The traders usually stopped shortly before reaching a fort to wash, shave, and repair their clothing—appearance was important.

At six o'clock in the morning of the 20th, we landed before the house amidst the rejoicing and firing of the people, who were animated with the prospect of again indulging themselves in the luxury of rum, of which they had been deprived since the beginning of May; as it is a practice throughout the North-West, neither to sell or give any rum to the natives during the summer. There was at this time only one chief with his people, the other two being hourly expected with their bands, and on the 21st and 22nd they all arrived except the war chief and fifteen men. [These were Beaver or Tsattine Indians, an Athapascan tribe of the middle Peace River. They were the first of the tribe that Mackenzie had seen.] As they very soon expressed their desire of the expected regale, I called them together, to the number of forty-two hunters, or men capable of bearing arms, to offer some advice, which would be equally advantageous to them and to us, and I strengthened my admonition with a nine gallon cask of reduced rum and a quantity of tobacco. At the same time I observed, that as I should not often visit them, I had instanced a greater degree of liberality than they had been accustomed to.

56   The number of people belonging to this establishment amounts to

about three hundred, of which, sixty are hunters. Although they appear from their language to be of the same stock as the Chepewyans, they differ from them in appearance, manners, and customs, as they had adopted those of their former enemies, the Knisteneaux: they speak their language, as well as cut their hair, paint, and dress like them, and possess their immoderate fondness for liquor and tobacco. This description, however, can be applied only to the men, as the women are less adorned even than those of the Chepewyan tribes. We could not observe, without some degree of surprize, the contrast between the neat and decent appearance of the men, and the nastiness of the women. I am disposed, however, to think that this circumstance is generally owing to the extreme submission and abasement of the latter: for I observed, that one of the chiefs allowed two of his wives more liberty and familiarity than were accorded to the others, as well as a more becoming exterior, and their appearance was proportionably pleasing. I shall, however, take a future opportunity to speak more at large on this subject.

There were frequent changes of the weather in the course of the day, and it froze rather hard in the night. The thickness of the ice in the morning was a sufficient notice for me to proceed. I accordingly gave the natives such good counsel as might influence their behaviour, communicated my directions to Mr. Finlay for his future conduct, and took my leave under several vollies of musketry, on the morning of the 23d. I had already dispatched my loaded canoes two days before, with directions to continue their progress without waiting for me.

Our course was South-South-East one mile and an half, South three quarters; East seven miles and an half, veering gradually to the West four miles and an half; South-East by South three miles, South-East three miles and an half, East-South-East to Long Point three miles, South-West one mile and a quarter, East by North four miles and three quarters, West three miles and an half, West-South-West one mile, East by South five miles and an half, South three miles and three quarters, South-East by South three miles, East-South-East three miles, East-North-East one mile, when there was a river that flowed in on the right [Notikewin River?]; East two miles and an half, East-South-East half a mile, South-East by South seven miles and an half, South two miles, South-South-East three miles and an half; in the course of which we passed an island South by West, where a rivulet flowed in on the right, one mile; East one mile and an half, South five miles, South-East by South four miles and an half, South-West one mile, South-East by East four miles and an half, West-South-West half a mile, South-West six miles and three quarters, South-East by South one mile and an half, South one mile and an half, South-East by South two miles, South-West three quarters of a mile, South-East by South two miles and an half, East by South one mile and three quarters, South two miles, South-East one mile and an half, South-South-East half a mile, East by South two miles and a half, North-East three miles, South-West by West short distance to the establishment of last year [A temporary post, later referred to as "the old fort of Mr. McLeod." It was about thirty miles north of Fort Fork.⁶], East-North-East four miles, South-South-East one mile and three quarters, South half a mile, South-East by South three quarters of a mile, North-East by East one mile, South three miles, South-South-East one mile and three quarters, South by East four miles and an half, South-West three miles South by East two miles, South by West one mile and an half, South-West two miles, South by West four miles and an half, South-West one mile and an half, and South by East three miles.

Here we arrived at the forks of the river; the Eastern branch [Smoky River] appearing to be not more than half the size of the Western one [Peace River]. We pursued the latter, in a course South-West by West six miles, and landed on the first of November at the place which was designed to be my winter residence: indeed, the weather had been so cold and disagreeable, that I was more than once apprehensive of our being stopped by the ice, and, after all, it required the utmost exertions of which my men were capable to prevent it; so that on their arrival they were quite exhausted. Nor were their labours at an end, for there was not a single hut to receive us; it was, however, now in my power to feed and sustain them in a more comfortable manner. [He was now at the site of his winter post, Fort

Fork. It was on the south (right) side of the Peace River, six miles above its junction with the Smoky River.⁷]

We found two men here who had been sent forward last spring, for the purpose of squaring timber for the erection of a house, and cutting pallisades, &c. to surround it. With them was the principal [Indian] chief of the place, and about seventy men, who had been anxiously waiting for our arrival, and received us with every mark of satisfaction and regard which they could express. If we might judge from the quantity of powder that was wasted on our arrival, they certainly had not been in want of ammunition, at least during the summer.

The banks of the river, from the falls, are in general lofty, except at low woody points, accidentally formed in the manner I have already mentioned: they also displayed, in all their broken parts, a face of clay, intermixed with stone; in some places there likewise appeared a black mould.

In the summer of 1788, a small spot was cleared at the Old Establishment [Fort Liard], which is situated on a bank thirty feet above the level of the river, and was sown with turnips, carrots, and parsnips. The first grew to a large size, and the others thrived very well. An experiment was also made with potatoes and cabbages, the former of which were successful; but for want of care the latter failed. The next winter the person who had undertaken this cultivation, suffered the potatoes, which had been collected for seed, to catch the frost, and none had been since brought to this place. There is not the least doubt but the soil would be very productive, if a proper attention were given to its preparation. In the fall of the year 1787, when I first arrived at Athabasca, Mr. Pond was settled on the banks of the Elk River, where he remained for three years, and had formed as fine a kitchen garden as I ever saw in Canada. [This was Peter Pond's "Old Establishment" on the Athabasca River, founded in 1778. The Peace River region now has a thriving agriculture.]

In addition to the wood which flourished below the fall, these banks produce the cypress tree [jackpine], arrow-wood [viburnum], 59 and the thorn [hawthorn]. On either side of the river, though invisible from it, are extensive plains, which abound in buffaloes, elks, wolves, foxes, and bears. At a considerable distance to the Westward is an immense ridge of high land or mountains, which take an oblique direction from below the falls, and are inhabited by great numbers of [mule] deer, which are seldom disturbed, but when the Indians go to hunt the beaver in those parts, and, being tired of the flesh of the latter, vary their food with that of the former. This ridge bears the name of the Deer Mountain. Opposite to our present situation, are beautiful meadows, with various animals grazing on them, and groves of poplars irregularly scattered over them.

My tent was no sooner pitched, than I summoned the Indians together, and gave each of them about four inches of Brazil tobacco, a dram of spirits, and lighted the pipe. As they had been very troublesome to my predecessor [Peter Pond], I informed them that I had heard of their misconduct, and was come among them to inquire into the truth of it. I added also that it would be an established rule with me to treat them with kindness, if their behaviour should be such as to deserve it; but, at the same time, that I should be equally severe if they failed in those returns which I had a right to expect from them. I then presented them with a quantity of rum, which I recommended to be used with discretion, and added some tobacco, as a token of peace. They, in return, made me the fairest promises; and, having expressed the pride they felt on beholding me in their country, took their leave.

I now proceeded to examine my situation; and it was with great satisfaction I observed that the two men who had been sent hither some time before us, to cut and square timber for our future operations, had employed the intervening period with activity and skill. They had formed a sufficient quantity of pallisades of eighteen feet long, and seven inches in diameter, to inclose a square spot of a hundred and twenty feet; they had also dug a ditch of three feet deep to receive them; and had prepared timber, planks, &c. for the erection

of a house.

I was, however, so much occupied in settling matters with the Indians, and equipping them for their winter hunting, that I could not
give my attention to any other object, till the 7th [of November],
when I set all hands at work to construct the fort, build the house,
and form store-houses. On the preceding day the river began to run
with ice, which we call the last of the navigation. On the 11th we
had a South-West wind, with snow. On the 16th the ice stopped in
the other fork [Smoky River], which was not above a league [two
and a half miles] from us, across the intervening neck of land. The
water in this branch continued to flow till the 22d, when it was ar-
rested also by the frost, so that we had a passage across the river,
which would last to the latter end of the succeeding April. This was
a fortunate circumstance, as we depended for our support upon what
the hunters could provide for us, and they had been prevented by the
running of the ice from crossing the river. They now, however, very
shortly procured us as much fresh meat as we required, though it
was for some time a toilsome business to my people, for as there was
not yet a sufficient quantity of snow to run sledges, they were under
the necessity of loading themselves with the spoils of the chase.

On the 27th the frost was so severe that the axes of the workmen
became almost as brittle as glass. The weather was very various until
the 2d of December, when my Farenheit's thermometer was injured
by an accident, which rendered it altogether useless. The following
table, therefore, from the 16th of November, to this unfortunate circumstance, is the only correct account of the weather which I can
offer.

In this situation, removed from all those ready aids which add so
much to the comfort, and indeed is a principal characteristic of
civilized life, I was under the necessity of employing my judgment
and experience in accessory circumstances, by no means connected
with the habits of my life, or the enterprise in which I was immediately engaged. I was now among a people who had no knowledge
whatever of remedial application to those disorders and accidents to
which man is liable in every part of the globe, in the distant wilder-

ness, as in the peopled city. They had not the least acquaintance with that primitive medicine which consists in an experience of the healing virtues of herbs and plants, and is frequently found among uncivilised and savage nations. This circumstance now obliged me to be their physician and surgeon, as a woman with a swelled breast, which had been lacerated with flint stones for the cure of it, pre-

Month and Year	Date	Hours A.M.	below o.	above o.	Wind.	Weather.	Hour.	below o.	above o.	Wind.	Weather.	Hour P.M.	below o.	above o.	Wind.	Weather.	
1792 Nov.	16	8½		10		clear	12	0	14		clear	6		15		cloudy	
	17	8½		17		clear	12		20		clear	6		23		ditto	
	18	9		19	E.S.E.		12		21	E.S.E.		6		14	E.S.E.	clear	
	19	8		5	N.W.	ditto	12		12	N.W.	ditto	6		9	N.W.	ditto	Strong wind.
	20	8½		4	——	ditto	12		14	——	ditto	6		19	——	cloudy	at 10 last night 1 below o.
	21	8		19	——		12		25	——		6		23	——		River stopped.
	22	9		27	——	cloudy	12		29	——	cloudy	6		28	——	cloudy	Ice drove, and water rises.
	23	8½		2	N.	clear	12		23	——	clear	6		15	N.	clear	Ice drove again.
	24	8	3		——	ditto	12	0	0	N.E.		6	1		N.E.	cloudy	
	25	8	14		——	ditto	12	4		——		6	2			clear	Snowed last night 2 inches.
	26	9	10		N.	ditto	12		2		N.		6	0	0	N.	ditto	
	27	8	2		——	ditto	12		2		——		6	1		S.W.	ditto	
	28	8	16		——	ditto	12	3		——		6	7		S.	ditto	After dark, over cast.
	29	7½		4	——	cloudy	12		13	——		6		7		ditto	Ditto, a little wind S.W.
	30	9		4	S.		12		13	S.	cloudy	5		16	S.	cloudy	
Dec.	1	9		10	——		12		19	S.E.		5		24	S.E.	ditto	Fell 3 inches snow last night.
	2	9		27	E.												

MACKENZIE'S TABLE OF WEATHER DATA

sented herself to my attention, and by cleanliness, poultices, and healing salve, I succeeded in producing a cure. One of my people also, who was at work in the woods, was attacked with a sudden pain near the first joint of his thumb, which disabled him from holding an axe. On examining his arm, I was astonished to find a narrow red stripe, about half an inch wide, from his thumb to his shoulder; the pain was violent, and accompanied with chilliness and shivering. This was a case that appeared to be beyond my skill, but it was necessary to do something towards relieving the mind of the patient, though I might be unsuccessful in removing his complaint. I accordingly prepared a kind of volatile liniment of rum and soap, with which I ordered his arm to be rubbed, but with little or no effect. He

62

was in a raving state throughout the night, and the red stripe not only increased, but was also accompanied with the appearance of several blotches on his body, and pains in his stomach: the propriety of taking some blood from him now occurred to me, and I ventured, from absolute necessity, to perform that operation for the first time, with an effect that justified the treatment. The following night afforded him rest, and in a short time he regained his former health and activity. [The man had blood poisoning (lymphangitis). The blood letting did not cure him, but the poultice may have helped.]

I was very much surprised on walking in the woods at such an inclement period of the year, to be saluted with the singing of birds, while they seemed by their vivacity to be actuated by the invigorating power of a more genial season. Of these birds the male was something less than the robin; part of his body is of a delicate fawn colour, and his neck, breast, and belly, of a deep scarlet; the wings are black, edged with fawn colour, and two white stripes running across them; the tail is variegated, and the head crowned with a tuft. The female is smaller than the male, and of a fawn colour throughout, except on the neck, which is enlivened by an hue of glossy yellow. [These probably were pine grosbeaks. Their singing was part of the false breeding activity that many birds show in the fall.] I have no doubt but they are constant inhabitants of this climate, as well as some other small birds which we saw, of a grey colour.

[December 23] I this day removed from the tent into the house which had been erected for me, and set all the men to begin the buildings intended for their own habitation. Materials sufficient to erect a range of five houses for them, of about seventeen by twelve feet, were already collected. It would be considered by the inhabitants of a milder climate as a great evil, to be exposed to the weather at this rigorous season of the year, but these people are inured to it, and it is necessary to describe in some measure the hardships which they undergo without a murmur, in order to convey a general notion of them.

The men who were now with me, left this place in the beginning of last May, and went to the Rainy Lake [in southern Manitoba; the outfitting point for Athabasca] in canoes, laden with packs of fur, which, from the immense length of the voyage, and other concurring circumstances, is a most severe trial of patience and perseverance: there they do not remain a sufficient time for ordinary repose, when they take a load of goods in exchange, and proceed on their return, in a great measure, day and night. They had been arrived near two months, and, all that time, had been continually engaged in very toilsome labour, with nothing more than a common shed to protect them from the frost and snow. Such is the life which these people lead; and is continued with unremitting exertion, till their strength is lost in premature old age.

The Canadians remarked, that the weather we had on the 25th, 26th, and 27th of this month, denoted such as we might expect in the three succeeding months. On the 29th, the wind being at North-East, and the weather calm and cloudy, a rumbling noise was heard in the air like distant thunder, when the sky cleared away in the South-West; from whence there blew a perfect hurricane, which lasted till eight. Soon after it commenced, the atmosphere became so warm that it dissolved all the snow on the ground; even the ice was covered with water, and had the same appearance as when it is breaking up in the spring. [This was a chinook wind.] From eight to nine the weather became calm, but immediately after a wind arose from the North-East with equal violence, with clouds, rain, and hail, which continued throughout the night and till the evening of the next day, when it turned to snow. One of the people who wintered at Fort Dauphin [Manitoba] in the year 1780, when the small-pox first appeared there, informed me, that the weather there was of a similar description.

[January 1, 1793] On January first my people, in conformity with the usual custom, awoke me at the break of day with the discharge of fire-arms, with which they congratulated the appearance of the new year. In return, they were treated with plenty of spirits, and when there is any flour, cakes are always added to their regales, which was the case on the present occasion. [It was not customary to celebrate Christmas, but the New Year's regale was traditional among the voyageurs.]

On my arrival here last fall, I found that one of the young Indians had lost the use of his right hand by the bursting of a gun, and that his thumb had been maimed in such a manner as to hang only by a small strip of flesh. Indeed, when he was brought to me, his wound was in such an offensive state, and emitted such a putrid smell, that it required all the resolution I possessed to examine it. His friends had done every thing in their power to relieve him; but as it consisted only in singing about him, and blowing upon his hand, the wound, as may be well imagined, had got into the deplorable state in which I found it. I was rather alarmed at the difficulty of the case, but as the young man's life was in a state of hazard, I was determined to risk my surgical reputation, and accordingly took him under my care. I immediately formed a poultice of bark, stripped from the roots of the spruce-fir [white spruce?], which I applied to the wound, having first washed it with the juice of the bark: this proved a very painful dressing: in a few days, however, the wound was clean, and the putrid flesh around it destroyed. I wished very much in this state of the business to have separated the thumb from the hand, which I well knew must be effected before the cure could be performed; but he would not consent to that operation, till, by the application of vitriol [probably copper sulphate], the flesh by which the thumb was suspended was shriveled almost to a thread. When I had succeeded in this object, I perceived that the wound was closing rather faster than I desired. The salve I applied on the occasion was made of the Canadian balsam [rosin of the balsam fir], wax, and tallow dropped from a burning candle into water. In short, I was so successful, that about Christmas my patient engaged in a hunting party, and brought me the tongue of an elk: nor was he finally ungrateful. When he left me I received the warmest acknowledgments, both from himself, and his relations with whom he departed, for my care of him. I certainly did not spare my time or attention on the occasion, as I regularly dressed his wound three times a day, during the course of a month.

On the 5th in the morning the weather was calm, clear, and very cold; the wind blew from the South-West, and in the course of the afternoon it began to thaw. I had already observed at Athabasca, that this wind never failed to bring us clear mild weather, whereas, when it blew from the opposite quarter, it produced snow. Here it is much more perceptible, for if it blows hard South-West for four hours, a thaw is the consequence, and if the wind is at North-East it brings sleet and snow. To this cause it may be attributed, that there is now so little snow in this part of the world. These warm winds come off the Pacific Ocean, which cannot, in a direct line, be very far from us; the distance being so short, that though they pass over mountains covered with snow, there is not time for them to cool. [Actually chinook winds are cooled as they cross the mountains, but on the eastern side of the mountains they are warmed again adiabatically as they descend to the plains.]

There being several of the natives at the house at this time, one of them, who had received an account of the death of his father, proceeded in silence to his lodge, and began to fire off his gun. As it was night, and such a noise being so uncommon at such an hour, especially when it was so often repeated, I sent my interpreter to inquire into the cause of it, when he was informed by the man himself, that this was a common custom with them on the death of a near relation, and was a warning to their friends not to approach, or intrude upon them, as they were, in consequence of their loss, become careless of life. The chief, to whom the deceased person was also related, appeared with his war-cap on his head, which is only worn on these solemn occasions, or when preparing for battle, and confirmed to me this singular custom of firing guns, in order to express their grief for the death of relations and friends.* The women

* When they are drinking together, they frequently present their guns to each other, when any of the parties have not other means of procuring rum. On such an occasion they always discharge their pieces, as a proof, I imagine,

alone indulge in tears on such occasions, the men considering it as a mark of pusillanimity and a want of fortitude to betray any personal tokens of sensibility or sorrow.

The Indians informed me, that they had been to hunt at a large lake, called by the Knisteneaux, the Slave Lake, which derived its name from that of its original inhabitants, who were called Slaves. They represented it as a large body of water, and that it lies about one hundred and twenty miles due East from this place. It is well known to the Knisteneaux, who are among the inhabitants of the plains on the banks of the Saskatchiwine [Saskatchewan] river; for formerly, when they used to come to make war in this country, they came in their canoes to that lake, and left them there; from thence there is a beaten path all the way to the Fork, or East branch of this river, which was their war-road. [This was Lesser Slave Lake, about sixty-five miles southeast of Fort Fork. It was hitherto unknown to the traders. The "East branch" was the Smoky River.]

[January 10] Among the people who were now here, there were two Rocky Mountain Indians, who declared, that the people to whom we had given that denomination, are by no means entitled to it, and that their country has ever been in the vicinity of our present situation. They said, in support of their assertion, that these people were entirely ignorant of those parts which are adjacent to the mountain, as well as the navigation of the river; that the Beaver Indians had greatly encroached upon them, and would soon force them to retire to the foot of these mountains. They represented themselves as the only real natives of that country then with me; and added, that the country, and that part of the river that intervenes between this place and the mountains, bear much the same appearance as that around us; that the former abounds with animals, but that the course of the latter is interrupted, near and in the mountains, by succesive rapids and considerable falls. These men also informed me, that there is another great river towards the mid-day sun, whose cur-

of their being in good order, and to determine the quantity of liquor they may propose to get in exchange for them.

rent runs in that direction, and that the distance from it is not great across the mountains.

These were western Beaver Indians, from the eastern slope of the Rocky Mountains. They brought extremely important news—there was a great river not far beyond the mountains. This was the first that Mackenzie had heard of the Fraser River, which was later to be so important to him. This was welcome news indeed, but the Indians also warned him of rapids and falls farther up the Peace.

The natives brought me plenty of furs. The small quantity of snow, at this time, was particularly favourable for hunting the beaver, as from this circumstance, those animals could, with the greater facility, be traced from their lodges to their lurking-places.

On the same day Mackenzie wrote Roderick: "I have been so attentive to the Companys affairs that I have not been able to do any thing for my own Amusement I worked once the distance between the Sun & Moon for the long^e. . . . I have not been able to get any certain information respecting the country beyond this. . . . I was thinking that if Mackay could be spared he would be of great Service to me should I undertake any Expedition but then I do not see any person who would undertake to open the road by Lake de Carribou —I would take Finlay with me but he is of too weak a constitution."[8]

Note that "should I undertake any expedition." He still is not sure what he will do, whether to go ahead with his plans or give it all up and go back to Athabasca in the spring. He has not been able to learn very much about what lies ahead, and he has doubts. If he does go he wants to have a reliable lieutenant with him, even if it means reducing the trading activities of the department.

On the 12th our hunter arrived, having left his mother-in-law, who was lately become a widow with three small children, and in actual labour of a fourth. Her daughter related this circumstance to the women here, without the least appearance of concern, though she represented her as in a state of great danger, which probably might proceed from her being abandoned in this unnatural manner; at the same time without any apparent consciousness of her own barbarous negligence: if the poor abandoned woman should die, she would most probably lament her with great outcries, and, perhaps, cut off one or two joints of her fingers as tokens of her grief. The Indians, indeed, consider the state of a woman in labour as among the most trifling occurrences of corporal pain to which human nature is subject, and they may be, in some measure, justified in this apparent insensibility from the circumstances of that situation among themselves. It is by no means uncommon in the hasty removal of their camps from one position to another, for a woman to be taken in labour, to deliver herself in her way, without any assistance or notice from her associates in the journey, and to overtake them before they complete the arrangements of their evening station, with her new-born babe on her back.

I was this morning threatened with a very unpleasant event, which, however, I was fortunately enabled to control. Two young Indians being engaged in one of their games, a dispute ensued, which rose to such an height, that they drew their knives, and if I had not happened to have appeared, they would, I doubt not, have employed them to very bloody purposes. So violent was their rage, that after I had turned them both out of the house, and severely reprimanded them, they stood in the fort for at least half an hour, looking at each other with a most vindictive aspect, and in sullen silence.

The game which produced this state of bitter enmity, is called that of the Platter, from a principal article of it. The Indians play at it in the following manner:

The instruments of it consist of a platter, or dish, made of wood 69 or bark, and six round, or square, but flat pieces of metal, wood, or stone, whose sides or surfaces are of different colours. These are put into the dish, and after being for some time shaken together, are thrown into the air, and received again in the dish with considerable dexterity; when, by the number that are turned up of the same mark or colour, the game is regulated. If there should be equal numbers, the throw is not reckoned; if two or four, the platter changes hands.

On the 13th, one of these people came to me, and presented in himself a curious example of Indian superstition. He requested me to furnish him with a remedy that might be applied to the joints of his legs and thighs, of which he had, in a great measure, lost the use for five winters. This affliction he attributed to his cruelty about that time, when having found a wolf with two whelps in an old Beaver lodge, he set fire to it and consumed them.

The winter had been so mild, that the swans had but lately left us, and at this advanced period there was very little snow on the ground: it was, however, at this time a foot and a half in depth, in the environs of the establishment below this, which is at the distance of about seventy leagues.

On the 28th the Indians were now employed in making their snow-shoes, as the snow had not hitherto fallen in sufficient quantity to render them necessary.

[February 2] The weather now became very cold, and it froze so hard in the night that my watch stopped; a circumstance that had never happened to this watch since my residence in the country.

There was a lodge of Indians here, who were absolutely starving with cold and hunger. They had lately lost a near relation, and had, according to custom, thrown away every thing belonging to them, and even exchanged the few articles of raiment which they possessed, in order, as I presume, to get rid of every thing that may bring the deceased to their remembrance. They also destroy every thing belonging to any deceased person, except what they consign to the grave with the late owner of them. We had some difficulty to make them comprehend that the debts of a man who dies should be discharged, if he left any furs behind him: but those who understand this principle of justice, and profess to adhere to it, never fail to prevent the appearance of any skins beyond such as may be necessary to satisfy the debts of their dead relation.

On the 8th I had an observation for the longitude. In the course of this day one of my men, who had been some time with the Indians, came to inform me that one of them had threatened to stab him; and on his preferring a complaint to the man with whom he now lived, and to whom I had given him in charge, he replied, that he had been very imprudent to play and quarrel with the young Indians out of his lodge, where no one would dare to come and quarrel with him; but that if he had lost his life where he had been, it would have been the consequence of his own folly. Thus, even among these children of nature, it appears that a man's house is his castle, where the protection of hospitality is rigidly maintained.

The hard frost which had prevailed from the beginning of February continued to the 16th of March, when the wind blowing from the South-West, the weather became mild.

On the 22d a wolf was so bold as to venture among the Indian lodges, and was very near carrying off a child.

I had another observation of Jupiter and his satellites for the longitude. On the 13th some [Canada?] geese were seen, and these birds are always considered as the harbingers of spring. On the 1st of April my hunters shot five of them. This was a much earlier period than I ever remember to have observed the visits of wild fowl in this part of the world. The weather had been mild for the last fortnight, and there was a promise of its continuance. On the 5th the snow had entirely disappeared.

At half past four this morning I was awakened to be informed that an Indian had been killed. I accordingly hastened to the camp, where I found two women employed in rolling up the dead body of a man, called the White Partridge, in a beaver robe, which I had lent him. He had received four mortal wounds from a dagger, two within the collar-bone, one in the left breast, and another in the small of the back, with two cuts across his head. The murderer, who had been my hunter throughout the winter, had fled; and it was pretended that several relations of the deceased were gone in pursuit of him. The history of this unfortunate event is as follows:—

These two men had been comrades for four years; the murderer had three wives, and the young man who was killed, becoming enamoured of one of them, the husband consented to yield her to him, with the reserved power of claiming her as his property, when it should be his pleasure. This connection was uninterrupted for near three years, when, whimsical as it may appear, the husband became jealous, and the public amour was suspended. The parties, however, made their private assignations, which caused the woman to be so ill treated by her husband, that the paramour was determined to take her away by force; and this project ended in his death. This is a very common practice among the Indians, and generally terminates in very serious and fatal quarrels. In consequence of this event all the Indians went away in great apparent hurry and confusion, and in the evening not one of them was to be seen about the fort.

The Beaver and Rocky Mountain Indians, who traded with us in this river, did not exceed an hundred and fifty men, capable of bearing arms, two thirds of whom call themselves Beaver Indians. The latter differ only from the former, as they have more or less imbibed the customs and manners of the Knisteneaux. As I have already observed, they are passionately fond of liquor, and in the moments of their festivity will barter any thing they have in their possession for it.

Though the Beaver Indians made their peace with the Knisteneaux, at Peace Point, as already mentioned, yet they did not secure a state of amity from others of the same nation, who had driven away the natives of the Saskatchiwine and Missinipy [Churchill] Rivers, and joined at the head water of the latter, called the Beaver River [a tributary of the Churchill in Saskatchewan]: from thence they proceeded West by the Slave Lake just described, on their war excursions, which they often repeated, even till the Beaver Indians had procured arms, which was in the year 1782. If it so happened that they missed them, they proceeded Westward till they were certain of wreaking their vengeance on those of the Rocky Mountain, who being without arms, became an easy prey to their blind and savage fury. All the European articles they possessed, previous to the year 1780, were obtained from the Knisteneaux and Chepewyans, who brought them from Fort Churchill, and for which they were made to pay an extravagant price. [Fort Churchill was the Hudson's Bay Company post on Hudson Bay at the mouth of the Churchill River, site of present-day Churchill, Manitoba.]

As late as the year 1786, when the first traders from Canada arrived on the banks of this river, the natives employed bows and snares, but at present very little use is made of the former, and the latter are no longer known. They still entertain a great dread of their natural enemies, but they are since become so well armed, that the others now call them their allies. The men are in general of a comely appearance, and fond of personal decoration. The women are of a contrary disposition, and the slaves of the men: in common with all the Indian tribes polygamy is allowed among them. They are very subject to jealousy, and fatal consequences frequently result from the indulgence of that passion. But notwithstanding the vigilance and severity which is exercised by the husband, it seldom happens that a woman is without her favourite, who, in the absence of the husband, exacts the same submission, and practices the same tyranny. And so premature is the tender passion, that it is sometimes known to invigorate so early a period of life as the age of eleven or twelve years. The women are not very prolific; a circumstance which may be attributed, in a great measure, to the hardships that they suffer, for except a few small dogs, they alone perform that labour which is allotted to beasts of burthen in other countries. It is not uncommon, while the men carry nothing but a gun, that their wives and daughters follow with such weighty burdens, that if they lay them down they cannot replace them, and that is a kindness which the men will not deign to perform; so that during their journeys 73 they are frequently obliged to lean against a tree for a small portion of temporary relief. When they arrive at the place which their tyrants have chosen for their encampment, they arrange the whole in a few minutes, by forming a curve of poles, meeting at the top, and expanding into circles of twelve or fifteen feet diameter at the bottom, covered with dressed skins of the moose sewed together. During these preparations, the men sit down quietly to the enjoyment of their pipes, if they happen to have any tobacco. But notwithstanding this abject state of slavery and submission, the women have a considerable influence on the opinion of the men in every thing except their own domestic situation.

These Indians are excellent hunters, and their exercise in that capacity is so violent as to reduce them in general to a very meagre appearance. Their religion is of a very contracted nature, and I never witnessed any ceremony of devotion which they had not borrowed from the Knisteneaux, their feasts and fasts being in imitation of that people. They are more vicious and warlike than the Chepewyans, from whence they sprang, though they do not possess their selfishness; for while they have the means of purchasing their necessaries, they are liberal and generous, but when those are exhausted they become errant beggars: they are, however, remarkable for their honesty, for in the whole tribe there were only two women and a man who had been known to have swerved from that virtue, and they were considered as objects of disregard and reprobation. They are afflicted with but few diseases, and their only remedies consist in binding the temples, procuring perspiration, singing, and blowing on the sick person, or affected part. When death overtakes any of them, their property, as I have before observed, is sacrificed and destroyed; nor is there any failure of lamentation or mourning on such occasion: they who are more nearly related to the departed person, black their faces, and sometimes cut off their hair; they also pierce their arms with knives and arrows. The grief of the females is carried to a still greater excess; they not only cut their hair, and cry and

howl, but they will sometimes, with the utmost deliberation, employ some sharp instrument to separate the nail from the finger, and then force back the flesh beyond the first joint, which they immediately amputate. But this extraordinary mark of affliction is only displayed on the death of a favourite son, an husband, or a father. Many of the old women have so often repeated this ceremony, that they have not a complete finger remaining on either hand. The women renew their lamentations at the graves of their departed relatives for a long succession of years. They appear, in common with all the Indian tribes, to be very fond of their children, but they are as careless in their mode of swaddling them in their infant state, as they are of their own dress: the child is laid down on a board, of about two feet long, covered with a bed of moss, to which it is fastened by bandages, the moss being changed as often as the occasion requires. The chief of the nation had no less than nine wives, and children in proportion.

When traders first appeared among these people, the Canadians were treated with the utmost hospitality and attention; but they have, by their subsequent conduct, taught the natives to withdraw that respect from them, and sometimes to treat them with indignity. They differ very much from the Chepewyans and Knisteneaux, in the abhorrence they profess of any carnal communication between their women and the white people. They carry their love of gaming to excess; they will pursue it for a succession of days and nights, and no apprehension of ruin, nor influence of domestic affection, will restrain them from the indulgence of it. They are a quick, lively, active people, with a keen, penetrating, dark eye; and though they are very susceptible of anger, are as easily appeased. The males eradicate their beards, and the females their hair in every part, except their heads, where it is strong and black, and without a curl. There are many old men among them, but they are, in general, ignorant of the space in which they have been inhabitants of the earth, though one of them told me that he recollected sixty winters.

An Indian in some measure explained his age to me, by relating that he remembered the opposite hills and plains, now interspersed 75 with groves of poplars, when they were covered with moss, and without any animal inhabitant but the rein-deer [caribou]. By degrees, he said, the face of the country changed to its present appearance, when the elk came from the East, and was followed by the buffalo; the rein-deer then retired to the long range of high lands that, at a considerable distance, run parallel with this river.[9]

On the 20th of April I had an observation of Jupiter and his satellites, for the longitude, and we were now visited by our summer companions the gnats and mosquitoes. On the other side of the river, which was yet covered with ice, the plains were delightful; the trees were budding, and many plants in blossom. Mr. Mackay brought me a bunch of flowers of a pink colour, and a yellow button, encircled with six leaves of a light purple. The change in the appearance of nature was as sudden as it was pleasing, for a few days only were passed away since the ground was covered with snow. On the 25th the river was cleared of the ice.

I now found that the death of the man called the White Partridge, had deranged all the plans which I had settled with the Indians for the spring hunting. They had assembled at some distance from the fort, and sent an embassy to me, to demand rum to drink, that they might have an opportunity of crying for their deceased brother. It would be considered as an extreme degradation in an Indian to weep when sober, but a state of intoxication sanctions all irregularities. On my refusal, they threatened to go to war, which, from motives of interest as well as humanity, we did our utmost to discourage; and as a second message was brought by persons of some weight among these people, and on whom I could depend, I thought it prudent to comply with the demand, on an express condition, that they would continue peaceably at home.

The month of April being now past, in the early part of which I was most busily employed in trading with the Indians, I ordered our old canoes to be repaired with bark, and added four new ones to them, when, with the furs and provisions I had purchased, six canoes were loaded and dispatched on the 8th of May for Fort Chepewyan.

I had, however, retained six of the men, who agreed to accompany me on my projected voyage of discovery. I also engaged my hunters, and closed the business of the year for the Company by writing my public and private dispatches.

One of the private dispatches was this letter to Roderick at Fort Chipewyan:

"I have been so vext and disturbed in mind since the beginning of this month that I cannot sit down to any thing steadily —The Indians in general have disappointed me in their hunt. I have had great trouble to procure young men to go along with me—none of them like the voyage—I at last got three; a fourth wanted to join but I would not take him and to be revenged he debauched my Guide—and both deserted last night—The two remaining lads know no more of the Country than I do myself—and it may be that they are on the eve of playing me the same trick—for there is no dependence to be put on the promises of any of these people—and without Indians I have very little hopes of succeeding. I mean getting out of the River— The Indian who deserted has been in another very large River to the westward of this River at a distance of two days march —but to find if there be such is the difficulty. At any rate we are too far advanced now not to make some attempt. In such a state of mind you may judge if the few letters I have written can be very correct. . . .

"I never was so undecided in my intentions as this year—regarding my going to the Portage or remaining in land. I weighed everything in my mind and over again—I cannot find that my opponent there can do me any injury without running the risk of greatly injuring his own interest—Therefore I fear nothing on that score. . . .

"With this weight on my mind—and my wishing to mix in the business at the Portage I would not have remained—had I any intention of continuing in this Country beyond the ensuing winter—Should I be successful I shall retire with greater advantage—should I not be successful I cannot be worse off than I am at present—I begin to think it is the height of folly in a man to reside in a Country of this kind—deprived of every comfort that can render life agreeable, especially when he has a competency to enjoy life in a civilized society which will or ought to be the case with me at that time. . . .

"I hardly know what am about therefore will conclude here till Tomorrow.

"Remember me kindly to those of our friends I do not write to—and plead my excuse. . . .

"I send you a couple of Guineas—the rest I take with me to traffik with the Russians. Alex.ʳ Mackay desires his compliments to you—I kept him so at work that he has no time to write you—May all happiness attend you adieu!" [10]

This letter reveals a great deal. Mackenzie was assailed by doubts and fears that threatened to stop him before he could start. The isolation and confinement of a frontier post in winter, coupled with the terrible loneliness of the leader, were almost too much for him. Nearly to the last he was undecided whether to go on, but now as so often before he chose the more difficult course. His only consolation was that he would have only one more year of the hated life of the trading post. This time, as in 1789, he expected to find Russian traders.

[May 9] Having ascertained, by various observations, the latitude of this place to be 56. 9. North, and longitude 117. 35. 15. West;—on the 9th day of May, I found, that my acrometer [chronometer] was one hour forty-six minutes slow to apparent time; the mean going of it I had found to be twenty-two seconds slow in twenty-four hours. Having settled this point, the canoe was put into the water; her dimensions were twenty-five feet long within, exclusive of the curves of stem and stern, twenty-six inches hold, and four feet nine inches beam. At the same time she was so light, that two men could carry her on a good road three or four miles without resting. In this slender vessel, we shipped provisions, goods for presents, arms, ammunition, and baggage, to the weight of three thousand pounds, and an equipage of ten people; viz. Alexander Mackay, Joseph Landry, Charles Ducette,* François Beaulieux, Baptist Bisson, François Courtois, and Jacques Beauchamp, with two Indians as hunters and interpreters.[11] One of them, when a boy, was used to be so idle, that he obtained the reputable name of Cancre, which he still possesses. With these persons I embarked at seven in the evening. My winter interpreter, with another person, whom I left here to take care of the fort, and supply the natives with ammunition during the summer, shed tears on the reflection of those dangers which we might encounter in our expedition, while my own people offered up their prayers that we might return in safety from it.

We began our voyage with a course South by West, against a strong current one mile and three quarters, South-West by South one mile, and landed before eight on an island for the night.

[May 10] The weather was clear and pleasant, though there was a keenness in the air; and at a quarter past three in the morning we continued our voyage, steering South-West three quarters of a mile, South-West by South one mile and a quarter, South three quarters of a mile, South-West by South one quarter of a mile, South-West by West one mile, South-West by South three miles, South by West three quarters of a mile, and South-West one mile. The canoe, being strained from its having been very heavily laden, became so leaky, that we were obliged to land, unload, and gum it. As this circumstance took place about twelve, I had an opportunity of taking an altitude, which made our latitude 55. 58. 48. [The canoes were made water-tight by sealing the seams with rosin from coniferous trees. A bag of rosin was always carried in the canoes; when they sprang a leak the rosin would be melted over a fire and used to reseal the seams.]

---

* Joseph Landry and Charles Ducette were with me in my former voyage.

When the canoe was repaired we continued our course, steering South-West by West one mile and an half, when I had the misfortune to drop my pocket compass into the water; West half a mile, West-South-West four miles and an half. Here, the banks are steep and hilly, and in some parts undermined by the river. Where the earth has given way, the face of the cliffs discovers numerous strata, consisting of reddish earth and small stones, bitumen [tar deposits], and a greyish earth, below which, near the water edge, is a red stone. Water issues from most of the banks, and the ground on which it spreads is covered with a thin white scurf, or particles of a saline substance: there are several of these salt springs [associated with deposits of natural gas]. At half past six in the afternoon the young men landed, when they killed an elk and wounded a buffalo. In this spot we formed our encampment for the night.

From the place which we quitted this morning, the West side of the river displayed a succession of the most beautiful scenery I had ever beheld. The ground rises at intervals to a considerable height, and stretching inwards to a considerable distance: at every interval or pause in the rise, there is a very gently-ascending space or lawn, which is alternate with abrupt precipices to the summit of the whole, or, at least as far as the eye could distinguish. This magnificent theatre of nature has all the decorations which the trees and animals of the country can afford it: groves of poplars in every shape vary the scene; and their intervals are enlivened with vast herds of elks and buffaloes: the former choosing the steeps and uplands, and the latter preferring the plains. At this time the buffaloes were attended with their young ones, who were frisking about them; and it appeared that the elks would soon exhibit the same enlivening circumstance. The whole country displayed an exuberant verdure; the trees that bear a blossom were advancing fast to that delightful appearance, and the velvet rind of their branches, reflecting the oblique rays of a rising or setting sun, added a splendid gaiety to the scene, which no expressions of mine are qualified to describe. The East side of the river consists of a range of high land covered with the white spruce and the soft [paper] birch, while the banks abound with the alder and the willow. The water continued to rise, and the current being proportionably strong, we made a greater use of setting poles than paddles.

[May 11] The weather was overcast. With a strong wind a-head, we embarked at four in the morning, and left all the fresh meat behind us, but the portion which had been assigned to the kettle; the canoe being already too heavily laden. Our course was West South-West one mile, where a small river flowed in from the East, named *Quiscatina Sepy,* or River with the High Banks; West half a mile, South half a mile, South-West by West three quarters of a mile, West one mile and a quarter, South-West a quarter of a mile, South-South-West half a mile, and West by South a mile and an half. Here I took a meridian altitude, which gave 55. 56. 3. North latitude. We then proceeded West three miles and an half, West-South-West, where the whole plain was on fire, one mile, West one mile, and the wind so strong a-head, that it occasioned the canoe to take in water, and otherwise impeded our progress. Here we landed to take time, with the mean of three altitudes, which made the watch slow, 1. 42. 10. apparent time. [By comparing local solar time with his watch, set for a known longitude, he could determine his present longitude.]

We now proceeded West-South-West, one mile and a quarter, where we found a chief of the Beaver Indians on a hunting party. I remained, however, in my canoe, and though it was getting late, I did not choose to encamp with these people, lest the friends of my hunters might discourage them from proceeding on the voyage. We, therefore, continued our course, but several Indians kept company with us, running along the bank and conversing with my people, who were so attentive to them, that they drove the canoe on a stony flat, so that we were under the necessity of landing to repair the damages, and put up for the night, though very contrary to my wishes. My hunters obtained permission to proceed with some of these people to their lodges, on the promise of being back by the break of day; though I was not without some apprehension respecting them. The chief, however, and another man, as well as several people from the lodges, joined us before we had completed the repair of the canoe; and they made out a melancholy story, that they had neither ammunition nor tobacco sufficient for their necessary supply during the summer. I accordingly referred him to the Fort, where plenty of those articles were left in the care of my interpreter, by whom they would be abundantly furnished, if they were active and industrious in pursuing their occupations. I did not fail, on this occasion, to magnify the advantages of the present expedition; observing, at the same time, that its success would depend on the fidelity and conduct of the young men who were retained by me to hunt. The chief also proposed to borrow my canoe, in order to transport himself and family across the river: several plausible reasons, it is true, suggested themselves for resisting his proposition; but when I stated to him, that, as the canoe was intended for a voyage of such consequence, no woman could be permitted to be embarked in it, he acquiesced in the refusal. It was near twelve at night when he took his leave, after I had gratified him with a present of tobacco.

[May 12] Some of the Indians passed the night with us, and I was informed by them, that, according to our mode of proceeding, we should, in ten days, get as far as the rocky mountains. The young men now returned, to my great satisfaction, and with the appearance of contentment: though I was not pleased when they dressed themselves in the clothes which I had given them before we left the Fort, as it betrayed some latent design.

At four in the morning we proceeded on our voyage, steering West three miles, including one of our course yesterday, North-West by North four miles, West two miles and an half, North-West by West a mile and an half, North by East two miles, North-West by West one mile, and North-North-West three miles. After a continuation of our course to the North for a mile and an half, we landed for the night on an island, where several of the Indians visited us, but unattended by their women, who remained in their camp, which was

at some distance from us.

The land on both sides of the river, during the two last days, is very much elevated, but particularly in the latter part of it, and, on the Western side, presents in different places, white, steep, and lofty cliffs. Our view being confined by these circumstances, we did not see so many animals as on the 10th. Between these lofty boundaries, the river becomes narrow, and in a great measure free from islands, for we had passed only four: the stream, indeed, was not more than two hundred to three hundred yards broad; whereas before these cliffs pressed upon it, its breadth was twice that extent and besprinkled with islands. We killed an elk, and fired several shots at animals from the canoe.

The greater part of this band being Rocky Mountain Indians [western Beavers], I endeavoured to obtain some intelligence of our intended route, but they all pleaded ignorance, and uniformly declared, that they knew nothing of the country beyond the first mountain: at the same time, they were of opinion, that, from the strength of the current and the rapids, we should not get there by water; though they did not hesitate to express their surprise at the expedition we had already made.

I inquired, with some anxiety, after an old man who had already given me an account of the country beyond the limits of his tribe, and was very much disappointed at being informed, that he had not been seen for upwards of a moon. This man had been at war on another large river beyond the Rocky Mountain, and described to me a fork of it between the mountains, the Southern branch of which he directed me to take: from thence, he said, there was a carrying-place of about a day's march for a young man to get to the other river. [The river beyond the Rocky Mountain was still the Peace, the southern branch was the Parsnip. The river on the other side of the portage was the Fraser. Now Mackenzie had one key to the voyage—which fork of the Peace to take.] To prove the truth of his relation, he consented, that his son, who had been with him in those parts, should accompany me; and he accordingly sent him to the Fort some days before my departure; but the preceding night he deserted with an-

83

other young man, whose application to attend me as a hunter being refused, he persuaded the other to leave me. I now thought it right to repeat to them what I had said to the chief of the first band, respecting the advantages which would be derived from the voyage, that the young men might be encouraged to remain with me; as without them I should not have attempted to proceed.

[May 13] The first object that presented itself to me this morning was the young man whom I have already mentioned, as having seduced away my intended guide. At any other time or place I should have chastised him for his past conduct, but in my situation it was necessary to pass over his offence, lest he should endeavour to exercise the same influence over those who were so essential to my service. Of the deserter he gave no satisfactory account, but continued to express his wish to attend me in his place, for which he did not possess any necessary qualifications.

The weather was cloudy, with an appearance of rain; and the Indians pressed me with great earnestness to pass the day with them, and hoped to prolong my stay among them by assuring me that the winter yet lingered in the rocky mountains: but my object was to lose no time, and having given the chief some tobacco for a small quantity of meat, we embarked at four, when my young men could not conceal their chagrin at parting with their friends, for so long a period as the voyage threatened to occupy. When I had assured them that in three moons we should return to them, we proceeded on our course,

West-North-West half a mile, West-South-West one mile and an half, West by North three miles, North-West by West two miles and an half, South-West by West half a mile, South-South-West a mile and an half, and South-West a mile and an half.

Here I had a meridian altitude, which gave 56. 17. 44. North latitude.

The last course continued a mile and an half, South by West three quarters of a mile, South-West by South three miles and an half, and West-South-West two miles and an half. Here the land lowered on both sides, with an increase of wood, and displayed great numbers of animals. The river also widened from three to five hundred yards, and was full of islands and flats. Having continued our course three miles, we made for the shore at seven, to pass the night.

At the place from whence we proceeded this morning, a river falls in from the North; there are also several islands, and many rivulets on either side, which are too small to deserve particular notice. We perceived along the river tracks of large bears, some of which were nine inches wide, and of a proportionate length. We saw one of their dens, or winter quarters, called *watee,* in an island, which was ten feet deep, five feet high, and six feet wide; but we had not yet seen one of those animals. The Indians entertain great apprehension of this kind of bear, which is called the grisly bear, and they never venture to attack it but in a party of at least three or four. Our hunters, though they had been much higher than this part of our voyage, by land, knew nothing of the river. One of them mentioned, that having been engaged in a war expedition, his party on their return made their canoes at some distance below us. The wind was North throughout the day, and at times blew with considerable violence.

The apprehensions which I had felt respecting the young men were not altogether groundless, for the eldest of them told me that his uncle had last night addressed him in the following manner—"My nephew, your departure makes my heart painful. The white people may be said to rob us of you. They are about to conduct you into the midst of our enemies, and you may never more return to us. Were you not with the Chief,* I know not what I should do, but he requires your attendance, and you must follow him."

[May 14] The weather was clear, and the air sharp, when we embarked at half past four. Our course was South by West one mile and an half, South-West by South half a mile, South-West. We here found it necessary to unload, and gum the canoe, in which operation we lost an hour; when we proceeded on the last course one mile and

---

* These people, as well as all the natives on this side of Lake Winipic [Lake Winnipeg, Manitoba], give the mercantile agent that distinguished appellation.

an half. I now took a meridian altitude, which gave 56. 11. 19. North latitude, and continued to proceed West-South-West two miles and an half. Here the Bear River [Pouce Coupé River], which is of a large appearance, falls in from the East; West three miles and an half, South-South-West one mile and an half, and South-West four miles and an half, when we encamped upon an island about seven in the evening. [That afternoon they had crossed the 120th meridian into what is now British Columbia. They made camp near Rolla Landing, B. C.[12]]

During the early part of the day, the current was not so strong as we had generally found it, but towards the evening it became very rapid, and was broken by numerous islands. We were gratified, as usual, with the sight of animals. The land on the West side is very irregular, but has the appearance of being a good beaver country; indeed we saw some of those animals in the river. Wood is in great plenty, and several rivulets added their streams to the main river. A goose was the only article of provision which we procured to day. Smoke was seen, but at a great distance before us.

[May 15] The rain prevented us from continuing our route till past six in the morning, when our course was South-West by West three quarters of a mile; at which time we passed a river on the left [Kiskatinaw River], West by South two miles and an half. The bank was steep, and the current strong. The last course continued one mile and an half, West-South-West two miles, where a river flowed in from the right [Beatton River], West by South one mile and an half, West-North-West one mile, and West by North two miles. Here the land takes the form of an high ridge, and cut our course, which was West for three miles, at right angles. We now completed the voyage of this day.

In the preceding night the water rose upwards of two inches, and had risen in this proportion since our departure. The wind, which was West-South-West, blew very hard throughout the day, and with the strength of the current, greatly impeded our progress. The river, in this part of it, is full of islands; and the land, on the South or left side, is thick with wood. Several rivulets also fall in from that quarter. At the entrance of the last river which we passed, there was a quantity of wood, which had been cut down by axes, and some by the beaver. This fall, however, was not made, in the opinion of my people, by any of the Indians with whom we were acquainted.

The land to the right is of a very irregular elevation and appearance, composed in some places of clay, and rocky cliffs, and others exhibiting stratas of red, green, and yellow colours. Some parts, indeed, offer a beautiful scenery, in some degree similar to that which we passed on the second day of our voyage, and equally enlivened with the elk and the buffalo, who were feeding in great numbers, and unmolested by the hunter. In an island which we passed, there was a large quantity of white [paper] birch, whose bark might be employed in the construction of canoes.

[May 16] The weather being clear, we reimbarked at four in the morning, and proceeded West by North three miles. Here the land again appeared as if it run across our course, and a considerable river discharged itself by various streams. According to the Rocky Mountain Indian, it is called the Sinew River [Pine River]. This spot would be an excellent situation for a fort or factory, as there is plenty of wood, and every reason to believe that the country abounds in beaver. [A fort was built there a few years later.] As for the other animals, they are in evident abundance, as in every direction the elk and the buffalo are seen in possession of the hills and the plains.

Our course continued West-North-West three miles and an half, North-West one mile and an half, South-West by West two miles; (the latitude was by observation 56. 16. 54.) North-West by North half a mile, West-North-West three quarters of a mile; a small river [Wilder Creek?] appearing on the right, North-West one mile and an half, West by North half a mile, West by South one mile and an half, West one mile; and at seven we formed our encampment.

Mr. Mackay, and one of the young men, killed two elks, and mortally wounded a buffalo, but we only took a part of the flesh of 87

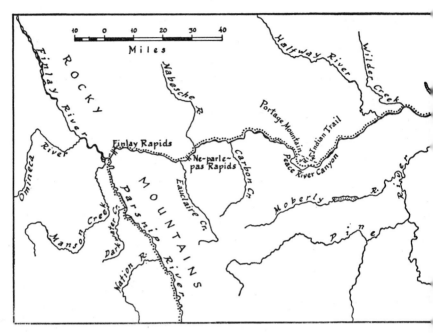

the former. The land above the spot where we encamped, spreads into an extensive plain [Bear Flat], and stretches on to a very high ridge, which, in some parts, presents a face of rock, but is principally covered with verdure, and varied with the poplar and white birch tree. The country is so crowded with animals as to have the appearance, in some places, of a stall-yard, from the state of the ground, and the quantity of dung which is scattered over it. The soil is black and light. We this day saw two grisly and hideous bears.

[May 17] It froze during the night, and the air was sharp in the morning, when we continued our course West-North-West three miles and an half, South-West by South two miles and an half, South-West by West one mile and an half, West three quarters of a mile, West-South-West one mile and a quarter, and South-West by South one mile and a half. At two in the afternoon the Rocky Mountains appeared in sight, with their summits covered with snow, bearing South-West by South: they formed a very agreeable object to every person in the canoe, as we attained the view of them much

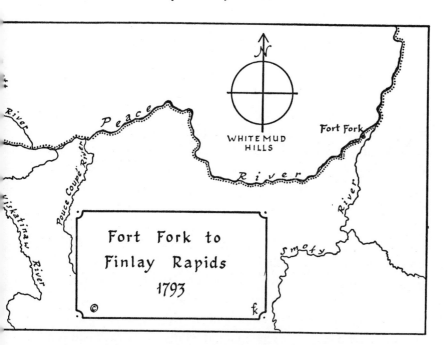

Fort Fork to
Finlay Rapids
1793

sooner than we expected. A small river [Halfway River] was seen on
our right, and we continued our progress South-West by South six
miles, when we landed at seven, which was our usual hour of encampment.

Mr. Mackay, who was walking along the side of the river, discharged his piece at a buffalo, when it burst near the muzzle, but
without any mischievous consequences. On the high grounds, which
were on the opposite side of the river, we saw a buffalo tearing up
and down with great fury, but could not discern the cause of his impetuous motions; my hunters conjectured that he had been wounded
with an arrow by some of the natives. We ascended several rapids in
the course of the day, and saw one bear.

[May 18] It again froze very hard during the night, and at four in
the morning we continued our voyage, but we had not proceeded
two hundred yards, before an accident happened to the canoe, which
did not, however, employ more than three quarters of an hour to
complete the repair. We then steered South by West one mile and 89

three quarters, South-West by South three miles, South-West by West one mile and a quarter, West by South three quarters of a mile, South-West half a mile, West by South one mile, South by West one mile and an half, South-South-West, where there is a small run of water from the right, three miles and an half, when the canoe struck on the stump of a tree, and unfortunately where the banks were so steep that there was no place to unload, except a small spot, on which we contrived to dispose the lading in the bow, which lightened the canoe so as to raise the broken part of it above the surface of the water; by which contrivance we reached a convenient situation. It required, however, two hours to complete the repair, when the weather became dark and cloudy, with thunder, lightning, and rain; we, however, continued the last course half a mile, and at six in the evening we were compelled by the rain to land for the night.

About noon we had landed on an island where there were eight [Indian] lodges of last year. The natives had prepared bark here for five canoes, and there is a road along the hills where they had passed. Branches were cut and broken along it; and they had also stripped off the bark of the trees, to get the interior rind, which forms a part of their food.

The current was very strong through the whole of the day, and the coming up along some of the banks was rendered very dangerous, from the continual falling of large stones from the upper parts of them. This place appears to be a particular pass for animals across the river, as there are paths leading to it on both sides, every ten yards.

In the course of the day we saw a ground hog, and two [double-crested] cormorants. The earth also appeared in several places to have been turned up by the bears, in search of roots.

[May 19] It rained very hard in the early part of the night, but the weather became clear towards the morning, when we embarked at our usual hour. As the current threatened to be very strong, Mr. Mackay, the two hunters, and myself, went on shore, in order to lighten the canoe, and ascended the hills, which are covered with cypress [lodgepole pine], and but little encumbered with underwood. We found a beaten path, and before we had walked a mile fell in with a herd of buffaloes, with their young ones; but I would not suffer the Indians to fire on them, from an apprehension that the report of their fowling pieces would alarm the natives that might be in the neighbourhood; for we were at this time so near the mountains, as to justify our expectation of seeing some of them. We, however, sent our dog after the herd, and a calf was soon secured by him. While the young men were skinning the animal, we heard two reports of fire-arms from the canoe, which we answered, as it was a signal for my return: we then heard another, and immediately hastened down the hill, with our veal, through a very close wood. There we met one of the men, who informed us that the canoe was at a small distance below, at the foot of a very strong rapid, and that, as several waterfalls appeared up the river, we should be obliged to unload and carry. I accordingly hastened to the canoe, and was greatly displeased that so much time had been lost, as I had given previous directions that the river should be followed as long as it was practicable. The last Indians whom we saw had informed us that at the first mountain there was a considerable succession of rapids, cascades, and falls, which they never attempted to ascend, and where they always passed over land the length of a day's march. My men imagined that the carrying place was at a small distance below us, as a path appeared to ascend a hill, where there were several lodges of the last year's construction. [This probably was the beginning of the Indian portage around the Peace River Canyon. If he had taken it he would have avoided a great deal of trouble.] The account which had been given me of the rapids, was perfectly correct: though by crossing to the other side, I must acknowledge with some risk, in such a heavy-laden canoe, the river appeared to me to be practicable, as far as we could see: the traverse [to the south (right) side of the river], therefore, was attempted, and proved successful. We now towed the canoe along an island [a long island in the river above Hudson Hope], and proceeded without any considerable difficulty till we reached the ex- 91 tremity of it, when the line could be no longer employed; and, in endeavouring to clear the point of the island, the canoe was driven with such violence on a stony shore, as to receive considerable injury. We now employed every exertion in our power to repair the breach that had been made, as well as to dry such articles of our loading as more immediately required it: we then transported the whole across the point, when we reloaded, and continued our course about three quarters of a mile. We could now proceed no further on this side of the water, and the traverse was rendered extremely dangerous, not only from the strength of the current, but by the cascades just below us, which, if we had got among them, would have involved us and the canoe in one common destruction. We had no other alternative than to return by the same course we came, or to hazard the traverse, the river on this side being bounded by a range of steep, over-hanging rocks, beneath which the current was driven on with resistless impetuosity from the cascades. Here are several islands of solid rock, covered with a small portion of verdure, which have been worn away by the constant force of the current, and occasionally, as I presume, of ice, at the water's edge, so as to be reduced in that part to one fourth the extent of the upper surface; presenting, as it were, so many large tables, each of which was supported by a pedestal of a more circumscribed projection. They are very elevated for such a situation, and afford an asylum for geese, which were at this time breeding on them. By crossing from one to the other of these islands, we came at length to the main traverse, on which we ventured, and were successful in our passage [to the north side]. Mr. Mackay, and the Indians, who observed our manoeuvres from the top of a rock, were in continual alarm for our safety, with which their own, indeed, may be said to have been nearly connected: however, the dangers that we encountered were very much augmented by the heavy loading of the canoe.

When we had effected our passage, the current on the West side was almost equally violent with that from whence we had just escaped, but the craggy bank being somewhat lower, we were enabled, with a line of sixty fathoms [three hundred sixty feet], to tow the canoe, till we came to the foot of the most rapid cascade we had hitherto seen. Here we unloaded, and carried every thing over a rocky point of a hundred and twenty paces. When the canoe was re-loaded, I, with those of my people who were not immediately em-ployed, ascended the bank, which was there, and indeed, as far as we could see it, composed of clay, stone, and a yellow gravel. My present situation was so elevated, that the men, who were coming up a strong point could not hear me, though I called to them with the utmost strength of my voice, to lighten the canoe of part of its lading. And here I could not but reflect, with infinite anxiety, on the hazard of my enterprise: one false step of those who were attached to the line, or the breaking of the line itself, would have at once consigned the canoe, and every thing it contained, to instant destruction: It, however, ascended the rapid in perfect security, but new dangers im-mediately presented themselves, for stones, both small and great, were continually rolling from the bank, so as to render the situation of those who were dragging the canoe beneath it extremely perilous; besides, they were at every step in danger, from the steepness of the ground, of falling into the water: nor was my solicitude diminished by my being necessarily removed at times from the sight of them.

In our passage through the woods, we came to an inclosure, which had been formed by the natives for the purpose of setting snares for the elk, and of which we could not discover the extent. After we had travelled for some hours through the forest, which consisted of the spruce, birch, and the largest poplars I had ever seen, we sunk down upon the river, where the bank is low, and near the foot of a moun-tain; between which, and an high ridge, the river flows in a channel of about one hundred yards broad; though, at a small distance below, it rushes on between perpendicular rocks [locally called Box Can-yon], where it is not much more than half that breadth. Here I re-mained, in great anxiety, expecting the arrival of the canoe, and after some time I sent Mr. Mackay with one of the Indians down the river in search of it, and with the other I went up it to examine what we 93 might expect in that quarter. In about a mile and a half I came to a part where the river washes the feet of lofty precipices, and presented, in the form of rapids and cascades, a succession of difficulties to our navigation. As the canoe did not come in sight we returned, and from the place where I had separated with Mr. Mackay, we saw the men carrying it over a small rocky point. We met them at the entrance of the narrow channel already mentioned; their difficulties had been great indeed, and the canoe had been broken, but they had persevered with success, and having passed the carrying-place, we proceeded with the line as far as I had already been, when we crossed over [to the south side] and encamped on the opposite beach; but there was no wood on this side of the water, as the adjacent country had been entirely over-run by fire. We saw several elks feeding on the edge of the opposite precipice, which was upwards of three hundred feet in height.

Our course to-day was about South-South-West two miles and an half, South-West half a mile, South-West by South one mile and an half, South by West half a mile, South-West half a mile, and West one mile and an half. There was a shower of hail, and some rain from flying clouds. I now dispatched a man with an Indian to visit the rapids above, when the latter soon left him to pursue a beaver, which was seen in the shallow water on the inside of a stony island; and though Mr. Mackay, and the other Indian joined him, the animal at length escaped from their pursuit. Several others were seen in the course of the day, which I by no means expected, as the banks are almost every where so much elevated above the channel of the river. Just as the obscurity of the night drew on, the man returned with an account that it would be impracticable to pass several points, as well as the super-impending promontories.

[May 20] The weather was clear with a sharp air, and we renewed our voyage at a quarter past four, on a course South-West by West three quarters of a mile. We now, with infinite difficulty, passed along the foot of a rock, which, fortunately, was not an hard stone, so that we were enabled to cut steps in it for the distance of twenty feet; from which, at the hazard of my life, I leaped on a small rock below, where I received those who followed me on my shoulders. In this manner four of us passed and dragged up the canoe, in which attempt we broke her. Very luckily, a dry tree had fallen from the rock above us, without which we could not have made a fire [to melt gum], as no wood was to be procured within a mile of the place. When the canoe was repaired, we continued towing it along the rocks to the next point, when we embarked, as we could not at present make any further use of the line, but got along the rocks of a round high island of stone, till we came to a small sandy bay. As we had already damaged the canoe, and had every reason to think that she soon would risk much greater injury, it became necessary for us to supply ourselves with bark, as our provision of that material article was almost exhausted; two men were accordingly sent to procure it, who soon returned with the necessary store.

Mr. Mackay, and the Indians who had been on shore, since we broke the canoe, were prevented from coming to us by the rugged and impassable state of the ground. We, therefore, again resumed our course with the assistance of poles, with which we pushed onwards till we came beneath a precipice, where we could not find any bottom; so that we were again obliged to have recourse to the line, the management of which was rendered not only difficult but dangerous, as the men employed in towing were under the necessity of passing on the outside of trees that grew on the edge of the precipice. We, however, surmounted this difficulty, as we had done many others, and the people who had been walking over land now joined us. They also had met with their obstacles in passing the mountain.

It now became necessary for us to make a traverse [to the north side], where the water was so rapid, that some of the people stripped themselves to their shirts that they might be the better prepared for swimming, in case any accident happened to the canoe, which they seriously apprehended; but we succeeded in our attempt without any other inconvenience, except that of taking in water. We now came to a cascade, when it was thought necessary to take out part of the lading. At noon we stopped to take an altitude, opposite to a small river that flowed in from the left: while I was thus engaged, the men went on shore to fasten the canoe, but as the current was not very strong, they had been negligent in performing this office; it proved, however, sufficiently powerful to sheer her off, and if it had not happened that one of the men, from absolute fatigue had remained and held the end of the line, we should have been deprived of every means of prosecuting our voyage, as well as of present subsistence. But notwithstanding the state of my mind on such an alarming circumstance, and an intervening cloud that interrupted me, the altitude which I took has been since proved to be tolerably correct, and gave 56. North latitude. Our last course was South-South-West two miles and a quarter.

We now continued our toilsome and perilous progress with the line West by North, and as we proceeded the rapidity of the current increased, so that in the distance of two miles we were obliged to unload four times, and carry every thing but the canoe: indeed, in many places, it was with the utmost difficulty that we could prevent her from being dashed to pieces against the rocks by the violence of the eddies. At five we had proceeded to where the river was one continued rapid. Here we again took every thing out of the canoe, in order to tow her up with the line, though the rocks were so shelving as greatly to increase the toil and hazard of that operation. At length, however, the agitation of the water was so great, that a wave striking on the bow of the canoe broke the line, and filled us with inexpressible dismay, as it appeared impossible that the vessel could escape from being dashed to pieces, and those who were in her from perishing. Another wave, however, more propitious than the former, drove her out of the tumbling water, so that the men were enabled to bring her ashore, and though she had been carried over rocks by these swells which left them naked a moment after, the canoe had received no material injury. The men were, however, in such a state from their late alarm, that it would not only have been unavailing but imprudent to have proposed any further progress at present, particularly as the river above us, as far as we could see, was one white sheet of foaming water.

That the discouragements, difficulties, and dangers, which had hitherto attended the progress of our enterprize, should have excited a wish in several of those who were engaged in it to discontinue the pursuit, might be naturally expected; and indeed it began to be muttered on all sides that there was no alternative but to return.

Instead of paying any attention to these murmurs, I desired those who had uttered them to exert themselves in gaining an ascent of the hill, and encamp there for the night. In the mean time I set off with one of the Indians, and though I continued my examination of the river almost as long as there was any light to assist me, I could see no end of the rapids and cascades: I was, therefore, perfectly satisfied, that it would be impracticable to proceed any further by water. We returned from this reconnoitring excursion very much fatigued, with our shoes worn out and wounded feet; when I found that, by felling trees on the declivity of the first hill, my people had contrived to ascend it.

He had been told about the rapids and he had seen the eastern end of the Indian carrying place, but he had not encountered anything like this canyon before and he did not realize what he was getting into. A few thousand years ago the original channel of the Peace was blocked by a glacial moraine and the river was forced into a new course. This course lay across a high ridge of resistant rock, east of the main body of the Rocky Mountains. Since then the river has cut a canyon 300 feet deep through this ridge, but in this canyon the river is much too violent to be navigated, dropping 225 feet in twenty-five miles.[18] It is worse in the upper canyon and relatively calm in the lower, so that Mackenzie was well into the canyon before he realized that he could not get through. The canyon is about twenty-five miles long, but it makes a bend. The Indian portage cut across this bend, and was only fourteen miles long.

This portage was north of the river and ran north of Portage Mountain. Mackenzie followed a shorter but much more difficult route south of Portage Mountain, between the mountain and the river. The Indian route was long used by the fur traders in later years, and the present road follows much the same route. Mackenzie was now camped at Grant Flat, about midway in the canyon.[14]

From the place where I had taken the altitude at noon, to the place where we made our landing, the river is not more than fifty yards wide, and flows between stupendous rocks, from whence huge fragments sometimes tumble down, and falling from such an height, dash into small stones, with sharp points, and form the beach between the rocky projections. Along the face of some of these precipices, there appears a stratum of a bitumenous substance which resembles coal; though while some of the pieces of it appeared to be excellent fuel, others resisted, for a considerable time, the action of fire, and did not emit the least flame. The whole of this day's course would have been altogether impracticable, if the water had been higher, which must be the case at certain seasons. We saw also several encampments of the Knisteneaux along the river, which must have been formed by them on their war excursions: a decided proof of the savage, bloodthirsty disposition of that people; as nothing less than such a spirit could impell them to encounter the difficulties of this almost inaccessible country, whose natives are equally unoffending and defenceless.

Mr. Mackay informed me, that in passing over the mountains, he observed several chasms in the earth that emitted heat and smoke, which diffused a strong sulphureous stench. I should certainly have visited this phaenomenon, if I had been sufficiently qualified as a naturalist, to have offered scientific conjectures or observations thereon. [There still are burning seams of coal in the Canyon.]

[May 21] It rained in the morning, and did not cease till about eight, and as the men had been very fatigued and disheartened, I suffered them to continue their rest till that hour. Such was the state of the river, as I have already observed, that no alternative was left us; nor did any means of proceeding present themselves to us, but the passage of the mountain over which we were to carry the canoe as well as the baggage. As this was a very alarming enterprize, I dispatched Mr. Mackay with three men and the two Indians to proceed in a straight course from the top of the mountain, and to keep the line of the river till they should find it navigable. If it should be their opinion, that there was no practicable passage in that direction, two of them were instructed to return in order to make their report; while the others were to go in search of the Indian carrying-place. While they were engaged in this excursion, the people who remained with me were employed in gumming the canoe, and making handles for the axes. At noon I got an altitude, which made our latitude 56. 0. 8. At three o'clock had time, when my watch was slow 1. 31. 32. apparent time.

At sun-set, Mr. Mackay returned with one of the men, and in about two hours was followed by the others. They had penetrated thick woods, asscended hills, and sunk into vallies, till they got beyond the rapids, which, according to their calculation, was a distance of three leagues. The two parties returned by different routes, but they both agreed, that with all its difficulties, and they were of a very alarming nature, the outward course was that which must be preferred. Unpromising, however, as the account of their expedition appeared, it did not sink them into a state of discouragement; and a kettle of wild rice, sweetened with sugar, which had been prepared for their return, with their usual regale of rum, soon renewed that courage which disdained all obstacles that threatened our progress: and they went to rest, with a full determination to surmount them on the morrow. I sat up in the hope of getting an observation of Jupiter and his first satellite, but the cloudy weather prevented my obtaining it.

[May 22] At break of day we entered on the extraordinary journey which was to occupy the remaining part of it. The men began, without delay, to cut a road up the mountain, and as the trees were but 99 of small growth, I ordered them to fell those which they found convenient, in such a manner, that they might fall parallel with the road, but, at the same time, not separate them entirely from the stumps, so that they might form a kind of railing on either side. The baggage was now brought from the waterside to our encampment. This was likewise from the steep shelving of the rocks, a very perilous undertaking, as one false step of any of the people employed in it, would have been instantly followed by falling headlong into the water. When this important object was attained, the whole of the party proceeded with no small degree of apprehension, to fetch the canoe, which, in a short time, was also brought to the encampment; and, as soon as we had recovered from our fatigue, we advanced with it up the mountain, having the line doubled and fastened successively as we went on to the stumps; while a man at the end of it, hauled it round a tree, holding it on and shifting it as we proceeded; so that we may be said, with strict truth, to have warped the canoe up the mountain: indeed by a general and most laborious exertion, we got every thing to the summit by two in the afternoon. At noon, the latitude was 56. 0. 47. North. At five, I sent the men to cut the road onwards, which they effected for about a mile, when they returned.

The weather was cloudy at intervals, with showers and thunder. At about ten, I observed an emersion of Jupiter's second satellite; time by the achrometer 8. 32. 20. by which I found the longitude to be 120. 29. 30. West from Greenwich.

[May 23] The weather was clear at four this morning, when the men began to carry. I joined Mr. Mackay, and the two Indians in the labour of cutting a road. The ground continued rising gently till noon, when it began to decline; but though on such an elevated situation, we could see but little, as mountains of a still higher elevation and covered with snow were seen far above us in every direction. In the afternoon the ground became very uneven; hills and deep defiles alternately presented themselves to us. Our progress, however, exceeded my expectation, and it was not till four in the afternoon that the carriers overtook us. At five, in a state of fatigue that may be more readily conceived than expressed, we encamped near a rivulet or spring that issued from beneath a large mass of ice and snow.

Our toilsome journey of this day I compute at about three miles; along the first of which the land is covered with plenty of wood consisting of large trees, encumbered with little underwood, through which it was by no means difficult to open a road, by following a well-beaten elk path: for the two succeeding miles we found the country overspread with the trunks of trees, laid low by fire some years ago; among which large copses had sprung up of a close growth, and intermixed with briars, so as to render the passage through them painful and tedious. The soil in the woods is light and of a dusky colour; that in the burned country is a mixture of sand and clay with small stones. The trees are spruce, red-pine, cypress, poplar, white birch, willow, alder, arrow-wood, red-wood, liard [balsam poplar], service-tree, bois-picant [devil's club], &c. I never saw any of the last kind before. It rises to about nine feet in height, grows in joints without branches, and is tufted at the extremity. The stem is of an equal size from the bottom to the top, and does not exceed an inch in diameter; it is covered with small prickles, which caught our trowsers, and working through them, sometimes found their way to the flesh. The shrubs are the gooseberry, the currant, and several kinds of briars.

[May 24] We continued our very laborious journey, which led us down some steep hills, and through a wood of tall pines. After much toil and trouble in bearing the canoe through the difficult passages which we encountered, at four in the afternoon we arrived at the river, some hundred yards above the rapids or falls, with all our baggage. I compute the distance of this day's progress to be about four miles; indeed I should have measured the whole of the way, if I had not been obliged to engage personally in the labour of making the road. But after all, the Indian carrying way, whatever may be its length, and I think it cannot exceed ten miles, will always be found more safe and expeditious than the passage which our toil and perseverance formed and surmounted. [They had now reached the head of the Canyon, and could travel by canoe again. Years later Cust's House would be established here to serve traders using Rocky Mountain Portage.]

Those of my people who visited this place on the 21st, were of opinion that the water had risen very much since that time. About two hundred yards below us the stream rushed with an astonishing but silent velocity, between perpendicular rocks, which are not more than thirty-five yards asunder: when the water is high, it runs over those rocks, in a channel three times that breadth, where it is bounded by far more elevated precipices. In the former are deep round holes [pot holes], some of which are full of water, while others are empty, in whose bottom are small round stones, as smooth as marble. Some of these natural cylinders would contain two hundred gallons. At a small distance below the first of these rocks, the channel widens in a kind of zig-zag progression; and it was really awful to behold with what infinite force the water drives against the rocks on one side, and with what impetuous strength it is repelled to the other: it then falls back, as it were, into a more strait but rugged passage, over which it is tossed in high, foaming, half-formed billows, as far as the eye could follow it.

The young men informed me that this was the place where their relations had told me that I should meet with a fall equal to that of Niagara: to exculpate them, however, from their apparent misinformation, they declared that their friends were not accustomed to utter falsehoods, and that the fall had probably been destroyed by the force of the water. It is, however, very evident that those people had not been here, or did not adhere to the truth. By the number of trees which appeared to have been felled with axes, we discovered that the Knisteneaux, or some tribes who are known to employ that instrument, had passed this way. We passed through a snare inclosure, but saw no animals, though the country was very much intersected by their tracks.

[May 25] It rained throughout the night, and till twelve this day; while the business of preparing great and small poles, and putting the canoe in order, &c. caused us to remain here till five in the afternoon. I now attached a knife, with a steel, flint, beads, and other trifling articles to a pole, which I erected, and left as a token of amity to the natives. When I was making this arrangement, one of my attendants, whom I have already described under the title of the Cancre, added to my assortment a small round piece of green wood, chewed at one end in the form of a brush, which the Indians use to pick the marrow out of bones. This he informed me was an emblem of a country abounding in animals. The water had risen during our stay here one foot and an half perpendicular height.

We now embarked, and our course was North-West one mile and three quarters. There were mountains on all sides of us, which were covered with snow: one in particular, on the South side of the river, rose to a great height. [This probably was Mount Gething. They were now coming into the Rocky Mountains proper.] We continued to proceed West three quarters of a mile, North-West one mile, and West-South-West a quarter of a mile, when we encamped for the night. The Cancre killed a small elk.

[May 26] The weather was clear and sharp, and between three and four in the morning we renewed our voyage, our first course being West by South three miles and an half, when the men complained of the cold in their fingers, as they were obliged to push on the canoe with the poles. Here a small river flowed in from the North [Aylard Creek?]. We now continued to steer West-South-West a quarter of a mile, West-North-West a mile and an half, and West two miles, when we found ourselves on a parallel with a chain of mountains on both sides the river, running South and North. The river, both yesterday and the early part of to-day, was from four to eight hundred yards wide, and full of islands, but was at this time diminished to about two hundred yards broad, and free from islands, with a smooth but strong current. Our next course was South-West two miles, when we encountered a rapid, and saw an encampment of the Knisteneaux. We now proceeded North-West by West one mile among islands, South-West by West three quarters of a mile, South-South-East one 103 mile, veered to South-West through islands three miles and an half, and South by East half a mile. Here a river [Carbon Creek] poured in on the left, which was the most considerable that we had seen since we had passed the mountain. At seven in the evening we landed and encamped.

Though the sun had shone upon us throughout the day, the air was so cold that the men, though actively employed, could not resist it without the aid of their blanket coats. This circumstance might in some degree be expected from the surrounding mountains, which were covered with ice and snow; but as they are not so high as to produce the extreme cold which we suffered, it must be more particularly attributed to the high situation of the country itself, rather than to the local elevation of the mountains, the greatest height of which does not exceed fifteen hundred feet; though in general they do not rise to half that altitude. But as I had not been able to take an exact measurement, I do not presume upon the accuracy of my conjecture. Towards the bottom of these heights, which were clear of snow, the trees were putting forth their leaves, while those in their middle region still retained all the characteristics of winter, and on their upper parts there was little or no wood.

[May 27] * The weather was clear, and we continued our voyage at the usual hour, when we successively found several rapids and points to impede our progress. At noon our latitude was 56. 5. 54. North. The Indians killed a stag; and one of the men who went to fetch it was very much endangered by the rolling down of a large stone from the heights above him.

[May 28] The day was very cloudy. The mountains on both sides of the river seemed to have sunk, in their elevation, during the voyage of yesterday. To-day they resumed their former altitude, and ran so

---

* From this day to the 4th of June, the courses of my voyage are omitted, as I lost the book that contained them. I was in the habit of sometimes indulging myself with a short doze in the canoe, and I imagine that the branches of the trees brushed my book from me, when I was in such a situation, which renders the account of these few days less distinct than usual.

close on either side of the channel, that all view was excluded of every thing but themselves. This part of the current was not broken by islands; but in the afternoon we approached cascades [Ne-parle-pas Rapids], which obliged us to carry our canoe and its lading for several hundred yards. Here we observed an encampment of the natives, though some time had elapsed since it had been inhabited. The greater part of the day was divided between heavy showers and small rain; and we took our station on the shore about six in the evening, about three miles above the last rapid.

[May 29] The rain was so violent throughout the whole of this day, that we did not venture to proceed. As we had almost expended the contents of a rum keg, and this being a day which allowed of no active employment, I amused myself with the experiment of inclosing a letter in it, and dispatching it down the stream, to take its fate. I accordingly introduced a written account of all our hardships, &c. carefully inclosed in bark, into the small barrel by the bung-hole, which being carefully secured, I consigned this epistolary cargo to the mercy of the current.

[May 30] We were alarmed this morning at break of day, by the continual barking of our dog, who never ceased from running backwards and forwards in the rear of our situation: when, however, the day advanced, we discovered the cause of our alarm to proceed from a wolf, who was parading a ridge a few yards behind us, and had been most probably allured by the scent of our small portion of fresh meat. The weather was cloudy, but it did not prevent us from renewing our progress at a very early hour. A considerable river [Eauclaire or Clearwater Creek] appeared from the left, and we continued our course till seven in the evening, when we landed at night where there was an Indian encampment.

[May 31] The morning was clear and cold, and the current very powerful. On crossing the mouth of a river [Bernard Creek] that flowed in from the right of us, we were very much endangered; indeed all the rivers which I have lately seen, appear to overflow their natural limits, as it may be supposed, from the melting of the mountain snow. The water is almost white, the bed of the river being of lime-stone. [The white color was caused by "glacial flour"—rock powdered by glaciers in the mountains.] The mountains are one solid mass of the same materials, but without the least shade of trees, or decoration of foliage. At nine the men were so cold that we landed, in order to kindle a fire, which was considered as a very uncommon circumstance at this season; a small quantity of rum, however, served as an adequate substitute; and the current being so smooth as to admit of the use of paddles, I encouraged them to proceed without any further delay. In a short time an extensive view opened upon us, displaying a beautiful sheet of water, that was heightened by the calmness of the weather, and a splendid sun. Here the mountains, which were covered with wood, opened on either side, so that we entertained the hope of soon leaving them behind us. When we had got to the termination of this prospect, the river was barred with rocks, forming cascades and small islands [Finlay Rapids]. To proceed onwards, we were under the necessity of clearing a narrow passage of the drift wood, on the left shore. Here the view convinced us that our late hopes were without foundation, as there appeared a ridge or chain of mountains, running South and North as far as the eye could reach.

Now they had passed through the Rocky Mountains, which are much lower here than farther south. They had expected to cross one mountain range and then have a clear route to the sea, but now they found that it would not be so easy. All of them were accustomed to the flat or rolling country to the east, and they could not conceive of the great jumble of high mountain ranges that lay between them and their goal. Perhaps it was just as well. The chain of mountains that lay ahead was the Omineca Mountains.

On advancing two or three miles, we arrived at the fork, one branch [Finlay River] running about West-North-West, and the other [Parsnip River] South-South-East. If I had been governed by my own judgment, I should have taken the former, as it appeared to me to be the most likely to bring us nearest to the part where I wished to fall on the Pacific Ocean; but the old man, whom I have already mentioned as having been frequently on war expeditions in this country, had warned me not, on any account, to follow it, as it was soon lost in various branches among the mountains, and that there was no great river than ran in any direction near it; but by following the latter, he said, we should arrive at a carrying-place to another large river, that did not exceed a day's march, where the inhabitants build houses, and live upon islands. There was so much apparent truth in the old man's narrative, that I determined to be governed by it; for I did not entertain the least doubt, if I could get into the other river, that I should reach the ocean.

I accordingly ordered my steersman to proceed at once to the East branch [Parsnip River], which appeared to be more rapid than the other, though it did not possess an equal breadth. These circumstances disposed my men and the Indians, the latter in particular being very tired of the voyage, to express their wishes that I should take the Western branch, especially when they perceived the difficulty of stemming the current, in the direction on which I had determined. Indeed the rush of water was so powerful, that we were the greatest part of the afternoon in getting two or three miles—a very tardy and mortifying progress, and which, with the voyage, was openly execrated by many of those who were engaged in it: and the inexpressible toil these people had endured, as well as the dangers they had encountered, required some degree of consideration; I therefore employed those arguments which were the best calculated to calm their immediate discontents, as well as to encourage their future hopes, though, at the same time, I delivered my sentiments in such a manner as to convince them that I was determined to proceed.

This was one of the major decisions of the voyage—whether to take the easier and more promising Finlay River to the   107 north or the less inviting Parsnip River to the south. Against his own judgment and that of his men Mackenzie decided to follow the directions of the old Indian. It was a difficult decision, but the right one. He could conceivably have gotten through to the sea via the Finlay, but men who know the country think it unlikely. Because of his decision he had to endure the complaints of his men, and even worse his own doubts, until he finally reached the great river that he was seeking.

[June 1] On the 1st of June we embarked at sun-rise, and towards noon the current began to slacken; we then put to shore, in order to gum the canoe, when a meridian altitude gave me 55. 42. 16. North latitude. We then continued our course, and towards the evening the current began to recover its former strength. Mr. Mackay and the Indians had already disembarked, to walk and lighten the boat. At sun-set we encamped on a point, being the first dry land which had been found on this side the river, that was fit for our purpose, since our people went on shore. In the morning we passed a large rapid river [Darkwater or Blackwater Creek], that flowed in from the right.

In no part of the North-West did I see so much beaver-work, within an equal distance, as in the course of this day. In some places they had cut down several acres of large poplars, and we saw also a great number of these active and sagacious animals. The time which these wonderful creatures allot for their labours, whether in erecting their curious habitations or providing food, is the whole of the interval between the setting and the rising sun.

Towards the dusky part of the evening we heard several discharges from the fowling pieces of our people, which we answered, to inform them of our situation; and some time after it was dark, they arrived in an equal state of fatigue and alarm: they were also obliged to swim across a channel in order to get to us, as we were situated on an island, though we were ignorant of the circumstance, till they came to inform us. One of the Indians was positive that he heard the discharge of fire arms above our encampment; and on comparing the number of our discharges with theirs, there appeared to be some foundation for his alarm, as we imagined that we heard two reports more than they acknowledged; and, in their turn, they declared that they had heard twice the number of those which we knew had proceeded from us. The Indians were therefore certain, that the Knisteneaux must be in our vicinity, on a war expedition, and consequently, if they were numerous, we should have had no reason to expect the least mercy from them in this distant country. Though I did not believe that circumstance, or that any of the natives could be in possession of fire-arms, I thought it right, at all events, we should be prepared. Our fusees [light muskets] were, therefore, primed and loaded, and, having extinguished our fire, each of us took his station at the foot of a tree, where we passed an uneasy and restless night.

[June 2] The succeeding morning being clear and pleasant, we proceeded at an early hour against a rapid current, intersected by islands. About eight we passed two large trees, whose roots having been undermined by the current, had recently fallen into the river; and, in my opinion, the crash of their fall had occasioned the noise which caused our late alarm. In this manner the water ravages the islands in these rivers, and by driving down great quantities of wood, forms the foundations of others. The men were so oppressed with fatigue, that it was necessary they should encamp at six in the afternoon. We, therefore, landed on a sandy island, which is a very uncommon object, as the greater part of the islands consist of a bottom of round stones and gravel, covered from three to ten feet with mud and old drift-wood. Beaver-work was as frequently seen as on the preceding day.

[June 3] On the 3d of June we renewed our voyage with the rising sun. At noon I obtained a meridian altitude, which gave 55. 22. 3. North latitude. I also took time, and the watch was slow 1. 30. 14. apparent time. According to my calculation, this place is about twenty-five miles South-East of the fork.*

[June 4] We embarked this morning at four in a very heavy fog. The water had been continually rising, and, in many places, over-flowed its banks. The current also was so strong, that our progress was very tedious, and required the most laborious exertions.

Our course was this day, South-South-East one mile, South-South-West half a mile, South-East three quarters of a mile, North-East by East three quarters of a mile, South-East half a mile, South-East by South one mile, South-South-East one mile three quarters, South-East by South half a mile, East by South a quarter of a mile, South-East three quarters of a mile, North-East by East half a mile, East by North a quarter of a mile, South-East half a mile, South-East by South a quarter of a mile, South-East by East half a mile, North-East by East half a mile, North-North-East three quarters of a mile, and South by East one mile and an half.

We could not find a place fit for an encampment, till nine at night, when we landed on a bank of gravel, of which little more appeared above water than the spot we occupied.

[June 5] This morning we found our canoe and baggage in the water, which had continued rising during the night. We then gummed the canoe, as we arrived at too late an hour to perform that operation on the preceding evening. This necessary business being completed, we traversed to the North shore, where I disembarked with Mr. Mackay and the hunters, in order to ascend an adjacent mountain, with the hope of obtaining a view of the interior part of the country. I directed my people to proceed with all possible dili-gence, and that, if they met with any accident, or found my return necessary, they should fire two guns. They also understood, that when they should hear the same signal from me, they were to an-swer, and wait for me, if I were behind them.

---

* I shall now proceed with my usual regularity, which, as I have already mentioned, has been, for some days, suspended, from the loss of my book of observation.

When we had ascended to the summit of the hill, we found that it extended onwards in an even, level country; so that, encumbered as we were with the thick wood, no distant view could be obtained: I therefore climbed a very lofty tree, from whose top I discerned on the right a ridge of mountains [Omineca Mountains?] covered with snow, bearing about North-West; from thence another ridge of high land, whereon no snow was visible, stretched towards the South; between which and the snowy hills [Rocky Mountains] on the East side, there appeared to be an opening, which we determined to be the course of the river.

Having obtained all the satisfaction that the nature of the place would admit, we proceeded forward to overtake the canoe, and after a warm walk came down upon the river, when we discharged our pieces twice, but received no answering signal. I was of opinion, that the canoe was before us, while the Indians entertained an opposite notion. I, however, crossed another point of land, and came again to the waterside about ten. Here we had a long view of the river, which circumstance excited in my mind some doubts of my former sentiments. We repeated our signals, but without any return; and as every moment now increased my anxiety, I left Mr. Mackay and one of the Indians at this spot to make a large fire, and send branches adrift down the current as notices of our situation, if the canoe was behind us, and proceeded with the other Indian across a very long point, where the river makes a considerable bend, in order that I might be satisfied if the canoe was a-head. Having been accustomed for the last fortnight to very cold weather, I found the heat of this day almost insupportable, as our way lay over a dry sand, which was relieved by no shade, but such as a few scattered cypresses could afford us. About twelve we arrived once more at the river, and the discharge of our pieces was as unsuccessful as it had hitherto been. The water rushed before us with uncommon velocity, and we also tried the experiment of sending fresh branches down it. To add to the disagreeableness of our situation, the gnats and musquitoes appeared in swarms to torment us. When we returned to our companions, we found that they had not been contented with remaining in the position where I left them, but had been three or four miles down the river, and were come back to their station, without having made any discovery of the people on the water.

Various very unpleasing conjectures at once perplexed and distressed us: the Indians, who are inclined to magnify evils of any and every kind, had at once consigned the canoe and every one on board it to the bottom, and were already settling a plan to return upon a raft, as well as calculating the number of nights that would be required to reach their home. As for myself, it will be easily believed, that my mind was in a state of extreme agitation; and the imprudence of my conduct in leaving the people in such a situation of danger and toilsome exertion, added a very painful mortification to the severe apprehensions I already suffered: it was an act of indiscretion which might have put an end to the voyage that I had so much at heart, and compelled me at length to submit to the scheme which my hunters had already formed for our return.

At half past six in the evening, Mr. Mackay and the Cancre set off to proceed down the river, as far as they could before the night came on, and to continue their journey in the morning to the place where we had encamped the preceding evening. I also proposed to make my excursion upwards; and, if we both failed of success in meeting the canoe, it was agreed that we should return to the place where we now separated.

In this situation we had wherewithal to drink in plenty, but with solid food we were totally unprovided. We had not seen even a partridge [grouse] throughout the day, and the tracks of rein-deer that we had discovered were of an old date. We were, however, preparing to make a bed of the branches of trees, where we should have had no other canopy than that afforded us by the heavens, when we heard a shot, and soon after another, which was the notice agreed upon, if Mr. Mackay and the Indian should see the canoe: that fortunate circumstance was also confirmed by a return of the signal from the people. I was, however, so fatigued from the heat and exercise of the day, as well as incommoded from drinking so much cold water, that I did not wish to remove till the following morning; but the Indian made such bitter complaints of the cold and hunger which he suffered, that I complied with his solicitations to depart, and it was almost dark when we reached the canoe, barefooted, and drenched with rain. But these inconveniences affected me very little, when I saw myself once more surrounded with my people. They informed me, that the canoe had been broken, and that they had this day experienced much greater toil and hardships than on any former occasion. I thought it prudent to affect a belief of every representation that they made, and even to comfort each of them with a consolatory dram: for, however difficult the passage might have been, it was too short to have occupied the whole day, if they had not relaxed in their exertions. The rain was accompanied with thunder and lightning.

It appeared from the various encampments which we had seen, and from several paddles we had found, that the natives frequent this part of the country at the latter end of the summer and the fall. The course to-day was nearly East-South-East two miles and an half, South by West one mile, South-South-East one mile and an half, East two miles, and South-East by South one mile.

[June 6] At half past four this morning we continued our voyage, our courses being South-East by South one mile, East by South three quarters of a mile, South-East by East two miles. The whole of this distance we proceeded by hauling the canoe from branch to branch. The current was so strong, that it was impossible to stem it with the paddles; the depth was too great to receive any assistance from the poles, and the bank of the river was so closely lined with willows and other trees, that it was impossible to employ the line. As it was past twelve before we could find a place that would allow of our landing, I could not get a meridian altitude. We occupied the rest of the day in repairing the canoe, drying our cloaths, and making paddles and poles to replace those which had been broken or lost.

[June 7] The morning was clear and calm, and since we had been 113

at this station the water had risen two inches; so that the current became still stronger, and its velocity had already been so great as to
justify our despair in getting up it, if we had not been so long accustomed to surmount it. I last night observed an emersion of Jupiter's first satellite, but inadvertently went to bed, without commiting
the exact time to writing; if my memory is correct, it was 8. 18. 10.
by the time-piece. The canoe, which had been little better than a
wreck, being now repaired, we proceeded

East two miles and a quarter, South-South-East half a mile, South-East a
quarter of a mile, where we landed to take an altitude for time. We continued our route at South-East by East three quarters of a mile, and landed
again to determine the latitude, which is 55. 2. 51. To this I add, 2. 45.
Southing, which will make the place of taking altitude for time 55. 5. 36.
with which I find that my time-piece was slow 1. 32. 23. apparent time,
and made the longitude obtained 122. 35. 50. West of Greenwich.

From this place we proceeded East by South four miles and an half,
East-South-East one mile and a half, in which space there falls in a small
river from the East; East half a mile, South-East a mile and an half, East
a quarter of a mile,

and encamped at seven o'clock. Mr. Mackay and the hunters walked
the greatest part of the day, and in the course of their excursion
killed a porcupine.* Here we found the bed of a very large bear quite
fresh. During the day several Indian encampments were seen, which
were of a late erection. The current had also lost some of its impetuosity during the greater part of the day.

[June 8] It rained and thundered throughout the night, and at
four in the morning we again encountered the current.

Our course was East a quarter of a mile, round to South by East along a
very high white sandy bank on the East shore three quarters of a mile,

---

* We had been obliged to indulge our hunters with sitting idle in the canoe,
lest their being compelled to share in the labour of navigating it should disgust
and drive them from us. We, therefore, employed them as much as possible on
shore, as well to procure provisions as to lighten the canoe.

South-South-East a quarter of a mile, South-South-West a quarter of a mile, South-South-East one mile and a quarter, South-East two miles, with a slack current; South-East by East two miles and a quarter, East a quarter of a mile, South-South-East a quarter of a mile, South-East by South four miles and an half, South-East one mile and an half, South-South-West half a mile, East-North-East half a mile, East-South-East a quarter of a mile, South-East by South one mile, South-East by East half a mile, East by South three quarters of a mile,

when the mountains were in full view, in this direction and East-ward. For the three last days we could only see them at short intervals and long distances; but till then, they were continually in sight on either side, from our entrance into the fork. Those to the left were at no great distance from us.

For the last two days we had been anxiously looking out for the carrying-place, but could not discover it, and our only hope was in such information as we should be able to procure from the natives. All that remained for us to do, was to push forwards till the river should be no longer navigable: it had now, indeed, overflowed its banks, so that it was eight at night before we could discover a place to encamp. Having found plenty of wild parsneps [cow parsnips], we gathered the tops, and boiled them with pemmican for our supper.

[June 9] The rain of this morning terminated in a heavy mist at half past five, when we embarked and steered

South-East one mile and an half, when it veered North-North-East half a mile, South-East three quarters of a mile, East by South three quarters of a mile, East-South-East a quarter of a mile, South-South-East a quarter of a mile, South-East by East one mile, North-East by East half a mile, South-East by East half a mile, South-East by South three quarters of a mile, South-East three quarters of a mile, East by South half a mile, South-East by East half a mile, East-North-East three quarters of a mile, when it veered to South-South-East half a mile, then back to East (when a blue mountain, clear of snow, appeared a-head) one mile and an half; North-

East by East half a mile, East by North one mile, when it veered to South-East half a mile, then on to North-West three quarters of a mile, and back to North-East by East half a mile, South by West a quarter of a mile, North-East by East to North-North-East half a mile, South-South-East a quarter of a mile, and East by North half a mile:

here we perceived a smell of fire, and in a short time heard people in the woods, as if in a state of great confusion, which was occasioned, as we afterwards understood, by their discovery of us. [These were Sekani Indians, and this probably was the tribe's first encounter with white men.] At the same time this unexpected circumstance produced some little discomposure among ourselves, as our arms were not in a state of preparation, and we were as yet unable to ascertain the number of the party. I considered, that if there were but few it would be needless to pursue them, as it would not be probable that we should overtake them in these thick woods; and if they were numerous, it would be an act of great imprudence to make the attempt, at least during their present alarm. I therefore ordered my people to strike off to the opposite side, that we might see if any of them had sufficient courage to remain; but, before we were half over the river, which, in this part, is not more than an hundred yards wide, two men appeared on a rising ground over against us, brandishing their spears, displaying their bows and arrows, and accompanying their hostile gestures with loud vociferations. My interpreter did not hesitate to assure them, that they might dispel their apprehensions, as we were white people, who meditated no injury, but were, on the contrary, desirous of demonstrating every mark of kindness and friendship. They did not, however, seem disposed to confide in our declarations, and actually threatened, if we came over before they were more fully satisfied of our peaceable intentions, that they would discharge their arrows at us. This was a decided kind of conduct which I did not expect; at the same time I readily complied with their proposition, and after some time had passed in hearing and answering their questions, they consented to our landing,

though not without betraying very evident symptoms of fear and dis-
trust. They, however, laid aside their weapons, and, when I stepped
forward and took each of them by the hand, one of them, but with
a very tremulous action, drew his knife from his sleeve, and presented it to me as a mark of his submission to my will and pleasure.
On our first hearing the noise of these people in the woods, we displayed our flag, which was now shewn to them as a token of friendship. They examined us, and every thing about us, with a minute
and suspicious attention. They had heard, indeed, of white men, but
this was the first time that they had ever seen an human being of a
complexion different from their own. The party had been here but a
few hours, nor had they yet erected their sheds; and, except the two
men now with us, they had all fled, leaving their little property behind them. To those which had given us such a proof of their confidence, we paid the most conciliating attentions in our power. One
of them I sent to recall his people, and the other, for very obvious
reasons, we kept with us. In the mean time the canoe was unloaded,
the necessary baggage carried up the hill, and the tents pitched.

Here I determined to remain till the Indians became so familiar-
ized with us, as to give all the intelligence which we imagined might
be obtained from them. In fact, it had been my intention to land
where I might most probably discover the carrying-place, which was
our more immediate object, and undertake marches of two or three
days, in different directions, in search of another river. If unsuccessful in this attempt, it was my purpose to continue my progress up the
present river, as far as it was navigable, and if we did not meet with
natives to instruct us in our further progress, I had determined to return to the fork, and take the other branch, with the hope of better
fortune. [He still was not sure that he had taken the right branch.
They had been struggling up the Parsnip for more than a week and
had seen no sign of the promised portage. If he failed to find it, he
would return to the forks and go up the Finlay.]

It was about three in the afternoon when we landed, and at five
the whole party of Indians were assembled. It consisted only of three 117

men, three women, and seven or eight boys and girls. With their scratched legs, bleeding feet, and dishevelled hair, as in the hurry of their flight they had left their shoes and leggins behind them, they displayed a most wretched appearance: they were consoled, however, with beads, and other trifles, which seemed to please them; they had pemmican also given them to eat, which was not unwelcome, and in our opinion, at least, superior to their own provision, which consisted entirely of dried fish.

The Sekanis were one of the most miserable groups of Indians. Their country was the bleak northern forest, with little fish and less game. They had formerly lived in the rich buffalo country east of the Rockies, but had been driven out by their stronger relatives, the Beavers. The salmon-rich country to the west was preëmpted by the Carriers. The Sekanis got a few European goods in trade with the Carriers, but could get no guns. They had to feed and defend themselves as well as they could with the meager resources of their country. It is not surprising that there were so few of them.

When I thought that they were sufficiently composed, I sent for the men to my tent, to gain such information respecting the country as I concluded it was in their power to afford me. But my expectations were by no means satisfied: they said that they were not acquainted with any river to the Westward, but that there was one from whence they were just arrived, over a carrying-place of eleven days march, which they represented as being a branch only of the river before us. Their ironwork they obtained from the people who inhabit the bank of that river, and an adjacent lake, in exchange for beaver skins, and dressed moose skins. They represented the latter as travelling, during a moon [month], to get to the country of other tribes, who live in houses, with whom they traffic for the same commodities; and that these also extend their journies in the same manner to the sea coast, or, to use their expression, the Stinking Lake, where they trade with people like us, who come there in vessels as big as islands. They added, that the people to the Westward, as they have been told, are very numerous. Those who inhabit the other branch they stated as consisting of about forty families, while they themselves did not amount to more than a fourth of that number; and were almost continually compelled to remain in their strong holds, where they sometimes perished with cold and hunger, to secure themselves from their enemies, who never failed to attack them whenever an opportunity presented itself. [This account is not clear. The Sekanis of the Parsnip River traded largely with the Carriers of the upper Fraser River,[15] and perhaps they had just come from there, though that is not a branch of the Parsnip.]

This account of the country, from a people who I had every reason to suppose were well acquainted with every part of it, threatened to disconcert the project on which my heart was set, and in which my whole mind was occupied. It occurred to me, however, that from fear, or other motives, they might be tardy in their communication; I therefore assured them that, if they would direct me to the river which I described to them, I would come in large vessels, like those that their neighbours had described, to the mouth of it, and bring them arms and ammunition in exchange for the produce of their country; so that they might be able to defend themselves against their enemies, and no longer remain in that abject, distressed, and fugitive state in which they then lived. I added also, that in the mean time, if they would, on my return, accompany me below the mountains, to a country which was very abundant in animals, I would furnish them and their companions with every thing they might want, and make peace between them and the Beaver Indians. But all these promises did not appear to advance the object of my inquiries, and they still persisted in their ignorance of any such river as I had mentioned, that discharged itself into the sea.

In this state of perplexity and disappointment, various projects presented themselves to my mind, which were no sooner formed than they were discovered to be impracticable, and were consequently abandoned. At one time I thought of leaving the canoe, and every thing it contained, to go over land, and pursue that chain of connexion by which these people obtain their iron-work; but a very brief course of reflection convinced me that it would be impossible for us to carry provisions for our support through any considerable part of such a journey, as well as presents, to secure us a kind reception among the natives, and ammunition for the service of the hunters, and to defend ourselves against any act of hostility. At another time my solicitude for the success of the expedition incited a wish to remain with the natives, and go to the sea by the way they had described; but the accomplishment of such a journey, even if no accident should interpose, would have required a portion of time which it was not in my power to bestow. In my present state of information, to proceed further up the river was considered as a fruitless waste of toilsome exertion; and to return unsuccessful, after all our labour, sufferings, and dangers, was an idea too painful to indulge. Besides, I could not yet abandon the hope that the Indians might not yet be sufficiently composed and confident, to disclose their real knowledge of the country freely and fully to me. Nor was I altogether without my doubts respecting the fidelity of my interpreter, who, being very much tired of the voyage, might be induced to withhold those communications which would induce me to continue it. I therefore continued my attentions to the natives, regaled them with such provisions as I had, indulged their children with a taste of sugar, and determined to suspend my conversation with them till the following morning. On my expressing a desire to partake of their fish, they brought me a few dried trout, well cured, that had been taken in the river which they lately left. One of the men also brought me five beaver skins, as a present.

[June 10] The solicitude that possessed my mind interrupted my repose; when the dawn appeared I had already quitted my bed, and was waiting with impatience for another conference with the natives. The sun, however, had risen before they left their leafy bowers, whither they had retired with their children, having most hospitably resigned their beds, and the partners of them, to the solicitations of my young men.

I now repeated my inquiries, but my perplexity was not removed by any favourable variation in their answers. About nine, however, one of them, still remaining at my fire, in conversation with the interpreters, I understood enough of his language to know that he mentioned something about a great river, at the same time pointing significantly up that which was before us. On my inquiring of the interpreter respecting that expression, I was informed that he knew of a large river [Fraser River] that runs towards the mid-day sun, a branch of which flowed near the source of that which we were now navigating; and that there were only three small lakes, and as many carrying-places, leading to a small river, which discharges itself into the great river, but that the latter did not empty itself into the sea. The inhabitants, he said, built houses, lived on islands, and were a numerous and warlike people. I desired him to describe the road to the other river, by delineating it with a piece of coal on a strip of bark, which he accomplished to my satisfaction. The opinion that the river did not discharge itself into the sea, I very confidently imputed to his ignorance of the country.

My hopes were now renewed, and an object presented itself which awakened my utmost impatience. To facilitate its attainment, one of the Indians was induced, by presents, to accompany me as a guide to the first inhabitants, which we might expect to meet on the small lakes in our way. I accordingly resolved to depart with all expedition, and while my people were making every necessary preparation, I employed myself in writing the following description of the natives around me:

They are low in stature, not exceeding five feet six or seven inches; and they are of that meagre appearance which might be expected in a people whose life is one succession of difficulties, in procuring subsistence. Their faces are round, with high cheek bones; and their eyes, which are small, are of a dark brown colour; the cartilage of their nose is perforated, but without any ornaments suspended from   121 it; their hair is of a dingy black, hanging loose and in disorder over their shoulders, but irregularly cut in front, so as not to obstruct the sight; their beards are eradicated, with the exception of a few straggling hairs, and their complexion is a swarthy yellow.

Their dress consists of robes made of the skins of the beaver, the ground hog, and the rein-deer, dressed in the hair, and of the moose-skin without it. All of them are ornamented with a fringe, while some of them have tassels hanging down the seams; those of the ground hog are decorated on the fur side with the tails of the animal, which they do not separate from them. Their garments they tie over the shoulders, and fasten them round the middle with a belt of green skin, which is as stiff as horn. Their leggins are long, and, if they were topped with a waistband, might be called trowsers: they, as well as their shoes, are made of dressed moose, elk, or rein-deer skin. The organs of generation they leave uncovered.

The women differ little in their dress from the men, except in the addition of an apron, which is fastened round the waist, and hangs down to the knees. They are in general of a more lusty make than the other sex, and taller in proportion, but infinitely their inferiors in cleanliness. A black artificial stripe crosses the face beneath the eye, from ear to ear, which I first took for scabs, from the accumulation of dirt on it. Their hair, which is longer than that of the men, is divided from the forehead to the crown, and drawn back in long plaits behind the ears. They have also a few white beads [dentalia shells [16]], which they get where they procure their iron; they are from a line [$\frac{1}{12}$ inch] to an inch in length, and are worn in their ears, but are not of European manufacture. These, with bracelets made of horn and bone, compose all the ornaments which decorate their persons. Necklaces of the grisly or white bear's claws, are worn exclusively by the men.

Their arms consist of bows made of [red] cedar, six feet in length, with a short iron spike at one end, and serve occasionally as a spear. Their arrows are well made, barbed, and pointed with iron, flint, stone, or bone; they are feathered, and from two to two feet and an half in length. They have two kinds of spears, but both are double edged, and of well polished iron; one of them is about twelve inches long, and two wide; the other about half the width, and two thirds of the length; the shafts of the first are eight feet in length, and the latter six. They have also spears made of bone. Their knives consist of pieces of iron, shaped and handled by themselves. Their axes are something like our adze, and they use them in the same manner as we employ that instrument. They were, indeed, furnished with iron in a manner that I could not have supposed, and plainly proved to me that their communication with those, who communicate with the inhabitants of the sea coast, cannot be very difficult; and, from their ample provision of iron weapons, the means of procuring it must be of a more [less?] distant origin than I had at first conjectured.

They have snares made of green skin, which they cut to the size of sturgeon twine, and twist a certain number of them together; and though when completed they do not exceed the thickness of cod-line, their strength is sufficient to hold a moose deer: they are from one and an half to two fathoms in length. Their nets and fishing lines are made of willow-bark and nettles; those made of the latter are finer and smoother than if made with hempen thread. Their hooks are small bones, fixed in pieces of wood split for that purpose, and tied round with fine watape, which has been particularly described in the former voyage. [He had described watape as "the divided roots of the spruce-fir, which the natives weave into a degree of compactness that renders it capable of containing a fluid. The different parts of the bark canoes are also sewed together with this kind of filament."] [17] Their kettles are also made of watape, which is so closely woven that they never leak, and they heat water in them, by putting red-hot stones into it. There is one kind of them, made of spruce-bark, which they hang over the fire, but at such a distance as to receive the heat without being within reach of the blaze; a very tedious operation. They have various dishes of wood and bark, spoons of horn and wood, and buckets; bags of leather and net-work, and baskets of bark, some of which hold their fishing-tackle, while others 123 are contrived to be carried on the back. They have a brown kind of earth in great abundance, with which they rub their clothes, not only for ornament but utility, as it prevents the leather from becoming hard after it has been wetted. They have spruce bark in great plenty, with which they make their canoes, an operation that does not require any great portion of skill or ingenuity, and is managed in the following manner.—The bark is taken off the tree the whole length of the intended canoe, which is commonly about eighteen feet, and is sewed with watape at both ends; two laths are then laid, and fixed along the edge of the bark which forms the gunwale; in these are fixed the bars, and against them bear the ribs or timbers, that are cut to the length to which the bark can be stretched; and, to give additional strength, strips of wood are laid between them: to make the whole water-tight, gum is abundantly employed. These vessels carry from two to five people. Canoes of a similar construction were used by the Beaver Indians within these few years, but they now very generally employ those made of the bark of the birch tree, which are by far more durable. Their paddles are about six feet long, and about one foot is occupied by the blade, which is in the shape of an heart.

Previous to our departure, the natives had caught a couple of trout, of about six pounds weight, which they brought me, and I paid them with beads. They likewise gave me a net, made of nettles, the skin of a moose-deer, dressed, and a white horn [of bighorn sheep?] in the shape of a spoon, which resembles the horn of the buffalo [musk ox] of the Copper-Mine River; but their description of the animal to which it belongs does not answer to that. My young men also got two quivers of excellent arrows, a collar of white [grizzly] bear's claws of a great length, horn bracelets, and other articles, for which they received an ample remuneration.

At ten we were ready to embark. I then took leave of the Indians, but encouraged them to expect us in two moons, and expressed an hope that I should find them on the road, with any of their relations whom they might meet. I also returned the beaver skins to the man
124 who had presented them to me, desiring him to take care of them

till I came back, when I would purchase them of him. Our guide expressed much less concern about the undertaking in which he had engaged, than his companions, who appeared to be affected with great solicitude for his safety.

We now pushed off the canoe from the bank, and proceeded East half a mile, when a river flowed in from the left, about half as large as that which we were navigating. We continued the same course three quarters of a mile, when we missed two of our fowling pieces, which had been forgotten, and I sent their owners back for them, who were absent on this errand upwards of an hour. We now proceeded North-East by East half a mile, North-East by North three quarters of a mile, when the current slackened: there was a verdant spot on the left, where, from the remains of some Indian timber-work, it appeared that the natives have frequently encamped. Our next course was East one mile, and we saw a ridge of mountains covered with snow to the South-East. The land on our right was low and marshy for three or four miles, when it rose into a range of heights that extended to the mountains.

We proceeded East-South-East a mile and an half, South-East by East one mile, East by South three quarters of a mile, South-East by East one mile, East by South half a mile, North-East by East one mile, South-East half a mile, East-North-East a mile and a quarter, South-South-East half a mile, North-North-East a mile and an half: here a river flowed in from the left which was about one-fourth part as large as that which received its tributary waters. We then continued East by South half a mile, to the foot of the mountain on the South of the above river. The course now veered short, South-West by West three quarters of a mile, East by South a quarter of a mile, South half a mile, South-East by South half a mile, South-West a quarter of a mile, East by South a quarter of a mile, veered to West-North-West a quarter of a mile, South-West one eighth of a mile, East-South-East one quarter of a mile, East one sixth of a mile, South-South-West one twelfth of a mile, East-South-East one eighth of a mile, North-East by East one third of a mile, East by North one twelfth of a mile, North-East by East one third of a mile, East one sixteenth of a mile, 125

South-East one twelfth of a mile, North-East by East one twelfth of a mile, East one eighth of a mile, and East-South-East half a mile,

when we landed at seven o'clock and encamped. During the greatest part of the distance we came to-day, the river runs close under the mountains on the left.

[June 11] The morning was clear and cold. On my interpreter's encouraging the guide to dispel all apprehension, to maintain his fidelity to me, and not to desert in the night, "How is it possible for me," he replied, "to leave the lodge of the Great Spirit!—"When he tells me that he has no further occasion for me, I will then return to my children." As we proceeded, however, he soon lost, and with good reason, his exalted notions of me.

At four we continued our voyage, steering East by South a mile and an half, East-South-East half a mile. A river appeared on the left, at the foot of a mountain, which, from its conical form, my young Indian called the Beaver Lodge Mountain. Having proceeded South-South-East half a mile, another river appeared from the right. We now came in a line with the beginning of the mountains we saw yesterday: others of the same kind ran parallel with them on the left side of the river, which was reduced to the breadth of fifteen yards, and with a moderate current.

We now steered East-North-East one eighth of a mile, South-East by South one eighth of a mile, East-South-East one sixth of a mile, South-West one eighth of a mile, East-South-East one eighth of a mile, South-South-East one sixth of a mile, North-East by East one twelfth of a mile, East-South-East half a mile, South-West by West one third of a mile, South-South-East one eighth of a mile, South-South-West one quarter of a mile, North-East one sixth of a mile, South by West one fourth of a mile, East three quarters of a mile, and North-East one quarter of a mile.

Here the mountain on the left appeared to be composed of a succession of round hills, covered with wood almost to their summits, which were white with snow, and crowned with withered trees.

126

We now steered East, in a line with the high lands on the right five miles; North one twelfth of a mile, North-East by North one eighth of a mile, South by East one sixteenth of a mile, North-East by North one fourth of a mile, where another river fell in from the right; North-East by East one sixth of a mile, East two miles and an half, South one twelfth of a mile, North-East half a mile, South-East one third of a mile, East one mile and a quarter, South-South-West one sixteenth of a mile, North-East by East half a mile, East one mile and three quarters, South and South-West by West half a mile, North-East half a mile, South one third of a mile, North-East by North one sixth of a mile, East by South one fourth of a mile, South one eighth of a mile, South-East three quarters of a mile.

The canoe had taken in so much water, that it was necessary for us to land here, in order to stop the leakage, which occasioned the delay of an hour and a quarter;

North-East a quarter of a mile, East-North-East a quarter of a mile, South-East by South a sixteenth of a mile, East by South a twelfth of a mile, North-East one sixth of a mile, East-South-East one sixteenth of a mile, South-West half a mile, North-East a quarter of a mile, East by South half a mile, South-South-East one twelfth of a mile, East half a mile, North-East by North a quarter of a mile, South-South-East a quarter of a mile, North-East by North one twelfth of a mile, where a small river flowed in from the left; South-East by East one twelfth of a mile, South by East a quarter of a mile, South-East one eighth of a mile, East one twelfth of a mile, North-East by North a quarter of a mile, South half a mile, South-East by South one eighth of a mile, North-East one fourth of a mile, South-East by East, and South-East by South one third of a mile, East-South-East, and North-North-East one third of a mile, and South by West, East and East-North-East one eighth of a mile.

Here we quitted the main branch, which, according to the information of our guide, terminates at a short distance, where it is supplied by the snow which covers the mountains. In the same direction is a valley which appears to be of very great depth, and is full of snow, that rises nearly to the height of the land, and forms a 127 reservoir of itself sufficient to furnish a river, whenever there is a moderate degree of heat. The branch which we left [Parsnip River] was not, at this time, more than ten yards broad, while that which we entered [an unnamed creek] was still less. Here the current was very trifling, and the channel so meandering, that we sometimes found it difficult to work the canoe forward. The straight course from this to the entrance of a small lake or pond [Arctic Lake [18]], is about East one mile. This entrance by the river into the lake was almost choked up by a quantity of drift-wood, which appeared to me to be an extraordinary circumstance; but I afterwards found that it falls down from the mountains. The water, however, was so high, that the country was entirely overflowed, and we passed with the canoe among the branches of trees. The principal wood along the banks is spruce, intermixed with a few white birch, growing on detached spots, the intervening spaces being covered with willow and alder. We advanced about a mile in the lake, and took up our station for the night at an old Indian encampment. Here we expected to meet with natives, but were disappointed; but our guide encouraged us with the hope of seeing some on the morrow. We saw beaver in the course of the afternoon, but did not discharge our pieces, from the fear of alarming the inhabitants; there were also swans in great numbers, with geese and ducks, which we did not disturb for the same reason. We observed also the tracks of moose deer that had crossed the river; and wild parsneps grew here in abundance, which have been already mentioned as a grateful vegetable. Of birds, we saw blue jays [Steller jays?], yellow birds, and one beautiful humming-bird: of the first and last, I had not seen any since I had been in the North-West.

[June 12] The weather was the same as yesterday, and we proceeded between three and four in the morning. We took up the net which we had set the preceding evening, when it contained a trout, one white fish, one carp [sucker], and three jub [chub?]. The lake is about two miles in length, East by South, and from three to five hundred yards wide. This I consider as the highest and Southern-

128

most source of the Unjigah, or Peace River, latitude 54. 24. North, longitude 121. West of Greenwich, which, after a winding course through a vast extent of country, receiving many large rivers in its progress, and passing through the Slave Lake, empties itself into the Frozen Ocean [Arctic Ocean], in 70. North latitude, and about 135 West longitude.

Mackenzie, Landry, and Ducette had now traveled the entire length of one of the continent's greatest river systems—from Athabasca via the Slave River, Great Slave Lake, and the Mackenzie River to the Arctic; and from Athabasca via the Peace River and the Parsnip River to the Continental Divide. Actually, they were not at the true source of the Parsnip, and the Finlay, not the Parsnip, is considered the source of the Peace (because it is longer), but it was a splendid achievement, both as a physical act and in historical significance. While they were ascending the Parsnip, an incident occurred on the coast that later almost cost them their lives.

Now they were about to cross the Continental Divide—the first Europeans to do so north of the plateaus of the Southwest. They were now entering not merely a new river system but a world very different from any they had known. It was a world of high mountains and dangerous rivers. There was little game, in comparison to the great herds east of the Rockies, but in compensation the rivers teemed with salmon at certain seasons. They were to find the Indians quite unlike the timid wandering tribes of the northern forests.

We landed and unloaded, where we found a beaten path leading over a low ridge of land [the Continental Divide] of eight hundred and seventeen paces in length to another small lake [Portage Lake]. The distance between the two mountains at this place is about a quarter of a mile, rocky precipices presenting themselves on both sides. A few large spruce trees and liards were scattered over the 129 carrying-place. There were also willows along the side of the water, with plenty of grass and weeds. The natives had left their old canoes here, with baskets hanging on the trees, which contained various articles. From the latter I took a net, some hooks, a [mountain] goat's horn, and a kind of wooden trap, in which, as our guide informed me, the ground hog is taken. I left, however, in exchange, a knife, some fire-steels, beads, awls &c. Here two streams tumble down the rocks from the right, and lose themselves in the lake which we had left [Arctic Lake]; while two others fall from the opposite heights, and glide into the lake which we were approaching [Portage Lake]; this being the highest point of land dividing these waters, and we are now going with the stream. This lake runs in the same course as the last, but is rather narrower, and not more than half the length. We were obliged to clear away some floating drift-wood to get to the carrying-place, over which is a beaten path of only an hundred and seventy-five paces long. The lake empties itself by a small river, which, if the channel were not interrupted by large trees that had fallen across it, would have admitted of our canoe with all its lading: the impediment, indeed, might have been removed by two axe-men in a few hours. On the edge of the water, we observed a large quantity of thick, yellow, scum or froth, of an acrid taste and smell.

We embarked on this lake [Pacific Lake], which is in the same course, and about the same size as that which we had just left, and from whence we passed into a small river [James Creek or Bad River], that was so full of fallen wood, as to employ some time, and require some exertion, to force a passage. At the entrance, it afforded no more water than was just sufficient to bear the canoe; but it was soon increased by many small streams which came in broken rills down the rugged sides of the mountains, and were furnished, as I suppose, by the melting of the snow. These accessory streamlets had all the coldness of ice. Our course continued to be obstructed by banks of gravel, as well as trees which had fallen across the river. We were obliged to force our way through the one, and to cut through the other, at a great expence of time and trouble. In many places the current was also very rapid and meandering. At four in the afternoon, we stopped to unload and carry, and at five we entered a small round lake [unnamed] of about one third of a mile in diameter. From the last lake to this is, I think, in a straight line, East by South six miles, though it is twice that distance by the winding of the river. We again entered the river, which soon ran with great rapidity, and rushed impetuously over a bed of flat stones. At half past six we were stopped by two large trees that lay across the river, and it was with great difficulty that the canoe was prevented from driving against them. Here we unloaded and formed our encampment.

The weather was cloudy and raw, and as the circumstances of this day's voyage had compelled us to be frequently in the water, which was cold as ice, we were almost in a benumbed state. Some of the people who had gone ashore to lighten the canoe, experienced great difficulty in reaching us, from the rugged state of the country; it was, indeed, almost dark when they arrived. We had no sooner landed than I sent two men down the river to bring me some account of its circumstances, that I might form a judgment of the difficulties which might await us on the morrow; and they brought back a fearful detail of rapid currents, fallen trees, and large stones. At this place our guide manifested evident symptoms of discontent: he had been very much alarmed in going down some of the rapids with us, and expressed an anxiety to return. He shewed us a mountain, at no great distance, which he represented as being on the other side of a river, into which this empties itself.

[June 13] At an early hour of this morning the men began to cut a road, in order to carry the canoe and lading beyond the rapid; and by seven they were ready. That business was soon effected, and the canoe reladen, to proceed with the current which ran with great rapidity. In order to lighten her, it was my intention to walk with some of the people; but those in the boat with great earnestness requested me to embark, declaring, at the same time, that, if they perished, I should perish with them. I did not then imagine in how 131

short a period their apprehension would be justified. We accordingly pushed off, and had proceeded but a very short way when the canoe struck, and notwithstanding all our exertions, the violence of the current was so great as to drive her sideways down the river, and break her by the first bar, when I instantly jumped into the water, and the men followed my example; but before we could set her straight, or stop her, we came to deeper water, so that we were obliged to re-embark with the utmost precipitation. One of the men who was not sufficiently active, was left to get on shore in the best manner in his power. We had hardly regained our situations when we drove against a rock which shattered the stern of the canoe in such a manner, that it held only by the gunwales, so that the steersman could no longer keep his place. The violence of this stroke drove us to the opposite side of the river, which is but narrow, when the bow met with the same fate as the stern. At this moment the foreman seized on some branches of a small tree in the hope of bringing up the canoe, but such was their elasticity that, in a manner not easily described, he was jerked on shore in an instant, and with a degree of violence that threatened his destruction. But we had no time to turn from our own situation to inquire what had befallen him; for, in a few moments, we came across a cascade which broke several large holes in the bottom of the canoe, and started all the bars, except one behind the scooping seat. If this accident, however, had not happened, the vessel must have been irretrievably overset. The wreck becoming flat on the water, we all jumped out, while the steersman, who had been compelled to abandon his place, and had not recovered from his fright, called out to his companions to save themselves. My peremptory commands superseded the effects of his fear, and they all held fast to the wreck; to which fortunate resolution we owed our safety, as we should otherwise have been dashed against the rocks by the force of the water, or driven over the cascades. In this condition we were forced several hundred yards, and every yard on the verge of destruction; but, at length, we most fortunately arrived in shallow
132 water and a small eddy, where we were enabled to make a stand,

from the weight of the canoe resting on the stones, rather than from any exertions of our exhausted strength. For though our efforts were short, they were pushed to the utmost, as life or death depended on them. This alarming scene, with all its terrors and dangers, occupied only a few minutes; and in the present suspension of it, we called to the people on shore to come to our assistance, and they immediately obeyed the summons. The foreman, however, was the first with us; he had escaped unhurt from the extraordinary jerk with which he was thrown out of the boat, and just as we were beginning to take our effects out of the water, he appeared to give his assistance. The Indians, when they saw our deplorable situation, instead of making the least effort to help us, sat down and gave vent to their tears. I was on the outside of the canoe, where I remained till every thing was got on shore, in a state of great pain from the extreme cold of the water; so that at length, it was with difficulty I could stand, from the benumbed state of my limbs.

The loss was considerable and important, for it consisted of our whole stock of balls, and some of our furniture; but these considerations were forgotten in the impressions of our miraculous escape. Our first inquiry was after the absent man, whom in the first moment of danger, we had left to get on shore, and in a short time his appearance removed our anxiety. We had, however, sustained no personal injury of consequence, and my bruises seemed to be in the greater proportion.

All the different articles were now spread out to dry. The powder had fortunately received no damage, and all my instruments had escaped. Indeed, when my people began to recover from their alarm, and to enjoy a sense of safety, some of them, if not all, were by no means sorry for our late misfortune, from the hope that it must put a period to our voyage, particularly as we were without a canoe, and all the bullets sunk in the river. It did not, indeed, seem possible to them that we could proceed under these circumstances. I listened, however, to the observations that were made on the occasion without replying to them, till their panic was dispelled and they had got 133 themselves warm and comfortable, with an hearty meal, and rum enough to raise their spirits.

I then addressed them, by recommending them all to be thankful for their late very narrow escape. I also stated, that the navigation was not impracticable in itself, but from our ignorance of its course; and that our late experience would enable us to pursue our voyage with greater security. I brought to their recollection, that I did not deceive them, and that they were made acquainted with the difficulties and dangers they must expect to encounter, before they engaged to accompany me. I also urged the honour of conquering disasters, and the disgrace that would attend them on their return home, without having attained the object of the expedition. Nor did I fail to mention the courage and resolution which was the peculiar boast of the North men; and that I depended on them, at that moment, for the maintenance of their character. I quieted their apprehension as to the loss of the bullets, by bringing to their recollection that we still had shot from which they might be manufactured. I at the same time acknowledged the difficulty of restoring the wreck of the canoe, but confided in our skill and exertion to put it in such a state as would carry us on to where we might procure bark, and build a new one. In short, my harangue produced the desired effect, and a very general assent appeared to go wherever I should lead the way.

Various opinions were offered in the present posture of affairs, and it was rather a general wish that the wreck should be abandoned, and all the lading carried to the river, which our guide informed us was at no great distance, and in the vicinity of woods where he believed there was plenty of bark. This project seemed not to promise that certainty to which I looked in my present operations; besides, I had my doubts respecting the views of my guide, and consequently could not confide in the representation he made to me. I therefore dispatched two of the men at nine in the morning, with one of the young Indians, for I did not venture to trust the guide out of my sight, in search of bark, and to endeavour, if it were possible, in the course of the day, to penetrate to the great river, into which that before us discharges itself in the direction which the guide had communicated. I now joined my people in order to repair, as well as circumstances would admit, our wreck of a canoe, and I began to set them the example.

At noon I had an altitude, which gave 54. 23. North latitude. At four in the afternoon I took time, with the hope that in the night I might obtain an observation of Jupiter, and his satellites, but I had not a sufficient horizon, from the propinquity of the mountains. The result of my calculation for time was 1. 38. 28. slow apparent time.

It now grew late, and the people who had been sent on the excursion already mentioned, were not yet returned; about ten o'clock, however, I heard a man halloo, and I very gladly returned the signal. In a short time our young Indian arrived with a small roll of indifferent bark: he was oppressed with fatigue and hunger, and his clothes torn to rags: he had parted with the other two men at sunset, who had walked the whole day, in a dreadful country, without procuring any good bark, or being able to get to the large river. His account of the river, on whose banks we were, could not be more unfavourable or discouraging; it had appeared to him to be little more than a succession of falls and rapids, with occasional interruptions of fallen trees.

Our guide became so dissatisfied and troubled in mind, that we could not obtain from him any regular account of the country before us. All we could collect from him was, that the river into which this empties itself is but a branch of a large river, the great fork being at no great distance from the confluence of this; and that he knew of no lake, or large body of still water, in the vicinity of these rivers. To this account of the country, he added some strange, fanciful, but terrifying descriptions of the natives, similar to those which were mentioned in the former voyage.

We had an escape this day, which I must add to the many instances of good fortune which I experienced in this perilous expedition. The powder had been spread out, to the amount of eighty pounds weight, to receive the air; and, in this situation, one of the 135 men carelessly and composedly walked across it with a lighted pipe in his mouth, but without any ill consequence resulting from such an act of criminal negligence. I need not add that one spark might have put a period to all my anxiety and ambition.

I observed several trees and plants on the banks of this river, which I had not seen to the North of the latitude 52. such as the [red] cedar, [Douglas] maple, [western] hemlock, &c. At this time the water rose fast, and passed on with the rapidity of an arrow shot from a bow.

[June 14] The weather was fine, clear, and warm, and at an early hour of the morning we resumed our repair of the canoe. At half past seven our two men returned hungry and cold, not having tasted food, or enjoyed the least repose for twenty-four hours, with their clothes torn into tatters, and their skin lacerated, in passing through the woods. Their account was the same as that brought by the Indian, with this exception, that they had reason to think they saw the river, or branch which our guide had mentioned; but they were of opinion that from the frequent obstructions in this river, we should have to carry the whole way to it, through a dreadful country, where much time and labour would be required to open a passage through it.

Discouraging as these accounts were, they did not, however, interrupt for a moment the task in which we were engaged, of repairing the canoe; and this work we contrived to complete by the conclusion of the day. The bark which was brought by the Indian, with some pieces of oil-cloth, and plenty of gum, enabled us to put our shattered vessel in a condition to answer our present purposes. The guide, who has been mentioned as manifesting continual signs of dissatisfaction, now assumed an air of contentment, which I attributed to a smoke that was visible in the direction of the river; as he naturally expected, if we should fall in with any natives, which was now very probable, from such a circumstance, that he should be released from a service which he had found so irksome and full of danger. I had an observation at noon, which made our latitude 54. 23. 43. North. I also took time, and found it slow apparent time 1. 38. 44.

[June 15] The weather continued the same as the preceding day, and according to the directions which I had previously given, my people began at a very early hour to open a road, through which we might carry a part of our lading; as I was fearful of risqing the whole of it in the canoe, in its present weak state, and in a part of the river which is full of shoals and rapids. Four men were employed to conduct her, lightened as she was of twelve packages. They passed several dangerous places, and met with various obstructions, the current of the river being frequently stopped by rafts to drift wood, and fallen trees, so that after fourteen hours hard labour we had not made more than three miles. Our course was South-East by East, and as we had not met with any accident, the men appeared to feel a renewed courage to continue their voyage. In the morning, however, one of the crew, whose name was Beauchamp, peremptorily refused to embark in the canoe. This being the first example of absolute disobedience which had yet appeared during the course of our expedition, I should not have passed it over without taking some very severe means to prevent a repetition of it; but as he had the general character of a simple fellow among his companions, and had been frightened out of what little sense he possessed by our late dangers, I rather preferred to consider him as unworthy of accompanying us, and to represent him as an object of ridicule and contempt for his pusillanimous behaviour; though, in fact, he was a very useful, active, and laborious man.

At the close of the day we assembled round a blazing fire, and the whole party, being enlivened with the usual beverage which I supplied on these occasions, forgot their fatigues and apprehensions; nor did they fail to anticipate the pleasure they should enjoy in getting clear of their present difficulties, and gliding onwards with a strong and steady stream, which our guide had described as the characteristic of the large river we soon expected to enter.

[June 16] The fine weather continued, and we began our work, as we had done the preceding day; some were occupied in opening a road, others were carrying, and the rest employed in conducting the   137 canoe. I was of the first party, and soon discovered that we had en-camped about half a mile above several falls, over which we could not attempt to run the canoe, lightened even as she was. This circum-stance rendered it necessary that the road should be made sufficiently wide to admit the canoe to pass; a tedious and toilsome work. In running her down a rapid above the falls, an hole was broken in her bottom, which occasioned a considerable delay, as we were destitute of the materials necessary for her effectual reparation. On my being informed of this misfortune, I returned, and ordered Mr. Mackay, with two Indians, to quit their occupation in making the road, and endeavour to penetrate to the great river, according to the direction which the guide had communicated, without paying any attention to the course of the river before us.

When the people had repaired the canoe in the best manner they were able, we conducted her to the head of the falls; she was then un-loaded and taken out of the water, when we carried her for a con-siderable distance through a low, swampy country. I appointed four men to this laborious office, which they executed at the peril of their lives, for the canoe was now become so heavy, from the additional quantity of bark and gum necessary to patch her up, that two men could not carry her more than an hundred yards, without being re-lieved; and as their way lay through deep mud, which was rendered more difficult by the roots and prostrate trunks of trees, they were every moment in danger of falling; and beneath such a weight, one false step might have been attended with fatal consequences. The other two men and myself followed, as fast as we could, with the lading. Thus did we toil till seven o'clock in the evening, to get to the termination of the road that had been made in the morning. Here Mr. Mackay and the Indian joined us, after having been at the river, which they represented as rather large. They had also ob-served, that the lower part of the river before us was so full of fallen wood, that the attempt to clear a passage through it, would be an unavailing labour. The country through which they had passed was morass, and almost impenetrable wood. In passing over one of the embarras [a pile of driftwood], our dog, which was following them, fell in, and it was with very great difficulty that he was saved, as the current had carried him under the drift. They brought with them two geese, which had been shot in the course of their expedition. To add to our perplexities and embarrassments, we were persecuted by musquitoes and sand-flies through the whole of the day.

The extent of our journey was not more than two miles South-East; and so much fatigue and pain had been suffered in the course of it, that my people, as might be expected, looked forward to a continuance of it with discouragement and dismay. I was, indeed, informed that murmurs prevailed among them, of which, however, I took no notice. When we were assembled together for the night, I gave each of them a dram, and in a short time they retired to the repose which they so much required. We could discover the termination of the mountains at a considerable distance on either side of us, which, according to my conjecture, marked the course of the great river. On the mountains to the East there were several fires, as their smokes were very visible to us. Excessive heat prevailed throughout the day.

[June 17] Having sat up till twelve last night, which had been my constant practice since we had taken our present guide, I awoke Mr. Mackay to watch him in turn. I then laid down to rest, and at three I was awakened to be informed that he had deserted. Mr. Mackay, with whom I was displeased on this occasion, and the Cancre, accompanied by the dog, went in search of him, but he had made his escape: a design which he had for some time meditated, though I had done every thing in my power to induce him to remain with me.

This misfortune did not produce any relaxation in our exertions. At an early hour of the morning we were all employed in cutting a passage of three quarters of a mile, through which we carried our canoe and cargo, when we put her into the water with her lading, but in a very short time were stopped by the drift-wood, and were obliged to land and carry. In short, we pursued our alternate journies, by land and water, till noon, when we could proceed no further, 139

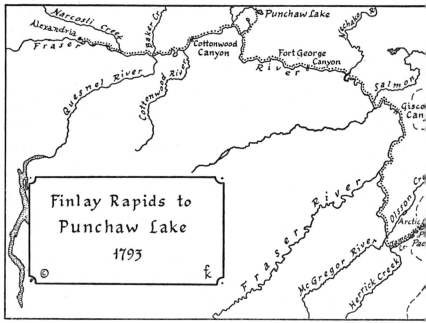

Finlay Rapids to Punchaw Lake 1793

from the various small unnavigable channels into which the river branched in every direction; and no other mode of getting forward now remained for us, but by cutting a road across a neck of land. I accordingly dispatched two men to ascertain the exact distance, and we employed the interval of their absence in unloading and getting the canoe out of the water. It was eight in the evening when we arrived at the bank of the great river. This journey was three quarters of a mile East-North-East, through a continued swamp, where, in many places, we waded up to the middle of our thighs. Our course in the small river was about South-East by East three miles. At length we enjoyed, after all our toil and anxiety, the inexpressible satisfaction of finding ourselves on the bank of a navigable river, on the West side of the first great range of mountains. [Mackenzie's route from James Creek to the Fraser River is not clear from his account. The general route is James Creek—Herrick Creek—McGregor River—Fraser River, but the identity of this "navigable river" and other places will have to be determined in the field.]

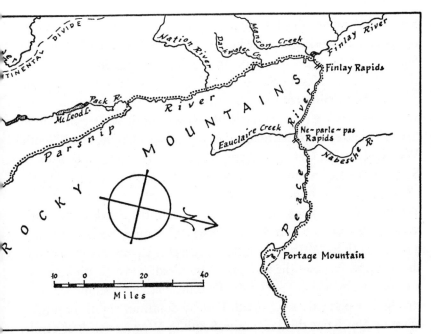

[June 18] It rained throughout the night and till seven in the morning; nor was I sorry that the weather gave me an excuse for indulging my people with that additional rest, which their fatigues, during the last three days, rendered so comfortable to them. Before eight, however, we were on the water, and driven on by a strong current, when we steered

East-South-East half a mile, South-West by South half a mile, South-South-East half a mile, South-West half a mile, went round to North-West half a mile, backed South-South-East three quarters of a mile, South-South-West half a mile, South by East a quarter of a mile, and South-West by South three quarters of a mile.

Here the water had fallen considerably, so that several mud and sand-banks were visible. There was also an hill ahead, West-South-West.

The weather was so hazy that we could not see across the river, which is here about two hundred yards wide. We now proceeded 141

South by West one third of a mile, when we saw a considerable quantity of beaver work along the banks; North-North-West half a mile, South-West by West one mile and an half, South-South-West one third of a mile, West by South one third of a mile, South by East half a mile. Mountains rose on the left, immediately above the river, whose summits were covered with snow; South-West half a mile, South a quarter of a mile, South-East one third of a mile, South-South-West half a mile. Here are several islands; we then veered to West by South a third of a mile, South-South-East a sixth of a mile. On the right, the land is high, rocky, and covered with wood, West-South-West one mile, a small river running in from the South-East, South-West half a mile, South three quarters of a mile, South-West half a mile, South by West half a mile. Here a rocky point protrudes from the left, and narrows the river to an hundred yards; South-East half a mile, East by South one eighth of a mile. The current now was very strong, but perfectly safe; South-East by South an eighth of a mile, West by North one third of a mile, South by West a twelfth of a mile, South-West one fourth of a mile. Here the high land terminates on one side of the river, while rocks rise to a considerable height immediately above the other, and the channel widens to an hundred and fifty yards, West by South one mile. The river now narrows again between rocks of a moderate height, North-North-East an eighth of a mile, veered to South-West an eighth of a mile, South and South-West half a mile. The country appeared to be low, as far as I could judge of it from the canoe, as the view is confined by woods at the distance of about an hundred yards from the banks.

Our course continued West by North two miles, North half a mile, North-West a quarter of a mile, South-West two miles, North-West three quarters of a mile; when a ridge of high land appeared in this direction, West one mile. A small river flowed in from the North, South a quarter of a mile, North-West half a mile, South-South-West two miles and an half, South-East three quarters of a mile; a rivulet lost itself in the main stream, West-North-West half a mile. Here the current slackened, and we proceeded South-South-West three quarters of a mile, South-West three quarters of a mile, South by East three quarters of a mile, South-East by East one mile, when it veered gradually to West-North-West half a mile; the river being full of islands. We proceeded due North, with little current, the river presenting a beautiful sheet of water for a mile and an half, South-West by West one mile, West-North-West one mile, when it veered round to South-East one mile, West by North one mile, South-East one mile, West by North three quarters of a mile, South one eighth of a mile,

when we came to an Indian cabin of late erection. Here was the great fork, of which our guide had informed us, and it appeared to be the largest branch from the South-East [Fraser River]. It is about half a mile in breadth, and assumes the form of a lake. The current was very slack, and we got into the middle of the channel, when we steered West, and sounded in sixteen feet water. A ridge of high land now stretched on, as it were, across our present direction: this course was three miles.

We then proceeded West-South-West two miles, and sounded in twenty-four feet water. Here the river narrowed and the current increased. We then continued our course North-North-West three quarters of a mile, a small river [Olsson Creek] falling in from the North-East. It now veered to South by West one mile and a quarter, West-South-West four miles and an half, West by North one mile and a quarter, North-West by West one mile, West a mile and a quarter: the land was high on both sides, and the river narrowed to an hundred and fifty, or two hundred yards; North-West three quarters of a mile, South-West by South two miles and an half: here its breadth again increased; South by West one mile, West-South-West half a mile, South-West by South three miles, South-South-East one mile, with a small river running in from the left; South with a strong current one mile, then East three quarters of a mile, South-West one mile, South-South-East a mile and an half; the four last distances being a continual rapid [Giscome Canyon]; South-West by West one mile East-North-East a mile and an half, East-South-East one mile, where a small river [Tay Creek] flowed in on the right; South-West by South two miles and an half, when another small river [Salmon River?] appeared 143 from the same quarter; South by East half a mile, and South-West by West one mile and a quarter:

here we landed for the night. When we had passed the last river we observed smoke rising from it, as if produced by fires that had been fresh lighted; I therefore concluded that there were natives on its banks; but I was unwilling to fatigue my people, by pulling back against the current in order to go in search of them.

This river appeared, from its high water-mark, to have fallen no more than one foot, while the smaller branch, from a similar measurement, had sunk two feet and an half. On our entering it, we saw a flock of ducks which were entirely white, except the bill and part of the wings. The weather was cold and raw throughout the day, and the wind South-West. We saw smoke rising in columns from many parts of the woods, and I should have been more anxious to see the natives, if there had been any person with me who could have introduced me to them; but as that object could not be then attained without considerable loss of time, I determined to pursue the navigation while it continued to be so favourable, and to wait till my return, if no very convenient opportunity offered in the mean time, to engage in an intercourse with them.

[June 19] The morning was foggy, and at three we were on the water. At half past that hour, our course was East by South three quarters of a mile, a small river flowing in from the right. We then proceeded South by East half a mile, and South-South-West a mile and an half. During the last distance, clouds of thick smoke rose from the woods, that darkened the atmosphere, accompanied with a strong odour of the gum of cypress and the spruce-fir.

Our courses continued to be South-West a mile and a quarter, North-West by West three quarters of a mile, South-South-East a mile and a quarter, East three quarters of a mile, South-West one mile, West by South three quarters of a mile, South-East by South three quarters of a mile, South by West half a mile, West by South three quarters of a mile, South by West two miles and an half.

In the last course there was an island, and it appeared to me, that the main channel of the river had formerly been on the other side of it. The banks were here composed of high white cliffs, crowned with pinnacles in very grotesque shapes.

We continued to steer South-East by South a mile and an half, South by East half a mile, East one mile and a quarter, South-East by East one mile, South by East three quarters of a mile, South-East by East one mile, South-South-East half a mile, East one mile and a quarter, South by East half a mile, East a mile and an half, South-South-East three miles, and South-West three quarters of a mile.

In the last course the rocks contracted in such a manner on both sides of the river, as to afford the appearance of the upper part of a fall or cataract.

> Mackenzie had passed one of the main tributaries of the Fraser, the Nechako River flowing in from the west, without noticing it. Now he was at the head of the Fort George or Red Rock Canyon, about sixteen miles south of Prince George, B. C. This is not a very formidable canyon, and he probably could have shot the rapids safely.

Under this apprehension we landed on the left shore, where we found a kind of foot-path, imperfectly traced, through which we conjectured that the natives occasionally passed with their canoes and baggage. On examining the course of the river, however, there did not appear to be any fall as we expected, but the rapids were of a considerable length and impassable for a light canoe. We had therefore no alternative but to widen the road so as to admit the passage of our canoe, which was now carried with great difficulty; as from her frequent repairs, and not always of the usual materials, her weight was such, that she cracked and broke on the shoulders of the men who bore her. The labour and fatigue of this undertaking, from eight till twelve, beggars all description, when we at length con- 145 quered this afflicting passage, of about half a mile, over a rocky and most rugged hill. Our course was South-South-West. Here I took a meridian altitude which gave me 53. 42. 20. North latitude. We, however, lost some time to put our canoe in a condition to carry us onwards. Our course was South a quarter of a mile to the next carrying-place, which was nothing more than a rocky point about twice the length of the canoe. From the extremity of this point to the rocky and almost perpendicular bank that rose on the opposite shore, is not more than forty or fifty yards. The great body of water, at the same time tumbling in successive cascades along the first carrying-place, rolls through this narrow passage in a very turbid current, and full of whirlpools. On the banks of the river there was great plenty of wild onions, which when mixed up with our pemmican was a great improvement of it; though they produced a physical effect on our appetites, which was rather inconvenient to the state of our provisions.

Here we embarked, and steered South-East by East three quarters of a mile. We now saw a smoke on the shore; but before we could reach land the natives had deserted their camp, which appeared to be erected for no more than two families. My two Indians were instantly dispatched in search of them, and, by following their tracks, they soon overtook them; but their language was mutually unintelligible, and all attempts to produce a friendly communication were fruitless. They no sooner perceived my young men than they prepared their bows and arrows, and made signs for them not to advance; and they thought it prudent to desist from proceeding, though not before the natives had discharged five arrows at them, which, however, they avoided, by means of the trees. When they returned with this account, I very much regretted that I had not accompanied them; and as these people could not be at any very great distance, I took Mr. Mackay, and one of the Indians with me in order to overtake them; but they had got so far that it would have been imprudent in me to have followed them. My Indians, who, I believe, were terrified at the manner in which these natives received them, informed me, that, besides their bows, arrows, and spears, they were armed with long knives, and that they accompanied their strange antics with menacing actions and loud shoutings. On my return, I found my people indulging their curiosity in examining the bags and baskets which the natives had left behind them. Some of them contained their fishing tackle, such as nets, lines, &c. others of a smaller size were filled with a red earth, with which they paint themselves. In several of the bags there were also sundry articles of which we did not know the use. I prevented my men from taking any of them; and for a few articles of mere curiosity, which I took myself, I left such things in exchange as would be much more useful to their owners.

> This was their first contact with the Carrier culture, which occupied most of the upper Fraser River. The Carrier Indians were so called because the widows carried part of their dead husband's bones on their backs, in mourning. The Carriers were prosperous, depending largely on the abundant supply of sockeye salmon that came to them yearly up the Fraser River from the sea.

At four we left this place, proceeding with the stream South-East three quarters of a mile, East-South-East one mile, South three quarters of a mile, South-South-West one mile, South by East three quarters of a mile, South-South-East one mile, South-South-West two miles, South-South-East three miles and a quarter, East by North one mile, South-South-East one mile and a quarter, with a rapid; South-South-West three quarters of a mile, South one mile and an half, South-East one mile and a quarter, South three quarters of a mile, and South-South-East one mile and an half.

At half past seven we landed for the night, where a small river flowed in from the right. The weather was showery, accompanied with several loud claps of thunder. The banks were overshadowed by lofty [Douglas?] firs, and wide-spreading [red] cedars.

[June 20] The morning was foggy, and at half past four we proceeded with a South wind, South-East by East two miles, South-South-East two miles and an half, and South-South-West two miles. The fog was so thick, that we could not see the length of our canoe, which rendered our progress dangerous, as we might have come suddenly upon a cascade or violent rapid. Our next course was West-North-West two miles and an half, which comprehended a rapid. Being close in with the left bank of the river, we perceived two red [mule] deer at the very edge of the water: we killed one of them, and wounded the other, which was very small. We now landed, and the Indians followed the wounded animal, which they soon caught, and would have shot another in the woods, if our dog, who followed them, had not disturbed it. From the number of their tracks it appeared that they abounded in this country. They are not so large as the elk of the Peace River, but are the real red deer, which I never saw in the North, though I have been told that they are to be found in great numbers in the plains along the Red, or Assiniboin River. [The Assiniboine River is a tributary of the Red River in southern Manitoba.] The bark had been stripped off many of the spruce trees, and carried away, as I presumed, by the natives, for the purpose of covering their cabins. We now got the venison on board, and continued our voyage South-West one mile, South a mile and an half, and West one mile. Here the country changed its appearance; the banks were but of a moderate height, from whence the ground continued gradually rising to a considerable distance, covered with poplars and cypresses, but without any kind of underwood. There are also several low points which the river, that is here about three hundred yards in breadth, sometimes overflows, and are shaded with the liard, the soft birch, the spruce, and the willow. For some distance before we came to this part of the river, our view was confined within very rugged, irregular, and lofty banks, which were varied with the poplar, different kinds of spruce fir, small birch trees, cedars, alders, and several species of the willow. Our next course was South-West by West six miles, when we landed at a deserted house, which 148 was the only Indian habitation of this kind that I had seen on this side of Mechilimakina. [Michilimackinac on Mackinac Island in Lake Huron, a major fur trading center and site of Iroquois-Huron villages.] It was about thirty feet long and twenty wide, with three doors, three feet high by one foot and an half in breadth. From this and other circumstances, it appears to have been constructed for three families. There were also three fire-places, at equal distances from each other; and the beds were on either side of them. Behind the beds was a narrow space in the form of a manger, and somewhat elevated, which was appropriated to the purpose of keeping fish. The wall of the house, which was five feet in height, was formed of very strait spruce timbers, brought close together, and laid into each other at the corners. The roof was supported by a ridge pole, resting on two upright forks of about ten feet high; that and the wall support a certain number of spars, which are covered with spruce bark; and the whole attached and secured by the fibres of the cedar. One of the gable ends is closed with split boards; the other with poles. Large rods are also fixed across the upper part of the building, where fish may hang and dry. To give the walls additional strength, upright posts are fixed in the ground, at equal distances, both within and without, of the same height as the wall, and firmly attached with bark fibres. Openings appear also between the logs in the wall, for the purpose, as I conjectured, of discharging their arrows at a besieging enemy; they would be needless for the purpose of giving light, which is sufficiently afforded by fissures between the logs of the building, so that it appeared to be constructed merely for a summer habitation. There was nothing further to attract our attention in or about the house, except a large machine, which must have rendered the taking off the roof absolutely necessary, in order to have introduced it. It was of a cylindrical form, fifteen feet long, and four feet and an half in diameter; one end was square, like the head of a cask, and a conical machine was fixed inwards to the other end, of similar dimensions; at the extremity of which was an opening of about seven inches diameter. This machine was certainly contrived to set in the river, to catch large fish, and very well adapted to that purpose; as 149 when they are once in, it must be impossible for them to get out, unless they should have strength sufficient to break through it. It was made of long pieces of split wood, rounded to the size of a small finger, and placed, at the distance of an inch asunder, on six hoops; to this was added a kind of boot of the same materials, into which it may be supposed that the fish are driven, when they are to be taken out. The house was left in such apparent order as to mark the design of its owners to return thither. It answered in every particular the description given us by our late guide, except that it was not situated on an island. [These were summer houses, where the Carriers lived during the salmon season. The large machine was a salmon trap built like a fyke net.]

We left this place, and steered South by East one mile and a quarter, when we passed where there had been another house, of which the ridge-pole and supporters alone remained: the ice had probably carried away the body of it. The bank was at this time covered with water, and a small river flowed in on the left. On a point we observed an erection that had the appearance of a tomb; it was in an oblong form, covered, and very neatly walled with bark. A pole was fixed near it, to which, at the height of ten or twelve feet, a piece of bark was attached, which was probably a memorial, or symbol of distinction. Our next course was South by West two miles and an half, when we saw a house on an island, South-East by East one mile and three quarters, in which we observed another island, with a house upon it. A river [West Road River] also flowed from the right, and the land was high and rocky, and wooded with the epinette [spruce].

Our canoe was now become so crazy, that it was a matter of absolute necessity to construct another; and as from the appearance of the country there was reason to expect that bark was to be found, we landed at eight, with the hope of procuring it. I accordingly dispatched four men with that commission, and at twelve they returned with a sufficient quantity to make the bottom of a canoe of five 150 fathom [thirty feet] in length, and four feet and an half in height.

At noon I had an observation, which gave me 53. 17. 28. North latitude.

We now continued our voyage South-East by South one mile and an half, East-South-East one mile, East-North-East half a mile, South-East two miles, South-East by South one mile, South-East six miles, and East-North-East. Here the river narrows between steep rocks, and a rapid [Cottonwood Canyon] succeeded, which was so violent that we did not venture to run it. I therefore ordered the loading to be taken out of the canoe, but she was now become so heavy that the men preferred running the rapid to the carrying her overland. Though I did not altogether approve of their proposition, I was unwilling to oppose it. Four of them undertook this hazardous expedition, and I hastened to the foot of the rapid with great anxiety, to wait the event, which turned out as I expected. The water was so strong, that although they kept clear of the rocks, the canoe filled, and in this state they drove half way down the rapid, but fortunately she did not overset; and having got her into an eddy, they emptied her, and in an half-drowned condition arrived safe on shore. The carrying-place is about half a mile over, with an Indian path across it. Mr. Mackay, and the hunters, saw some deer on an island above the rapid; and had that discovery been made before the departure of the canoe, there is little doubt but we should have added a considerable quantity of venison to our stock of provisions. Our vessel was in such a wretched condition, as I have already observed, that it occasioned a delay of three hours to put her in a condition to proceed. At length we continued our former course, East-North-East a mile and an half, when we passed an extensive Indian encampment; East-South-East one mile, where a small river [Cottonwood River] appeared on the left; South-East by South one mile and three quarters, East by South half a mile, East by North one mile, and saw another house on an island; South half a mile, West three quarters of a mile, South-West half a mile, where the cliffs of white and red clay appeared like the ruins of ancient castles. Our canoe now veered gradually to East-North-East one mile and an half, when we landed 151 in a storm of rain and thunder, where we perceived the remains of Indian houses. It was impossible to determine the wind in any part of the day, as it came ahead in all our directions.

[June 21] As I was very sensible of the difficulty of procuring provisions in this country, I thought it prudent to guard against any possibility of distress of that kind on our return; I therefore ordered ninety pounds weight of pemmican to be buried in an hole, sufficiently deep to admit of a fire over it without doing any injury to our hidden treasure, and which would, at the same time, secure it from the natives of the country, or the wild animals of the woods.

The morning was very cloudy, and at four o'clock we renewed our voyage, steering

South by East one mile and a quarter, East-South-East half a mile, South by East one mile and an half, East half a mile, South-East two miles, where a large river [Quesnel River] flowed in from the left, and a smaller one [Baker Creek] from the right. We then continued South by West three quarters of a mile, East by South a mile and an half, South three quarters of a mile, South-East by East one mile, South by East half a mile, South-East three quarters of a mile, South-East by South half a mile, South-East by East half a mile,

the cliffs of blue and yellow clay displaying the same grotesque shapes as those which we passed yesterday, South-South-East a mile and an half, South by East two miles. The latitude by observation was 52. 47. 51. North.

Here we perceived a small new canoe, that had been drawn up to the edge of the woods, and soon after another appeared, with one man in it, which came out of a small river [Narcosli Creek]. He no sooner saw us than he gave the whoop, to alarm his friends, who immediately appeared on the bank, armed with bows and arrows, and spears. They were thinly habited, and displayed the most outrageous antics. Though they were certainly in a state of great apprehension, they manifested by their gestures that they were resolved to attack us, if we should venture to land. I therefore ordered the men to stop the way of the canoe, and even to check her drifting with the current, as it would have been extreme folly to have approached these savages before their fury had in some degree subsided. My interpreters, who understood their language, informed me that they threatened us with instant death if we drew nigh the shore; and they followed the menace by discharging a volley of arrows, some of which fell short of the canoe, and others passed over it, so that they fortunately did us no injury. As we had been carried by the current below the spot where the Indians were, I ordered my people to paddle to the opposite side of the river, without the least appearance of confusion, so that they brought me abreast of them. My interpreters, while we were within hearing, had done every thing in their power to pacify them, but in vain. We also observed that they had sent off a canoe with two men, down the river, as we concluded, to communicate their alarm, and procure assistance. This circumstance determined me to leave no means untried that might engage us in a friendly intercourse with them, before they acquired additional security and confidence, by the arrival of their relations and neighbours, to whom their situation would be shortly notified.

I therefore formed the following adventurous project, which was happily crowned with success. I left the canoe, and walked by myself along the beach, in order to induce some of the natives to come to me, which I imagined they might be disposed to do, when they saw me alone, without any apparent possibility of receiving assistance from my people, and would consequently imagine that a communication with me was not a service of danger. At the same time, in order to possess the utmost security of which my situation was susceptible, I directed one of the Indians to slip into the woods, with my gun and his own, and to conceal himself from their discovery; he also had orders to keep as near me as possible, without being seen; and if any of the natives should venture across, and attempt to shoot me from the water, it was his instructions to lay him low: at the same time he was particularly enjoined not to fire till I had discharged one or both of the pistols that I carried in my belt. If, how- 153 ever, any of them were to land, and approach my person, he was immediately to join me. In the mean time my other interpreter assured them that we entertained the most friendly disposition, which I confirmed by such signals as I conceived would be comprehended by them. I had not, indeed, been long at my station, and my Indian in ambush behind me, when two of the natives came off in a canoe, but stopped when they had got within an hundred yards of me. I made signs for them to land, and as an inducement, displayed looking glasses, beads, and other alluring trinkets. At length, but with every mark of extreme apprehension, they approached the shore, stern foremost, but would not venture to land. I now made them a present of some beads, with which they were going to push off, when I renewed my entreaties, and, after some time, prevailed on them to come ashore, and sit down by me. My hunter now thought it right to join me, and created some alarm in my new acquaintance. It was, however, soon removed, and I had the satisfaction to find that he and these people perfectly understood each other.[19] I instructed him to say every thing that might tend to soothe their fears and win their confidence. I expressed my wish to conduct them to our canoe, but they declined my offer; and when they observed some of my people coming towards us, they requested me to let them return; and I was so well satisfied with the progress I had made in my intercourse with them, that I did not hesitate a moment in complying with their desire. During their short stay, they observed us, and every thing about us, with a mixture of admiration and astonishment. We could plainly distinguish that their friends received them with great joy on their return, and that the articles which they carried back with them were examined with a general and eager curiosity; they also appeared to hold a consultation, which lasted about a quarter of an hour, and the result was, an invitation to come over to them, which was cheerfully accepted. Nevertheless, on our landing, they betrayed evident signs of confusion, which arose probably from the quickness of our movements, as the prospect of a friendly communication had

154 so cheered the spirits of my people, that they paddled across the river

with the utmost expedition. The two men, however, who had been with us, appeared, very naturally, to possess the greatest share of courage on the occasion, and were ready to receive us on our landing; but our demeanor soon dispelled all their apprehensions, and the most familiar communication took place between us. When I had secured their confidence, by the distribution of trinkets among them, and treated the children with sugar, I instructed my interpreters to collect every necessary information in their power to afford me.

According to their account, this river, whose course is very extensive, runs towards the mid-day sun; and that at its mouth, as they had been informed, white people were building houses. [This probably was a distorted rumor of the Nootka settlement.] They represented its current to be uniformly strong, and that in three places it was altogether impassable, from the falls and rapids, which poured along between perpendicular rocks that were much higher and more rugged than any we had yet seen, and would not admit of any passage over them. But besides the dangers and difficulties of the navigation, they added, that we should have to encounter the inhabitants of the country, who were very numerous. They also represented their immediate neighbours as a very malignant race, who lived in large subterraneous recesses. [The immediate neighbors were Shuswap Indians. In winter they lived in partly underground "keekwillie" houses.] And when they were made to understand that it was our design to proceed to the sea, they dissuaded us from prosecuting our intention, as we should certainly become a sacrifice to the savage spirit of the natives. These people they described as possessing iron, arms, and utensils, which they procured from their neighbours to the Westward, and were obtained by a commercial progress from people like ourselves, who brought them in great canoes.

Such an account of our situation, exaggerated as it might be in some points, and erroneous in others, was sufficiently alarming, and awakened very painful reflections; nevertheless it did not operate on my mind so as to produce any change in my original determination. 155

My first object, therefore, was to persuade two of these people to accompany me, that they might secure for us a favourable reception from their neighbours. To this proposition they assented, but expressed some degree of dissatisfaction at the immediate departure, for which we were making preparation; but when we were ready to enter the canoe, a small one was seen doubling the point below, with three men in it. We thought it prudent to wait for their arrival, and they proved to be some of their relations, who had received the alarm from the messengers, which I have already mentioned as having been sent down the river for that purpose, and who had passed on, as we were afterwards informed, to extend the notice of our arrival. Though these people saw us in the midst of their friends, they displayed the most menacing actions, and hostile postures. At length, however, this wild, savage spirit appeared to subside, and they were persuaded to land. One of them, who was a middle-aged person, whose agitations had been less frequent than those of his companions, and who was treated with particular respect by them all, inquired who we were, whence we came, whither we were going, and what was the motive of our coming into that country. When his friends had satisfied him as far as they were able respecting us, he instantly advised us to delay our departure for that night, as their relations below, having been by this time alarmed by the messengers, who had been sent for that purpose, would certainly oppose our passage, notwithstanding I had two of their own people with me. He added, that they would all of them be here by sun-set, when they would be convinced, as he was, that we were good people, and meditated no ill designs against them.

Such were the reasons which this Indian urged in favour of our remaining till the next morning; and they were too well founded for me to hesitate in complying with them; besides, by prolonging my stay till the next morning, it was probable that I might obtain some important intelligence respecting the country through which I was to pass, and the people who inhabited it. I accordingly ordered the canoe to be unloaded, taken out of the water, and gummed. My tent

156

was also pitched, and the natives were now become so familiar, that I was obliged to let them know my wish to be alone and undisturbed.

My first application to the native whom I have already particularly mentioned, was to obtain from him such a plan of the river as he should be enabled to give me; and he complied with this request with a degree of readiness and intelligence that evidently proved it was by no means a new business to him. In order to acquire the best information he could communicate, I assured him, if I found his account correct, that I should either return myself, or send others to them, with such articles as they appeared to want: particularly arms and ammunition, with which they would be able to prevent their enemies from invading them. I obtained, however, no addition to what I already knew, but that the country below us, as far as he was acquainted with it, abounded in animals, and that the river produced plenty of fish.

Our canoe was now become so weak, leaky, and unmanageable, that it became a matter of absolute necessity to construct a new one; and I had been informed, that if we delayed that important work till we got further down the river, we should not be able to procure bark. I therefore dispatched two of my people, with an Indian, in search of that necessary material. The weather was so cloudy that I could not get an observation.*

I passed the rest of the day in conversing with these people: they consisted of seven families, containing eighteen men; they were clad in leather, and had some beaver and rabbit-skin blankets. They had not been long arrived in this part of the country, where they proposed to pass the summer, to catch fish for their winter provision: for this purpose they were preparing machines similar to that which we found in the first Indian house we saw and described. The fish which they take in them are large, and only visit this part of the river at certain seasons. These people differ very little, if at all, either in their appearance, language, or manners, from the Rocky-Mountain In-

---

* The observation, already mentioned, I got on my return.

dians. The men whom I sent in search of bark, returned with a certain quantity of it, but of a very indifferent kind. We were not gratified with the arrival of any of the natives whom we expected from a lower part of the river.

[June 22] At six in the morning we proceeded on our voyage, with two of the Indians, one of them in a small pointed canoe, made after the fashion of the Esquimaux, and the other in our own. This precaution was necessary in a two-fold point of view, as the small canoe could be sent ahead to speak to any of the natives that might be seen down the river, and, thus divided, would not be easy for them both to make their escape. Mr. Mackay also embarked with the Indian, which seemed to afford him great satisfaction, and he was thereby enabled to keep us company with diminution of labour.

Our courses were South-South-East a mile and an half, South-East half a mile, South by East four miles and an half, South-East by South half a mile, South by West half a mile, South-East by East one mile, South-South-West a mile and an half, South by East one mile and a quarter.

The country on the right presented a very beautiful appearance: it rose at first rather abruptly to the height of twenty-five feet, when the precipice was succeeded by an inclined plain to the foot of another steep; which was followed by another extent of gently-rising ground: these objects, which were shaded with groves of fir, presenting themselves alternately to a considerable distance.

We now landed near an house, the roof of which alone appeared above ground; but it was deserted by its inhabitants who had been alarmed at our approach. We observed several men in the second steep, who displayed the same postures and menacing actions as those which we have so lately described. Our conductors went to them immediately on an embassy of friendship, and, after a very vociferous discourse, one of them was persuaded to come to us, but presented a very ferocious aspect: the rest, who were seven in number, soon followed his example. They held their bows and arrows in their hands, and appeared in their garments, which were fastened round the neck, but left the right arm free for action. A cord fastened a blanket or leather covering under the right armpit, so that it hung upon the left shoulder, and might be occassionally employed as a target, that would turn an arrow which was nearly spent. As soon as they had recovered from their apprehensions, ten women made their appearance, but without any children, whom, I imagine, they had sent to a greater distance, to be out of the reach of all possible danger. I distributed a few presents among them, and left my guides to explain to them the object of my journey, and the friendliness of my designs, with which they had themselves been made acquainted; their fears being at length removed, I gave them a specimen of the use to which we applied our fire-arms: at the same time, I calmed their astonishment, by the assurance, that, though we could at once destroy those who did us injury, we could equally protect those who shewed us kindness. Our stay here did not exceed half an hour, and we left these people with favourable impressions of us.

From this place we steered East by North half a mile, South by East three quarters of a mile, and South by West a mile and an half, when we landed again on seeing some of the natives on the high ground, whose appearance was more wild and ferocious than any whom we had yet seen. Indeed I was under some apprehension that our guides, who went to conciliate them to us, would have fallen a prey to their savage fury. At length, however, they were persuaded to entertain a more favourable opinion of us, and they approached us one after another, to the number of sixteen men, and several women. I shook hands with them all, and desired my interpreters to explain that salutation as a token of friendship. As this was not a place where we could remain with the necessary convenience, I proposed to proceed further, in search of a more commodious spot. They immediately invited us to pass the night at their lodges, which were at no great distance, and promised, at the same time, that they would in the morning send two men to introduce us to the next nation, who were very numerous, and ill-disposed towards strangers. As we were 159 pushing from the shore, we were very much surprised at hearing a woman pronounce several words in the Knisteneaux language. She proved to be a Rocky-Mountain native, so that my interpreters perfectly understood her. She informed us that her country is at the forks of this river, and that she had been taken prisoner by the Knisteneaux, who had carried her across the mountains. [Apparently she was a Sekani from near the mouth of the McGregor River. She had been taken prisoner by a party of Cree raiders from east of the Rockies.] After having passed the greatest part of the summer with them, she had contrived to escape, before they had reached their own country, and had re-crossed the mountains, when she expected to meet her own friends: but after suffering all the hardships incident to such a journey, she had been taken by a war-party of the people with whom she then was, who had driven her relations from the river into the mountains. She had since been detained by her present husband, of whom she had no cause to complain; nevertheless she expressed a strong desire to return to her own people. I presented her with several useful articles, and desired her to come to me at the lodges, which she readily engaged to do. We arrived thither before the Indians, and landed, as we had promised. It was now near twelve at noon, but on attempting to take an altitude I found the angle too great for my sextant. [This village is supposed to have been at the site of the the future Fort Alexandria, B. C.]

The natives whom we had already seen, and several others, soon joined us, with a greater number of women than I had yet seen; but I did not observe the female prisoner among them. There were thirty-five of them, and my remaining store of presents was not sufficient to enable me to be very liberal to so many claimants. Among the men I found four of the adjoining nation [Shuswaps], and a Rocky-Mountain [Sekani?] Indian, who had been with them for some time. As he was understood by my interpreters, and was himself well acquainted with the language of the strangers, I possessed the means of obtaining every information respecting the country, which it might be in their power to afford me. For this purpose I selected an elderly man from the four strangers, whose countenance had prepossessed me in his favour. I stated to these people, as I had already done to those from whom I had hitherto derived information, the objects of my voyage, and the very great advantages which they would receive from my successful termination of it. They expressed themselves very much satisfied at my communication, and assured me that they would not deceive me respecting the subject of my inquiry. An old man also, who appeared to possess the character of a chief, declared his wish to see me return to his land, and that his two young daughters should then be at my disposal. I now proceeded to request the native whom I had particularly selected, to commence his information, by drawing a sketch of the country upon a large piece of bark, and he immediately entered on the work, frequently appealing to, and sometimes asking the advice of, those around him. He described the river as running to the East of South, receiving many rivers, and every six or eight leagues encumbered with falls and rapids, some of which were very dangerous, and six of them impracticable. The carrying-places he represented as of great length, and passing over hills and mountains. He depicted the lands of three other tribes, in succession, who spoke different languages [probably the Shuswaps, Lillooets, and Thompsons]. Beyond them he knew nothing either of the river or country, only that it was still a long way to the sea; and that, as he had heard, there was a lake before they reached the water, which the natives did not drink. As far as his knowledge of the river extended, the country on either side was level, in many places without wood, and abounding in red [mule] deer, and some of a small fallow kind [probably mule deer fawns]. Few of the natives, he said, would come to the banks for some time; but that at a certain season they would arrive there in great numbers, to fish. They now procured iron, brass, copper, and trinkets, from the Westward; but formerly these articles were obtained from the lower parts of the river, though in small quantities. A knife was produced which had been brought from that quarter. The blade was ten inches long, and an inch and an half broad, but 161 with a very blunted edge. The handle was of horn. We understood that this instrument had been obtained from white men, long before they had heard that any came to the Westward. One very old man observed, that as long as he could remember, he was told of white people to the Southward; and that he had heard, though he did not vouch for the truth of the report, that one of them had made an attempt to come up the river, and was destroyed. [The first white trade goods to reach them had come up the Fraser from ships in the Strait of Georgia, but now the Carriers were trading via the overland route to Bella Coola. There is no record of the unsuccessful attempt to ascend the Fraser, but it may well have happened.]

These people describe the distance across the country as very short to the Western ocean; and, according to my own idea, it cannot be above five or six degrees. If the assertion of Mr. Mears be correct, it cannot be so far, as the inland sea which he mentions within Nootka, must come as far East as 126 West longitiude. [Captain John Mears was an English trader of questionable character who had published unreliable reports of his explorations on the Northwest coast. It is actually about 4½° from Alexandria to Bella Coola, about 6° to the open sea.] They assured us that the road was not difficult, as they avoided the mountains, keeping along the low lands between them, many parts of which are entirely free from wood. According to their account, this way is so often travelled by them, that their path is visible throughout the whole journey, which lies along small lakes and rivers. It occupied them, they said, no more than six nights, to go to where they meet the people [Bella Coola Indians] who barter iron, brass, copper, beads, &c. with them, for dressed leather, and beaver, bear, lynx, fox, and marten skins. The iron is about eighteen inches of two-inch bar. To this they give an edge at one end, and fix it to an handle at right angles, which they employ as an axe. When the iron is worn down, they fabricate it into points for their arrows and spikes. Before they procured iron they employed bone and horn for those purposes. The copper and brass they convert into collars, armbands, bracelets, and other ornaments. They sometimes also point their arrows with those metals. They had been informed by those whom they meet to trade with, that the white people, from whom these articles are obtained, were building houses [at Nootka?] at the distance of three days, or two nights journey from the place where they met last fall. With this route they all appeared to be well acquainted.

I now requested that they would send for the female prisoner whom I saw yesterday, but I received only vague and evasive answers: they probably apprehended, that it was our design to take her from them. I was, however, very much disappointed at being prevented from having an interview with her, as she might have given me a correct account of the country beyond the forks of the river, as well as of the pass through the mountains from them.

My people had listened with great attention to the relation which had been given me, and it seemed to be their opinion, that it would be absolute madness to attempt a passage through so many savage and barbarous nations. My situation may, indeed, be more easily conceived than expressed: I had no more than thirty days provision remaining, exclusive of such supplies as I might obtain from the natives, and the toil of our hunters, which, however, was so precarious as to be matter of little dependence: besides, our ammunition would soon be exhausted, particularly our ball, of which we had not more than an hundred and fifty, and about thirty pounds weight of shot, which, indeed, might be converted into bullets, though with great waste.

The more I heard of the river, the more I was convinced it could not empty itself into the ocean to the North of what is called the River of the West, so that with its windings, the distance must be very great. Such being the discouraging circumstances of my situation, which were now heightened by the discontents of my people, I could not but be alarmed at the idea of attempting to get to the discharge of such a rapid river, especially when I reflected on the tardy progress of my return up it, even if I should meet with no obstruction from the natives; a circumstance not very probable, from the num- 163 bers of them which would then be on the river; and whom I could have no opportunity of conciliating in my passage down, for the reasons which have been already mentioned. At all events, I must give up every expectation of returning this season to Athabasca. Such were my reflections at this period; but instead of continuing to indulge them, I determined to proceed with resolution, and set future events at defiance. At the same time I suffered myself to nourish the hope that I might be able to penetrate with more safety, and in a shorter period, to the ocean by the inland western communication.

To carry this project into execution I must have returned a considerable distance up the river, which would necessarily be attended with a very serious inconvenience, if I passed over every other; as in a voyage of this kind, a retrograde motion could not fail to cool the ardour, slacken the zeal, and weaken the confidence of those, who have no greater inducement in the undertaking, than to follow the conductor of it. Such was the state of my mind at this period, and such the circumstances by which it was distressed and distracted.

To the people who had given me the foregoing information, I presented some beads, which they preferred to any other articles in my possession, and I recompensed in the same manner two of them who communicated to me the following vocabulary in the languages of the Nagailer [Carrier] and Atnah [Shuswap] tribes.

	The Nagailer, or Carrier-Indians	The Atnah, or Chin-Indians
Eye,	Nah,	Thloustin.
Hair,	Thigah,	Cahowdin.
Teeth,	Gough,	Chliough.
Nose,	Nenzeh,	Pisax.
Head,	Thie,	Scapacay.
Wood,	Dekin,	Shedzay.
Hand,	Lah,	Calietha.
Leg,	Kin,	Squacht.
Tongue,	Thoula,	Dewhasjisk.

	The Nagailer, or Carrier-Indians	The Atnah, or Chin-Indians
Ear,	Zach,	Ithlinah.
Man,	Dinay,	Scuynlouch.
Woman,	Chiqoui,	Smosledgensk.
Beaver,	Zah,	Schugh.
Elk,	Yezey,	Oikoy-Beh.
Dog,	Sleing,	Scacah.
Ground-hog,	Thidnu,	Squaiquais.
Iron,	Thlisitch,	Soucoumang.
Fire,	Coun,	Teuck.
Water,	Tou,	Shaweliquoih.
Stone,	Zeh,	Ishehoineah.
Bow,	Nettuny,	Isquoinah.
Arrow,	Igah,	Squaili.
Yes,	Nesi,	Amaig.
Plains,	Thoughoud,	Spilela.
Come here,	Andezei,	Thla-elyeh.

The Atnah language has no affinity to any with which I am acquainted; but the Nagailer differs very little from that spoken by the Beaver Indians, and is almost the same as that of the Chepewyans. [The Chipewyans, Beavers, Sekanis, and Carriers all spoke closely related Athapascan languages, but the Shuswaps spoke a very different Salishan language. According to Adrien Morice these vocabularies are worthless.]

We had a thunder-storm with heavy rain; and in the evening when it had subsided, the Indians amused us with singing and dancing, in which they were joined by the young women. Four men now arrived whom we had not yet seen; they had left their families at some distance in the country, and expressed a desire that we should visit them there.

[June 23] After a restless night, I called the Indians together, from 165 whom I yesterday received the intelligence which has been already mentioned, in the hope that I might obtain some additional information. From their former account they did not make the least deviation; but they informed me further, that where they left this river, a small one [West Road River] from the Westward falls into it, which was navigable for their canoes during four days, and from thence they slept but two nights, to get to the people with whom they trade, and who have wooden canoes much larger than ours, in which they go down a river to the sea. They continued to inform me, that if I went that way we must leave our own canoe behind us; but they thought it probable that those people would furnish us with another. From thence they stated the distance to be only one day's voyage with the current to the lake whose water is nauseous, and where they had heard that great canoes came two winters ago, and that the people belonging to them, brought great quantities of goods and built houses.

At the commencement of this conversation, I was very much surprised by the following question from one of the Indians: "What," demanded he, "can be the reason that you are so particular and anxious in your inquiries of us respecting a knowledge of this country: do not you white men know every thing in the world?" This interrogatory was so very unexpected, that it occasioned some hesitation before I could answer it. At length, however, I replied, that we certainly were acquainted with the principal circumstances of every part of the world; that I knew where the sea is, and where I myself then was, but that I did not exactly understand what obstacles might interrupt me in getting to it; with which he and his relations must be well acquainted, as they had so frequently surmounted them. Thus I fortunately preserved the impression in their minds, of the superiority of white people over themselves.

It was now, however, absolutely necessary that I should come to a final determination which route to take; and no long interval of reflection was employed, before I preferred to go over land: the comparative shortness and security of such a journey, were alone sufficient to determine me. I accordingly proposed to two of the Indians to accompany me and one of them readily assented to my proposition.

He has now made his second major decision. It was based on what he knew of the country—a little about the coast from the accounts of European mariners, and some highly questionable reports about the interior of the country from the Indians. The perils of the river had to be weighed against those of the overland route, and on the basis of the Indians' tales the latter seemed less formidable. It was a reasonable decision, but it may not have been the best one. The Indians seem to have magnified the dangers of the river route and to have minimized the distance to the coast by the overland route. The Fraser is certainly one of the most vicious rivers on the continent, but Simon Fraser's party went down it and returned without loss of life, fifteen years later. It took Fraser about a month to reach the sea from the place where Mackenzie turned back, and the return trip took less time. The Indians had told Mackenzie that it took them no more than six nights on the overland route to reach the Bella Coola Indians on the coast, but the round trip took Mackenzie a month. In other words, he probably would have had time to return to Athabasca that season.

But he could not know this. In fact, what he knew of the coast actually misled him. The year before, Captain Robert Gray, an American trader, had discovered and entered the Columbia River at about 46° north latitude. Mackenzie could not have heard of this, but he probably had heard that the Spanish mariner Bruno Heceta had sighted a river there. Heceta had not really discovered the Columbia, but he was in the bay at the mouth and believed that a river flowed into the bay. Mackenzie may have been thinking of this, or he may have been thinking of the mythical River of the West that 167 men had been assuming for centuries. He says that he was convinced that the river he was on "could not empty itself into the ocean to the North of what is called the River of the West." If he had been right the journey would have been prohibitively long, but he was not right. No one guessed it at the time except a few Spanish mariners he had never heard of, but there was another great river, the Fraser. This is the river that Mackenzie was on, and it reaches the sea at about 49°, more than two hundred miles north of the Columbia.

I now called those of my people about me, who had not been present at my consultation with the natives; and after passing a warm eulogium on their fortitude, patience, and perseverance, I stated difficulties that threatened our continuing to navigate the river, the length of time it would require, and the scanty provision we had for such a voyage: I then proceeded for the foregoing reasons to propose a shorter route, by trying the over-land road to the sea. At the same time, as I knew from experience the difficulty of retaining guides, and as many circumstances might occur to prevent our progress in that direction, I declared my resolution not to attempt it, unless they would engage, if we could not after all proceed over land, to return with me, and continue our voyage to the discharge of the waters, whatever the distance might be. At all events, I declared, in the most solemn manner, that I would not abandon my design of reaching the sea, if I made the attempt alone, and that I did not despair of returning in safety to my friends.

This proposition met with the most zealous return, and they unanimously assured me, that they were as willing now as they had ever been, to abide by my resolutions, whatever they might be, and to follow me wherever I should go. I therefore requested them to prepare for an immediate departure, and at the same time gave notice to the man who had engaged to be our guide, to be in readiness to accompany us. When our determination to return up the river was made known, several of the natives took a very abrupt departure; but to those who remained, I gave a few useful articles, explaining to them at the same time, the advantages that would result to them, if their relations conducted me to the sea along such a road as they had described. I had already given a moose skin to some of the women for the purpose of making shoes, which were now brought us; they were well sewed but ill shaped, and a few beads were considered as a sufficient renumeration for the skill employed on them. Mr. Mackay, by my desire, engraved my name, and the date of the year on a tree.

When we were ready to depart, our guide proposed, for the sake of expedition, to go over land to his lodge, that he might get there before us, to make some necessary preparation for his journey. I did not altogether relish his design, but was obliged to consent: I thought it prudent, however, to send Mr. Mackay, and the two Indians along with him. Our place of rendezvous was the subterraneous house which we passed yesterday.

At ten in the morning we embarked, and went up the current much faster than I expected with such a crazy vessel as that which carried us. We met our people at the house as had been appointed; but the Indian still continued to prefer going on by land, and it would have been needless for me to oppose him. He proceeded, therefore, with his former companions, whom I desired to keep him in good humour by every reasonable gratification. They were also furnished with a few articles that might be of use if they should meet with strangers.

In a short time after we had left the house, I saw a wooden canoe coming down the river, with three natives in it, who, as soon as they perceived us, made for the shore, and hurried into the woods. On passing their vessel, we discovered it to be one of those which we had seen at the lodges. A severe gust of wind, with rain, came from the South-South-East. This we found to be a very prevalent wind in these parts. We soon passed another wooden canoe drawn stern foremost on the shore; a circumstance which we had not hitherto observed. The men worked very hard, and though I imagined we went ahead very fast, we could not reach the lodges, but landed for the night at nine, close to the encampment of two families of the natives whom we had formerly seen at the lodges. I immediately went and sat down with them, when they gave me some roasted fish; two of my men who followed me were gratified also with some of their provisions. The youngest of the two natives now quitted the shed, and did not return during the time I remained there. I endeavoured to explain to the other by signs, the cause of my sudden return, which he appeared to understand. In the mean time my tent was pitched, and on my going to it, I was rather surprised that he did not follow me, as he had been constantly with me during the day and night I had passed with his party on going down. We, however, went to rest in a state of perfect security; nor had we the least apprehension for the safety of our people who were gone by land.

[June 24] We were in our canoe by four this morning, and passed by the Indian hut, which appeared in a state of perfect tranquillity. We soon came in sight of the point where we first saw the natives, and at eight were much surprised and disappointed at seeing Mr. Mackay and our two Indians coming alone from the ruins of an house that had been partly carried away by the ice and water, at a short distance below the place where we had appointed to meet. Nor was our surprise and apprehension diminished by the alarm which was painted in their countenances. When we had landed, they informed me that they had taken refuge in that place, with the determination to sell their lives, which they considered in the most imminent danger, as dear as possible. In a very short time after they had left us, they met a party of Indians, whom we had known at this place, and were probably those whom we had seen to land from their canoe. They appeared to be in a state of extreme rage, and had their bows bent, with their arrows across them. The guide stopped to ask them some questions, which my people did not understand, and then set off with his utmost speed. Mr. Mackay, however, did not leave him till they were both exhausted with running. When the young man came up, he then said, that some treacherous design was medi-

170

tated against them, as he was induced to believe from the declaration of the natives, who told him that they were going to do mischief, but refused to name the enemy. The guide then conducted them through very bad ways, as fast as they could run; and when he was desired to slacken his pace, he answered that they might follow him in any manner they pleased, but that he was impatient to get to his family, in order to prepare shoes, and other necessaries, for his journey. They did not, however, think it prudent to quit him, and he would not stop till ten at night. On passing a track that was but lately made, they began to be seriously alarmed, and on inquiring of the guide where they were, he pretended not to understand them. They then all laid down, exhausted with fatigue, and without any kind of covering: they were cold, wet, and hungry, but dared not light a fire, from the apprehension of an enemy. This comfortless spot they left at dawn of day, and, on their arrival at the lodges, found them deserted, the property of the Indians being scattered about, as if abandoned for ever. The guide then made two or three trips into the woods, calling aloud, and bellowing like a madman. At length he set off in the same direction as they came, and had not since appeared. To heighten their misery, as they did not find us at the place appointed, they concluded that we were all destroyed, and had already formed their plan to take to the woods, and cross in as direct a line as they could proceed to the waters of the Peace River, a scheme which could only be suggested by despair. They intended to have waited for us till noon, and if we did not appear by that time, to have entered without further delay on their desperate expedition.

This alarm among the natives was a very unexpected as well as perilous event, and my powers of conjecture were exhausted in searching for the cause of it. A general panic seized all around me, and any further prosecution of the voyage was now considered by them as altogether hopeless and impracticable. But without paying the least attention to their opinions or surmises, I ordered them to take every thing out of the canoe, except six packages: when that was done, I left four men to take care of the lading, and returned with 171 the others to our camp of last night, where I hoped to find the two men, with their families, whom we had seen there, and to be able to bring them to lodge with us, when I should wait the issue of this mysterious business. This project, however, was disappointed, for these people had quitted their sheds in the silence of the night, and had not taken a single article of their little property with them.

These perplexing circumstances made a deep impression on my mind, not as to our immediate safety, for I entertained not the least apprehension of the Indians I had hitherto seen, even if their whole force should have been combined to attack us; but these untoward events seemed to threaten the prosecution of my journey, and I could not reflect on the possibility of such a disappointment but with sensations little short of agony. Whatever might have been the wavering disposition of the people on former occasions, they were now decided in their opinions as to the necessity of returning without delay; and when we came back to them, their cry was—"Let us reimbark, and be gone." This, however, was not my design, and in a more peremptory tone than I usually employed, they were ordered to unload the canoe, and take her out of the water. On examining our property, several articles appeared to be missing, which the Indians must have purloined; and among them were an axe, two knives, and the young men's bag of medicines. We now took a position that was the best calculated for defence, got our arms in complete order, filled each man's flask of powder, and distributed an hundred bullets, which were all that remained, while some were employed in melting down shot to make more. The weather was so cloudy that I had not an opportunity of taking an observation.

While we were employed in making these preparations, we saw an Indian in a canoe come down the river, and land at the huts, which he began to examine. On perceiving us he stood still, as if in a state of suspense, when I instantly dispatched one of my Indians towards him, but no persuasions could induce him to have confidence in us; he even threatened that he would hasten to join his friends, who would come and kill us. At the conclusion of this menace he disappeared. On the return of my young man with this account of the interview, I pretended to discredit the whole, and attributed it to his own apprehensions and alarms. This, however, he denied, and asked with a look and tone of resentment, whether he had ever told me a lie? Though he was but a young man, he said, he had been on war excursions before he came with me, and that he should no longer consider me as a wise man, which he had hitherto done.

To add to our distresses we had not an ounce of gum for the reparation of the canoe, and not one of the men had sufficient courage to venture into the woods to collect it. In this perplexing situation I entertained the hope that in the course of the night some of the natives would return, to take away a part at least of the things which they had left behind them, as they had gone away without the covering necessary to defend them from the weather and the flies. I therefore ordered the canoe to be loaded, and dropped to an old house, one side of which, with its roof, had been carried away by the water; but the three remaining angles were sufficient to shelter us from the woods. I then ordered two strong piquets to be driven into the ground, to which the canoe was fastened, so that if we were hard pressed we had only to step on board and push off. We were under the necessity of making a smoke to keep off the swarms of flies, which would have otherwise tormented us; but we did not venture to excite a blaze, as it would have been a mark for the arrows of the enemy. Mr. Mackay and myself, with three men kept alternate watch, and allowed the Indians to do as they fancied. I took the first watch, and the others laid down in their clothes by us. I also placed a centinel at a small distance, who was relieved every hour. The weather was cloudy, with showers of rain.

[June 25] At one I called up the other watch and laid down to a small portion of broken rest. At five I arose, and as the situation which we left yesterday was preferable to that which we then occupied, I determined to return to it. On our arrival Mr. Mackay informed me that the men had expressed their dissatisfaction to him in a very unreserved manner, and had in very strong terms declared their resolution to follow me no further in my proposed enterprize. I did not appear, however, to have received such communications from him, and continued to employ my whole thoughts in contriving means to bring about a reconciliation with the natives, which alone would enable me to procure guides, without whose assistance it would be impossible for me to proceed, when my darling project would end in disappointment.

At twelve we saw a man coming with the stream upon a raft, and he must have discovered us before we perceived him, as he was working very hard to get to the opposite shore, where he soon landed, and instantly fled into the woods. I now had a meridional altitude, which gave 60. 23. natural horizon, (the angle being more than the sextant could measure with the artificial horizon), one mile and an half distant; and the eye five feet above the level of the water, gave 52. 47. 51. North latitude.

While I was thus employed, the men loaded the canoe without having received any orders from me, and as this was the first time they had venture to act in such a decided manner, I naturally concluded, that they had preconcerted a plan for their return. I thought it prudent, however, to take no notice of this transaction, and to wait the issue of future circumstances. At this moment our Indians perceived a person in the edge of the woods above us, and they were immediately dispatched to discover who it was. After a short absence they returned with a young woman whom we had seen before: her language was not clearly comprehended by us, so that we could not learn from her, at least with any degree of certainty, the cause of this unfortunate alarm that had taken place among the natives. She told us that her errand was to fetch some things which she had left behind her; and one of the dogs whom we found here, appeared to acknowledge her as mistress. We treated her with great kindness, gave her something to eat, and added a present of such articles as we thought might please her. On her expressing a wish to leave us, we readily consented to her departure, and indulged the hope that her

174

reception would induce the natives to return in peace, and give us an opportunity to convince them, that we had no hostile designs whatever against them. On leaving us, she went up the river without taking a single article of her own, and the dog followed. The wind was changeable throughout the day, and there were several showers in the course of it.

Though a very apparent anxiety prevailed among the people for their departure, I appeared to be wholly inattentive to it, and at eight in the evening I ordered four men to step into the canoe, which had been loaded for several hours, and drop down to our guard-house, and my command was immediately obeyed: the rest of us proceeded there by land. When I was yet a considerable distance from the house, and thought it impossible for an arrow to reach it, having a bow and quiver in my hand, I very imprudently let fly an arrow, when, to my astonishment and infinite alarm, I heard it strike a log of the house. The men who had just landed imagined that they were attacked by an enemy from the woods. Their confusion was in proportion to their imaginary danger, and on my arrival I found that the arrow had passed within a foot of one of the men; though it had no point, the weapon, incredible as it may appear, had entered an hard, dry log of wood upwards of an inch. But this was not all: for the men readily availed themselves of this circumstance, to remark upon the danger of remaining in the power of a people possessed of such means of destruction. Mr. Mackay having the first watch, I laid myself down in my cloak.

[June 26] About midnight a rustling noise was heard in the woods which created a general alarm, and I was awakened to be informed of the circumstance, but heard nothing. At one I took my turn of the watch, and our dog continued unceasingly to run backwards and forwards along the skirts of the wood in a state of restless vigilance. At two in the morning the centinel informed me, that he saw something like an human figure creeping along on all-fours about fifty paces above us. After some time had passed in our search, I at length discovered that his information was true, and it appeared to me that 175 a bear had occasioned the alarm; but when day appeared, it proved to be an old, grey-haired, blind man, who had been compelled to leave his hiding-place by extreme hunger, being too infirm to join in the flight of the natives to whom he belonged. When I put my hand on this object of decaying nature, his alarm was so great, that I expected it would have thrown him into convulsions. I immediately led him to our fire which had been just lighted, and gave him something to eat, which he much wanted, as he had not tasted food for two days. When his hunger was satisfied, and he had got warm and composed, I requested him to acquaint me with the cause of that alarm which had taken place respecting us among his relations and friends, whose regard we appeared to have conciliated but a few days past. He replied, that very soon after we had left them, some natives arrived from above, who informed them that we were enemies; and our unexpected return, in direct contradiction to our own declarations, confirmed them in that opinion. They were now, he said, so scattered, that a considerable time would elapse, before they could meet again. We gave him the real history of our return, as well as of the desertion of our guide, and, at the same time, stated the impossibility of our proceeding, unless we procured a native to conduct us. He replied, that if he had not lost his sight, he would with the greatest readiness have accompanied us on our journey. He also confirmed the accounts which we had received of the country, and the route to the Westward. I did not neglect to employ every argument in my power, that he might be persuaded of our friendly dispositions to the inhabitants wheresoever we might meet them.

At sun-rise we perceived a canoe with one man in it on the opposite side of the river, and at our request, the blind man called to him to come to us, but he returned no answer, and continued his course as fast as he could paddle down the current. He was considered as a spy by my men, and I was confirmed in that opinion, when I saw a wooden canoe drifting with the stream close in to the other shore, where it was more than probable that some of the natives might be concealed. It might, therefore, have been an useless enterprise, or perhaps fatal to the future success of our undertaking, if we had pursued these people, as they might, through fear, have employed their arms against us, and provoked us to retaliate.

The old man informed me, that some of the natives whom I had seen here were gone up the river, and those whom I saw below had left their late station to gather a root in the plains, which, when dried, forms a considerable article in their winter stock of provisions. He had a woman, he said, with him, who used to see us walking along the small adjoining river, but when he called her he received no answer, so that she had probably fled to join her people. He informed me, also, that he expected a considerable number of his tribe to come on the upper part of the river to catch fish for their present support, and to cure them for their winter store; among whom he had a son and two brothers.

In consequence of these communications, I deemed it altogether unnecessary to lose any more time at this place, and I informed the old man that he must accompany me for the purpose of introducing us to his friends and relations, and that if we met with his son or brothers, I depended upon him to persuade them, or some of their party, to attend us as guides in our meditated expedition. He expressed his wishes to be excused from this service, and in other circumstances we should not have insisted on it, but, situated as we were, we could not yield to his request.

At seven in the morning we left this place, which I named Deserter's River or Creek [Narcosli Creek]. Our blind guide was, however, so averse to continuing with us, that I was under the very disagreeable necessity of ordering the men to carry him into the canoe; and this was the first act during my voyage, that had the semblance of violent dealing. He continued to speak in a very loud tone, while he remained, according to his conjecture, near enough to the camp to be heard, but in a language that our interpreters did not understand. On asking him what he said, and why he did not speak in a language known to us, he replied, that the woman understood him better in that which he spoke, and he requested her, if she heard him, 177 to come for him to the carrying-place, where he expected we should leave him.

At length our canoe was become so leaky, that it was absolutely unfit for service; and it was the unremitting employment of one person to keep her clear of water: we, therefore, inquired of the old man where we could conveniently obtain the articles necessary to build a new one; and we understood from him that, at some distance up the river, we should find plenty of bark and cedar.

At ten, being at the foot of a rapid, we saw a small canoe coming down with two men in it. We thought it would be impossible for them to escape, and therefore struck off from the shore with a design to intercept them, directing the old man at the same time to address them; but they no sooner perceived us, than they steered into the strength of the current, where I thought that they must inevitably perish; but their attention appeared to be engrossed by the situation of their canoe, and they escaped without making us the least reply.

About three in the afternoon we perceived a lodge at the entrance of a considerable river [Quesnel River] on the right, as well as the tracks of people in the mud at the mouth of a small river [Baker Creek] on the left. As they appeared to be fresh, we landed, and endeavoured to trace them, but without success. We then crossed over to the lodge, which was deserted, but all the usual furniture of such buildings remained untouched.

Throughout the whole of this day the men had been in a state of extreme ill humour, and as they did not choose openly to vent it upon me, they disputed and quarrelled among themselves. About sun-set the canoe struck upon the stump of a tree, which broke a large hole in her bottom; a circumstance that gave them an opportunity to let loose their discontents without reserve. I left them as soon as we had landed, and ascended an elevated bank, in a state of mind which I scare wish to recollect, and shall not attempt to describe. At this place there was a subterraneous house, where I determined to pass the night. The water had risen since we had passed down, and it was with the utmost exertion that we came up several points in the course of the day.

[June 27] We embarked at half past four, with very favourable weather, and at eight we landed, where there was an appearance of our being able to procure bark; we, however, obtained but a small quantity. At twelve we went on shore again, and collected as much as was necessary for our purpose. It now remained for us to fix on a proper place for building another canoe, as it was impossible to proceed with our old one, which had become an absolute wreck. At five in the afternoon we came to a spot well adapted to the business in which we were about to engage. It was on a small island not much encumbered with wood, though there was plenty of the spruce kind on the opposite land, which was only divided from us by a small channel. We now landed, but before the canoe was unloaded, and the tent pitched, a violent thunder-storm came on, accompanied with rain, which did not subside till the night had closed in upon us. Two of our men who had been in the woods for axe-handles, saw a deer, and one of them shot at it, but unluckily missed his aim. A net was also prepared and set in the eddy at the end of the island.

[June 28] At a very early hour of the morning every man was employed in making preparations for building another canoe, and different parties went in search of wood, watape, and gum. At two in the afternoon they all returned successful, except the collectors of gum, and of that article it was feared we should not obtain here a sufficient supply for our immediate wants. After a necessary portion of time allotted for refreshment, each began his respective work. I had an altitude at noon, which made us in 53. 2. 32. North latitude.

[June 29] The weather continued to be fine. At five o'clock we renewed our labour, and the canoe was got in a state of considerable forwardness. The conductor of the work, though a good man, was remarkable for the tardiness of his operations, whatever they might be, and more disposed to eat than to be active; I, therefore, took this opportunity of unfolding my sentiments to him, and thereby discovering to all around me the real state of my mind, and the resolutions

I had formed for my future conduct. After reproaching him for his general inactivity, but particularly on the present occasion, when our time was so precious, I mentioned the apparent want of economy both of himself and his companions, in the article of provisions. I informed him that I was not altogether a stranger to their late conversations, from whence I drew the conclusion that they wished to put an end to the voyage. If that were so, I expressed my wish that they would be explicit, and tell me at once of their determination to follow me no longer. I concluded, however, by assuring him, that whatever plan they had meditated to pursue, it was my fixed and unalterable determination to proceed, in spite of every difficulty that might oppose, or danger that should threaten me. The man was very much mortified at my addressing this remonstrance particularly to him; and replied, that he did not deserve my displeasure more than the rest of them. My object being answered, the conversation dropped, and the work went on.

About two in the afternoon one of the men perceived a canoe, with two natives in it, coming along the inside of the island, but the water being shallow, it turned back, and we imagined that on perceiving us they had taken the alarm; but we were agreeably surprised on seeing them come up the outside of the island, when we recognized our guide, and one of the natives whom we had already seen. The former began immediately to apologize for his conduct, and assured me that since he had left me, his whole time had been employed in searching after his family, who had been seized with the general panic, that had been occasioned by the false reports of the people who had first fled from us. He said it was generally apprehended by the natives that we had been unfriendly to their relations above, who were expected upon the river in great numbers at this time; and that many of the Atnah or Chin nation, had come up the river to where we had been, in the hope of seeing us, and were very much displeased with him and his friends for having neglected to give them an early notice of our arrival there. He added, that the two men whom we had seen yesterday, or the day before, were just returned from their rendezvous, with the natives of the sea coast, and had brought a message from his brother-in-law, that he had a new axe for him, and not to forget to bring a moose skin dressed in exchange, which he actually had in his canoe. He expected to meet him, he said, at the other end of the carrying-place.

This was as pleasing intelligence as we had reason to expect, and it is almost superfluous to observe that we stood in great need of it. I had a meridian altitude, which gave 53. 3. 7. North latitude. I also took time in the fore and afternoon, that gave a mean of 1. 37. 42. Achrometer slow apparent time, which, with an observed immersion of Jupiter's first satellite, made our longitude 122. 48. West of Greenwich.

The blind old man gave a very favourable account of us to his friends, and they all three were very merry together during the whole of the afternoon. That our guide, however, might not escape from us during the night, I determined to watch him.

[June 30] Our strangers conducted themselves with great good-humour throughout the day. According to their information we should find their friends above and below the carrying-place. They mentioned, also, that some of them were not of their tribe, but are allied to the people of the sea coast, who trade with the white men. I had a meridian altitude, that gave 53. 3. 17. North latitude.

[July 1] Last night I had the first watch, when one of my Indians proposed to sit up with me, as he understood, from the old man's conversation, that he intended, in the course of the night, to make his escape. Accordingly at eleven I extinguished my light, and sat quietly in my tent, from whence I could observe the motions of the natives. About twelve, though the night was rather dark, I observed the old man creeping on his hands and knees towards the water-side. We accordingly followed him very quietly to the canoe, and he would have gone away with it, if he had not been interrupted in his design. On upbraiding him for his treacherous conduct, when he had been treated with so much kindness by us, he denied the intention of which we accused him, and declared that his sole object was to as- 181 suage his thirst. At length, however, he acknowledged the truth, and when we brought him to the fire, his friends, who now awoke, on being informed of what had passed, reprobated his conduct, and asked him how he could expect that the white people would return to this country, if they experienced such ungrateful treatment. The guide said, for his part, he was not a woman, and would never run away through fear. But notwithstanding this courageous declaration, at one I awakened Mr. Mackay, related to him what had passed, and requested him not to indulge himself in sleep till I should rise. It was seven before I awoke, and on quitting my tent I was surprised at not seeing the guide and his companion, and my apprehensions were increased when I observed that the canoe was removed from its late situation. To my inquiries after them, some of the men very composedly answered that they were gone up the river, and had left the old man behind them. Mr. Mackay also told me, that while he was busily employed on the canoe, they had got to the point before he had observed their departure. The interpreter now informed me that at the dawn of day the guide had expressed his design, as soon as the sun was up, to go and wait for us, where he might find his friends. I hoped this might be true; but that my people should suffer them to depart without giving me notice, was a circumstance that awakened very painful reflections in my breast. The weather was clear in the forenoon. My observation this day gave 53. 3. 32. North latitude.

At five in the afternoon our vessel was completed, and ready for service. She proved a stronger and better boat than the old one, though had it not been for the gum obtained from the latter, it would have been a matter of great difficulty to have procured a sufficiency of that article to have prevented her from leaking. The remainder of the day was employed by the people in cleaning and refreshing themselves, as they had enjoyed no relaxation from their labour since we landed on this spot.

The old man having manifested for various and probably very
fallacious reasons, a very great aversion to accompany us any further,

it did not appear that there was any necessity to force his inclination. We now put our arms in order, which was soon accomplished, as they were at all times a general object of attention.

[July 2] It rained throughout the night, but at half past three we were ready to embark, when I offered to conduct the old man where he had supposed we should meet his friends, but he declined the proposition. I therefore directed a few pounds of pemmican to be left with him for his immediate support, and took leave of him and the place, which I named Canoe Island. [This island probably no longer exists.] During our stay there we had been most cruelly tormented by flies, particularly the sand-fly, which I am disposed to consider as the most tormenting insect of its size in nature. I was also compelled to put the people upon short allowance, and confine them to two meals a-day; a regulation peculiarly offensive to a Canadian voyager. One of these meals was composed of the dried rows [roes] of fish, pounded, and boiled in water, thickened with a small quantity of flour, and fattened with a bit of grain. These articles, being brought to the consistency of an hasty pudding, produced a substantial and not unpleasant dish. The natives are very careful of the rows of fish, which they dry, and preserve in baskets made of bark. Those we used were found in the huts of the first people who fled from us. During our abode in Canoe Island, the water sunk three perpendicular feet. I now gave the men a dram each, which could not but be considered, at this time, as a very comfortable treat. They were, indeed, in high spirits, when they perceived the superior excellence of the new vessel, and reflected that it was the work of their own hands.

At eleven we arrived at the rapids [Cottonwood Canyon], and the foreman, who had not forgotten the fright he suffered on coming down it, proposed that the canoe and lading should be carried over the mountain. I threatened him with taking the office of foreman on myself, and suggested the evident change there was in the appearance of the water since we passed it, which upon examination had sunk four feet and an half. As the water did not seem so strong on the West side, I determined to cross over, having first put Mr. Mac- 183 kay and our two hunters on shore to try the woods for game. We accordingly traversed, and got up close along the rocks to a considerable distance with the paddles, when we could proceed no further without assistance from the line; and to draw it across a perpendicular rock, for the distance of fifty fathoms, appeared to be an insurmountable obstacle. The general opinion was to return, and carry on the other side; I desired, however, two of the men to take the line, which was seventy fathoms in length, with a small roll of bark, and endeavour to climb up the rocks, from whence they were to descend on the other side of that which opposed our progress; they were then to fasten the end of the line to the roll of bark, which the current would bring to us; this being effected, they would be able to draw us up. This was an enterprise of difficulty and danger, but it was crowned with success; though to get to the water's edge above, the men were obliged to let themselves down with the line, run round a tree, from the summit of the rock. By a repetition of the same operation, we at length cleared the rapid, with the additional trouble of carrying the canoe, and unloading at two cascades. We were not more than two hours getting up this difficult part of the river, including the time employed in repairing an hole which had been broken in the canoe, by the negligence of the steersman.

Here we expected to meet with the natives, but there was not the least appearance of them, except that the guide, his companion, and two others, had apparently passed the carrying-place. We saw several fish leap out of the water, which appeared to be of the salmon kind. The old man, indeed, had informed us that this was the season when the large fish begin to come up the river. Our hunters returned, but had not seen the track of any animal. We now continued our journey; the current was not strong, but we met with frequent impediments from the fallen trees, which lay along the banks. We landed at eight in the evening, and suffered indescribable inconveniences from the flies.

[July 3] It had rained hard in the night, and there was some small rain in the morning. At four we entered our canoe, and at ten we came to a small river [West Road River], which answered to the description of that whose course the natives said, they follow in their journies towards the sea coast; we therefore put into it, and endeavoured to discover if our guide had landed here; but there were no traces of him or of any others. My former perplexities were now renewed. If I passed this river, it was probable that I might miss the natives; and I had reason to suspect that my men would not consent to return thither. As for attempting the woods without a guide, to introduce us to the first inhabitants, such a determination would be little short of absolute madness. At length, after much painful reflection, I resolved to come at once to a full explanation with my people, and I experienced a considerable relief from this resolution. Accordingly, after repeating the promise they had so lately made me, on our putting back up the river, I represented to them that this appeared to me to be the spot from which the natives took their departure for the sea coast, and added, withal, that I was determined to try it; for though our guide had left us, it was possible that, while we were making the necessary preparations, he or some others might appear, to relieve us from our present difficulties. I now found, to my great satisfaction, that they had not come to any fixed determination among themselves, as some of them immediately assented to undertake the woods with me. Others, however, suggested that it might be better to proceed a few leagues further up the river, in expectation of finding our guide, or procuring another, and that after all we might return hither. This plan I very readily agreed to adopt, but before I left this place, to which I gave the name of the West-Road River, I sent some of the men into the woods, in different directions, and went some distance up the river myself, which I found to be navigable only for small canoes. Two of the men found a good beaten path, leading up a hill just behind us, which I imagined to be the great road.

At four in the afternoon we left this place, proceeding up the [Fraser] river; and had not been upon the water more than three quarters of an hour, when we saw two canoes coming with the 185 stream. No sooner did the people in them perceive us than they landed, and we went on shore at the same place with them. They proved to be our guide, and six of his relations. He was covered with a painted beaver robe, so that we scarcely knew him in his fine habiliment. He instantly desired us to acknowledge that he had not disappointed us, and declared, at the same time, that it was his constant intention to keep his word. I accordingly gave him a jacket, a pair of trowsers, and an handkerchief, as a reward for his honourable conduct. The strangers examined us with the most minute attention, and two of them, as I was now informed, belonged to the people whom we first saw, and who fled with so much alarm from us. They told me, also, that they were so terrified on that occasion, as not to approach their huts for two days; and that when they ventured thither, they found the greater part of their property destroyed, by the fire running in the ground. According to their account, they were of a different tribe, though I found no difference in their language from that of the Nagailas or Carriers. They are called Nascud Denee. Their lodges were at some distance, on a small lake, where they take fish, and if our guide had not gone for them there, we should not have seen an human being on the river. They informed me that the road by their habitation is the shortest, and they proposed that we should take it. [These Indians were Naskotins, a branch of the Carriers.]

[July 4] At an early hour this morning, and at the suggestion of our guide, we proceeded to the landing-place that leads to the strangers lodges. Our great difficulty here was to procure a temporary separation from our company, in order to hide some articles we could not carry with us, and which it would have been imprudent to leave in the power of the natives. Accordingly Mr. Mackay, and one of our Indians embarked with them, and soon run out of our sight. At our first hiding-place we left a bag of pemmican, weighing ninety pounds, two bags of wild rice, and a gallon keg of gunpowder. Previous to our putting these articles in the ground, we rolled them up in oil cloth and dressed leather. In the second hiding-place, and guarded with the same rollers, we hid two bags of Indian corn, or maize, and a bale of different articles of merchandise. When we had completed this important object, we proceeded till half past eight, when we landed at the entrance of a small rivulet, where our friends were waiting for us.

Here it was necessary that we should leave our canoe, and whatever we could not carry on our backs. In the first place, therefore, we prepared a stage, on which the canoe was placed bottom upwards, and shaded by a covering of small trees and branches, to keep her from the sun. We then built an oblong hollow square, ten feet by five, of green logs, wherein we placed every article it was necessary for us to leave here, and covered the whole with large pieces of timber.

While we were eagerly employed in this necessary business, our guide and his companions were so impatient to be gone, that we could not persuade the former to wait till we were prepared for our departure, and we had some difficulty in persuading another of the natives to remain, who had undertook to conduct us where the guide had promised to wait our arrival.

At noon we were in a state of preparation to enter the woods, an undertaking of which I shall not here give any preliminary opinion, but leave those who read it to judge for themselves.

We carried on our backs four bags and an half of pemmican, weighing from eighty-five to ninety pounds each, a case with my instruments, a parcel of goods for presents, weighing ninety pounds, and a parcel containing ammunition of the same weight. Each of the Canadians had a burden of about ninety pounds, with a gun, and some ammunition. The Indians had about forty-five pounds weight of pemmican to carry, besides their gun, &c. with which they were very much dissatisfied, and if they had dared would have instantly left us. They had hitherto been very much indulged, but the moment was now arrived when indulgence was no longer practicable. My own load, and that of Mr. Mackay, consisted of twenty-two pounds of pemmican, some rice, a little sugar, &c. amounting in the whole 187 to about seventy pounds each, besides our arms and ammunition. I had also the tube of my telescope swung across my shoulder, which was a troublesome addition to my burthen. It was determined that we should content ourselves with two meals a day, which were regulated without difficulty, as our provisions did not require the ceremony of cooking. [They had seen the beginning of the main trail near the mouth of the West Road River, but they had come about ten miles farther up the Fraser to go with one of the Indians to his village on a side trail. Now they were ready to begin the overland journey to the coast.]

In this state of equipment we began our journey, as I have already mentioned, about twelve at noon, the commencement of which was a steep ascent of about a mile; it lay along a well-beaten path, but the country through which it led was rugged and ridgy, and full of wood. When we were in a state of extreme heat, from the toil of our journey, the rain came on, and continued till the evening, and even when it ceased the underwood continued its drippings upon us.

About half past six we arrived at an Indian camp of three fires, where we found our guide, and on his recommendation we determined to remain there for the night. The computed distance of this day's journey was about twelve geographical miles; the course about West.

At sun-set an elderly man and three other natives joined us from the Westward. The former bore a lance that very much resembled a serjeant's halberd. He had lately received it, by way of barter, from the natives of the Sea-Coast, who procured it from the white men. We should meet, he said, with many of his countrymen who had just returned from thence. According to his report, it did not require more than six days journey, for people who are not heavily laden, to reach the country of those with whom they bartered their skins for iron, &c. and from thence it is not quite two day's march to the sea. They proposed to send two young men on before us, to notify to the different tribes that we were approaching, that they might not be surprised at our appearance, and be disposed to afford us a friendly reception. This was a measure which I could not but approve, and endeavoured by some small presents to prepossess our couriers in our favour.

These people live but poorly at this season, and I could procure no provision from them, but a few small dried fish, as I think, of the carp kind. They had several European articles; and one of them had a strip of fur, which appeared to me to be of the sea otter. He obtained it from the natives of the coast, and exchanged it with me for some beads and a brass cross.

We retired to rest in as much security as if we had been long habituated to a confidence in our present associates: indeed, we had no alternative; for so great were the fatigues of the day in our mode of travelling, that we were in great need of rest at night.

[July 5] We had no sooner laid ourselves down to rest last night, than the natives began to sing, in a manner very different from what I had been accustomed to hear among savages. It was not accompanied either with dancing, drum, or rattle; but consisted of soft, plaintive tones, and a modulation that was rather agreeable: it had somewhat the air of church music. As the natives had requested me not to quit them at a very early hour in the morning, it was five before I desired that the young men, who were to proceed with us, should depart, when they prepared to set off: but, on calling to our guide to conduct us, he said, that he did not intend to accompany us any further, as the young men would answer our purpose as well as himself. I knew it would be in vain to remonstrate with him, and therefore submitted to his caprice without a reply. However, I thought proper to inform him, that one of my people had lost his dag, or poignard [dagger], and requested his assistance in the recovery of it. He asked me what I would give him to conjure it back again, and a knife was agreed to be the price of his necromantic exertions. Accordingly, all the dags and knives in the place were gathered together, and the natives formed a circle round them; the conjurer also remaining in the middle. When this part of the ceremony was arranged, he began to sing, the rest joining in the chorus;   189 and after some time he produced the poignard which was stuck in the ground, and returned it to me.

At seven we were ready to depart; when I was surprised to hear our late guide propose, without any solicitation on our part, to resume his office; and he actually conducted us as far as a small lake, where we found an encampment of three families. The young men who had undertaken to conduct us were not well understood by my interpreters, who continued to be so displeased with their journey, that they performed this part of their duty with great reluctance. I endeavoured to persuade an elderly man of this encampment to accompany us to the next tribe, but no inducement of mine could prevail on him to comply with my wishes. I was, therefore, obliged to content myself with the guides I had already engaged, for whom we were obliged to wait some time, till they had provided shoes for their journey. I exchanged two halfpence here, one of his present Majesty, and the other of the State of Massachuset's Bay, coined in 1787. They hung as ornaments in children's ears.

My situation here was rendered rather unpleasant by the treatment which my hunters received from these people. The former, it appeared, were considered as belonging to a tribe who inhabit the mountains, and are the natural enemies of the latter. We had also been told by one of the natives, of a very stern aspect, that he had been stabbed by a relation of theirs, and pointed to a scar as the proof of it. I was, therefore, very glad to proceed on my journey.

Our guides conducted us along the lake through thick woods, and without any path, for about a mile and an half, when we lost sight of it. This piece of water is about three miles long and one broad. [This is supposed to have been Punchaw Lake.] We then crossed a creek and entered upon a beaten track, through an open country, sprinkled with cypress trees. At twelve the sky became black, and an heavy gust with rain shortly followed, which continued for upwards of an hour. When we perceived the approaching storm, we fixed our thin, light oil-cloth to screen us from it. On renewing our march, as the bushes were very wet, I desired our guides, they having no burdens, to walk in front, and beat them as they went: this task they chose to decline, and accordingly I undertook it. Our road now lay along a lake, and across a creek that ran into it. The guides informed me, that this part of the country abounds in beaver: many traps were seen along the road which had been set for lynxes and martens. About a quarter of a mile from the place where we had been stopped by the rain, the ground was covered with hail, and as we advanced, the hailstones increased in size, some of them being as big as musket-balls. In this manner was the ground whitened for upwards of two miles. At five in the afternoon we arrived on the banks of another lake, when it again threatened rain; and we had already been sufficiently wetted in the course of the day, to look with complacency towards a repetition of it: we accordingly fixed our shed [tent], the rain continuing with great violence through the remainder of the day: it was, therefore, determined that we should stop here for the night.

In the course of the day we passed three winter huts; they consisted of low walls, with a ridge-pole, covered with the branches of the Canadian balsam-tree [fir]. One of my men had a violent pain in his knee, and I asked the guides to take a share of his burden, as they had nothing to carry but their beaver robes, and bows and arrows, but they could not be made to understand a word of my request.

[July 6] At four this morning I arose from my bed, such as it was. As we must have been in a most unfortunate predicament if our guides should have deserted us in the night, by way of security, I proposed to the youngest of them to sleep with me, and he readily consented. These people have no covering but their beaver garments, and that of my companions was a nest of vermin. I, however, spread it under us, and having laid down upon it, we covered ourselves with my camblet cloak. My companion's hair being greased with fish-oil, and his body smeared with red earth, my sense of smelling, as well as that of feeling, threatened to interrupt my rest; but these inconveniences yielded to my fatigue, and I passed a night of sound repose. 191

I took the lead in our march, as I had done yesterday, in order to clear the branches of the wet which continued to hang upon them. We proceeded with all possible expedition through a level country with but little under-wood; the larger trees were of the [Douglas] fir kind. At half past eight we fell upon the road [main trail], which we first intended to have taken from the Great River [Fraser River], and must be shorter than that which we had travelled. The West-road river was also in sight, winding through a valley. We had not met with any water since our encampment of last night, and though we were afflicted with violent thirst, the river was at such a distance from us, and the descent to it so long and steep, that we were compelled to be satisfied with casting our longing looks towards it. There appeared to be more water in the river here, than at its discharge. The Indian account, that it is navigable for their canoes, is, I believe, perfectly correct.

Our guides now told us, that as the road was very good and well traced, they would proceed to inform the next tribe that we were coming. This information was of a very unpleasant nature; as it would have been easy for them to turn off the road at a hundred yards from us, and, when we had passed them, to return home. I proposed that one of them should remain with us, while two of my people should leave their loads behind and accompany the other to the lodges. But they would not stay to hear our persuasions, and were soon out of sight.

I now desired the Cancre to leave his burden, take a small quantity of provision, with his arms and blanket, and follow me. I also told my men to come on as fast as they could, and that I would wait for them as soon as I had formed an acquaintance with the natives of the country before us. We accordingly followed our guides with all the expedition in our power, but did not overtake them till we came to a family of natives, consisting of one man, two women, and six children, with whom we found them. These people betrayed no signs of fear at our appearance, and the man willingly conversed with my

interpreter, to whom he made himself more intelligible than our guides had been able to do. They, however, had informed him of the object of our journey. He pointed out to us one of his wives, who was a native of the sea coast, which was not a very great distance from us. This woman was more inclined to corpulency than any we had yet seen, was of low stature, with an oblong face, grey eyes, and a flattish nose. She was decorated with ornaments of various kinds, such as large blue beads, either pendant from her ears, encircling her neck, or braided in her hair: she also wore bracelets of brass, copper, and horn. Her garments consisted of a kind of tunic, which was covered with a robe of matted bark, fringed round the bottom with skin of the sea otter. None of the women whom I had seen since we crossed the mountain wore this kind of tunic; their blankets being merely girt round the waist. She had learned the language of her husband's tribe, and confirmed his account, that we were at no great distance from the sea. They were on their way, she said, to the great river to fish. Age seemed to be an object of great veneration among these people, for they carried an old woman by turns on their backs who was quite blind and infirm, from the very advanced period of her life.

Our people having joined us and rested themselves, I requested our guides to proceed, when the elder of them told me that he should not go any further, but that these people would send a boy to accompany his brother, and I began to think myself rather fortunate, that we were not deserted by them all.

About noon we parted, and in two hours we came up with two men and their families: when we first saw them they were sitting down, as if to rest themselves; but no sooner did they perceive us than they rose up and seized their arms. The boys who were behind us immediately ran forward and spoke to them, when they laid by their arms and received us as friends. They had been eating green berries and dried fish. We had, indeed, scarcely joined them, when a woman and a boy came from the river with water, which they very hospitably gave us to drink. The people of this party had a very sickly appearance, which might have been the consequence of disease, or that indolence which is so natural to them, or of both. One of the women had a tattooed line along the chin, of the same length as her mouth.

The lads now informed me that they would go no further, but that these men would take their places; and they parted from their families with as little apparent concern, as if they were entire strangers to each other. One of them was very well understood by my interpreter, and had resided among the natives of the sea coast, whom he had left but a short time. According to his information, we were approaching a river [Dean River or Bella Coola River], which was neither large nor long, but whose banks are inhabited; and that in the bay which the sea forms at the mouth of it, a great wooden canoe, with white people, arrives about the time when the leaves begin to grow: I presume in the early part of May.

After we parted with the last people, we came to an uneven, hilly, and swampy country, through which our way was impeded by a considerable number of fallen trees. At five in the afternoon we were overtaken by a heavy shower of rain and hail, and being at the same time very much fatigued, we encamped for the night near a small creek. Our course, till we came to the river [West Road River], was about South-West ten miles, and then West twelve or fourteen miles. I thought it prudent, by way of security, to submit to the same inconveniences I have already described, and shared the beaver robe of one of my guides during the night.

[July 7] I was so busily employed in collecting intelligence from our conductors, that I last night forgot to wind up my time-piece, and it was the only instance of such an act of negligence since I left Fort Chepewyan, on the 11th [10th] of last October. At five we quitted our station, and proceeded across two mountains, covered with spruce, poplar, white birch, and other trees. We then descended into a level country, where we found a good road through woods of cypress. We then came to two small lakes, at the distance of about fourteen miles. Course about West. Through them the river passes, and our road kept in a parallel line with it on a range of elevated

194

ground. [The trail had left the West Road River and turned up the Euchiniko River. After crossing the Euchiniko they crossed a ridge and dropped again into the valley of the West Road River, which flowed through these two small lakes.] On observing some people before us, our guides hastened to meet them, and, on their approach, one of them stepped forward with an axe in his hand. This party consisted only of a man, two women, and the same number of children. The eldest of the women, who probably was the man's mother, was engaged, when we joined them, in clearing a circular spot, of about five feet in diameter, of the weeds that infested it; nor did our arrival interrupt her employment, which was sacred to the memory of the dead. The spot to which her pious care was devoted, contained the grave of a husband and a son, and whenever she passed this way, she always stopped to pay this tribute of affection.

As soon as we had taken our morning allowance, we set forwards, and about three we perceived more people before us. After some alarm we came up with them. They consisted of seven men, as many women, and several children. Here I was under the necessity of pro-curing another guide, and we continued our route on the same side of the river, till six in the evening, when we crossed it. It was knee deep, and about an hundred yards over. I wished now to stop for the night, as we were all of us very much fatigued, but our guide recom-mended us to proceed onwards to a family of his friends, at a small distance from thence, where we arrived at half past seven. He had gone forward, and procured us a welcome and quiet reception. There being a net hanging to dry, I requested the man to prepare and set it in the water, which he did with great expedition, and then presented me with a few small dried fish. Our course was South-West about twelve miles, part of which was an extensive swamp, that was seldom less than knee deep. In the course of the afternoon we had several showers of rain. I had attempted to take an altitude, but it was past meridian. The water of the river before the lodge was quite still, and expanded itself into the form of a small lake. In many other places, indeed, it had assumed the same form.

[July 8] It rained throughout the night, and it was seven in the morning before the weather would allow us to proceed. The guide brought me five small boiled fish, in a platter made of bark; some of them were of the carp kind, and the rest of a species for which I am not qualified to furnish a name. Having dried our clothes, we set off on our march about eight, and our guide very cheerfully continued to accompany us; but he was not altogether so intelligible as his predecessors in our service. We learned from him, however that this lake [Kluskoil Lake], through which the river [West Road River] passes, extends to the foot of the mountain, and that he expected to meet nine men, of a tribe [a branch of the Carriers] which inhabits the North side of the river.

In this part of our journey we were surprised with the appearance of several regular basons [basins], some of them furnished with water, and the others empty; their slope from the edge to the bottom formed an angle of about forty-five degrees, and their perpendicular depth was about twelve feet. Those that contained water, discovered gravel near their edges, while the empty ones were covered with grass and herbs, among which we discovered mustard and mint. There were also several places from whence the water appears to have retired, which are covered with the same soil and herbage.

We now proceeded along a very uneven country, the upper parts of which were covered with poplars, a little under-wood, and plenty of grass: the intervening vallies were watered with rivulets. From these circumstances, and the general appearance of vegetation, I could not account for the apparent absence of animals of every kind.

At two in the afternoon we arrived at the largest river [still the West Road River] that we had seen since we left our canoe, and which forced its way between and over the huge stones that opposed its current. Our course was about South-South-West sixteen miles along the river, which might here justify the title of a lake [Euchiniko Lakes, expansions of the West Road River]. The road was good, and our next course, which was West by South, brought us onward

196

ten miles, where we encamped, fatigued and wet, it having rained three parts of the day. This river abounds with fish, and must fall into the great river, further down than we had extended our voyage.

[July 9] A heavy and continued rain fell throughout great part of the night, and as we were in some measure exposed to it, time was required to dry our clothes; so that it was half past seven in the morning before we were ready to set out. As we found the country so destitute of game, and foreseeing the difficulty of procuring provisions for our return, I thought it prudent to conceal half a bag of pemmican: having sent off the Indians, and all my people except two, we buried it under the fire-place, as we had done on a former occasion. We soon overtook our party, and continued our route along the river or lake. About twelve I had an altitude, but it was inaccurate from the cloudiness of the weather. We continued our progress till five in the afternoon, when the water began to narrow, and in about half an hour we came to a ferry, where we found a small raft. At this time it began to thunder, and torrents of rain soon followed, which terminated our journey for the day. Our course was about South, twenty-one miles from the lake already mentioned. We now discovered the tops of mountains, covered with snow, over very high intermediate land. [These mountains were either the Coast Range or one of the outlying ranges to the east of it.] We killed a white-head [bald eagle] and a grey [?] eagle, and three grey partridges [grouse]; we saw also two otters in the river, and several beaver lodges along it. When the rain ceased, we caught a few small fish, and repaired the raft for the service of the ensuing day.

[July 10] At an early hour of this morning we prepared to cross the water. The traverse is about thirty yards, and it required five trips to get us all over. At a short distance below, a small river falls in, that comes from the direction in which we were proceeding. [They had crossed to the south side of the West Road River and were about to leave it to follow the trail up the Kluskus River, which flows into the West Road from the west. The Kluskus flows through several lakes, the Kluskus Lakes.]

It is a rapid for about three hundred yards, when it expands into a lake, along which our road conducted us, and beneath a range of beautiful hills, covered with verdure. At half past eight we came to the termination of the lake, where there were two houses that occupied a most delightful situation, and as they contained their necessary furniture, it seemed probable that their owners intended shortly to return. Near them were several graves or tombs, to which the natives are particularly attentive, and never suffer any herbage to grow upon them. In about half an hour we reached a place where there were two temporary huts, that contained thirteen men, with whom we found our guide, who had preceded us in order to secure a good reception. The buildings were detached from each other, and conveniently placed for fishing in the lake. Their inhabitants called themselves Sloua-cuss-Dinais [the Kluskus, a branch of the Carriers], which denomination, as far as my interpreter could explain it to me, I understood to mean Red-fish Men. They were much more cleanly, healthy, and agreeable in their appearance, than any of the natives whom we had passed; nevertheless, I have no doubt that they are the same people, from their name alone, which is of the Chepewyan language. My interpreters, however, understood very little of what they said, so that I did not expect much information from them. Some of them said it was a journey of four days to the sea, and others were of opinion that it was six; and there were among them who extended it to eight; but they all uniformly declared that they had been to the coast. They did not entertain the smallest apprehension of danger from us, and, when we discharged our pieces, expressed no sensation but that of astonishment, which, as may be supposed, was proportionably increased when one of the hunters shot an eagle, at a considerable distance. At twelve I obtained an altitude, which made our latitude 53. 4. 32. North, being not so far South as I expected.

I now went, accompanied by one of my men, an interpreter, and the guide, to visit some huts at the distance of a mile. On our arrival the inhabitants presented us with a dish of boiled trout, of a small kind. The fish would have been excellent if it had not tasted of the kettle, which was made of the bark of the white spruce, and of the dried grass with which it was boiled. Besides this kind of trout, red and white carp and jub, are the only fish I saw as the produce of these waters.

These people appeared to live in a state of comparative comfort: they take a greater share in the labour of the women, than is common among the savage tribes, and are, as I was informed, content with one wife. Though this circumstance may proceed rather from the difficulty of procuring subsistence, than any habitual aversion to polygamy.

My present guide now informed me, that he could not proceed any further, and I accordingly engaged two of these people to succeed him in that office; but when they desired us to proceed on the beaten path without them, as they could not set off till the following day, I determined to stay that night, in order to accommodate myself to their convenience. I distributed some trifles among the wives and children of the men who were to be our future guides, and returned to my people. We came back by a different way, and passed by two buildings, erected between four trees, and about fifteen feet from the ground, which appeared to me to be intended as magazines for winter provisions. At four in the afternoon we proceeded with considerable expedition, by the side of the lake, till six, when we came to the end of it: we then struck off through a much less beaten track, and at half past seven stopped for the night. Our course was about West-South-West thirteen miles, and West six miles.

[July 11] I passed a most uncomfortable night: the first part of it I was tormented with flies, and in the latter deluged with rain. In the morning the weather cleared, and as soon as our clothes were dried, we proceeded through a morass. This part of the country had been laid waste by fire, and the fallen trees added to the pain and perplexity of our way. An high, rocky ridge stretched along our left. [This ridge is the northern front of a basaltic plateau south of the West Road River.] Though the rain returned, we continued our 199 progress till noon, when our guides took to some trees for shelter. We then spread our oil-cloth, and, with some difficulty, made a fire. About two the rain ceased, when we continued our journey through the same kind of country which we had hitherto passed. At half past three we came in sight of a lake [Tsacha Lake]; the land, at the same time gradually rising to a range of mountains [either the Itcha or Ilgachuz Mountains] whose tops were covered with snow. We soon after observed two fresh tracks, which seemed to surprise our guides, but they supposed them to have been made by the inhabitants of the country who were come into this part of it to fish. At five in the afternoon we were so wet and cold, (for it had at intervals continued to rain,) that we were compelled to stop for the night. We passed seven rivulets and a creek in this day's journey. As I had hitherto regulated our course by the sun, I could not form an accurate judgment of this route, as we had not been favoured with a sight of it during the day; but I imagine it to have been nearly in the same direction as that of yesterday. Our distance could not have been less than fifteen miles.

Our conductors now began to complain of our mode of travelling, and mentioned their intention of leaving us; and my interpreters, who were equally dissatisfied, added to our perplexity by their conduct. Besides these circumstances, and the apprehension that the distance from the sea might be greater than I had imagined, it became a matter of real necessity that we should begin to diminish the consumption of our provisions, and to subsist upon two-thirds of our allowance; a proposition which was as unwelcome to my people, as it was necessary to be put into immediate practice.

[July 12] At half past five this morning we proceeded on our journey, with cloudy weather, and when we came to the end of the lake several tracks were visible that led to the side of the water; from which circumstance I concluded, that some of the natives were fishing along the banks of it. This lake is not more than three miles long, and about one broad. [Tsacha Lake is much longer—Mackenzie saw only the western end.] We then passed four smaller lakes, the two first being on our right, and those which preceeded on our left. A small river also flowed across our way from the right, and we passed it over a beaver-dam. A larger lake now appeared on our right, and the mountains on each side of us were covered with snow. [The large lake was Tsetzi Lake. The mountains were outliers of the Coast Range.] We afterwards came to another lake on our right, and soon reached a river, which our guides informed us was the same that we had passed on a raft. [This was Cluchuta Lake. Before they reached it the main trail to Bella Coola turned off to the left, but they did not take it.[20] He had now come to the West Road River again, and was about to cross it to the north side.] They said it was navigable for canoes from the great river [Fraser River], except two rapids, one of which we had seen. At this place it is upwards of twenty yards across, and deep water. One of the guides swam over to fetch a raft which was on the opposite side; and having increased its dimensions, we crossed at two trips, except four of the men, who preferred swimming.

Here our conductors renewed their menace of leaving us, and I was obliged to give them several articles, and promise more, in order to induce them to continue till we could procure other natives to succeed them. At four in the afternoon we forded the same river [This was a tributary of the West Road River. They were north of the West Road and would not see it again], and being with the guides at some distance before the rest of the people, I sat down to wait for them, and no sooner did they arrive, than the former set off with so much speed, that my attempt to follow them proved unsuccessful. One of my Indians, however, who had no load, overtook them, when they excused themselves to him by declaring, that their sole motive for leaving us, was to prevent the people, whom they expected to find, from shooting their arrows at us. At seven o'clock, however, we were so fatigued, that we encamped without them: the mountains covered with snow now appeared to be directly before us. As we were collecting wood for our fire, we discovered a cross road, where it appeared that people had passed within seven or eight days. In short, our situa- 201 tion was such as to afford a just cause of alarm, and that of the people with me was of a nature to defy immediate alleviation. It was necessary, however, for me to attempt it; and I rested my principles of encouragement on a representation of our past perplexities and unexpected relief, and endeavoured to excite in them the hope of similar good fortune. I stated to them, that we could not be at a great distance from the sea, and that there were but few natives to pass, till we should arrive among those, who being accustomed to visit the sea coast, and, having seen white people, would be disposed to treat us with kindness. Such was the general tenor of reasoning I employed on the occasion, and I was happy to find that it was not offered in vain.

The weather had been cloudy till three in the afternoon, when the sun appeared; but surrounded, as we were, with snow-clad mountains, the air became so cold, that the violence of our exercise, was not sufficient to produce a comfortable degree of warmth. Our course to-day was from West to South, and at least thirty-six miles. The land in general was very barren and stony, and lay in ridges, with cypress trees scattered over them. We passed several swamps, where we saw nothing to console us but a few tracks of deer.

[July 13] The weather this morning was clear but cold, and our scanty covering was not sufficient to protect us from the severity of the night. About five, after we had warmed ourselves at a large fire, we proceeded on our dubious journey. In about an hour we came to the edge of a wood, when we perceived a house, situated on a green spot, and by the side of a small river [Ulgako Creek or a tributary]. The smoke that issued from it informed us that it was inhabited. I immediately pushed forward toward this mansion, while my people were in such a state of alarm, that they followed me with the utmost reluctance. On looking back I perceived that we were in an Indian defile [narrow passage], of fifty yards in length. I, however, was close upon the house before the inhabitants perceived us, when the women and children uttered the most horrid shrieks, and the only man who appeared to be with them, escaped out of a back door, which I reached in time to prevent the women and children from following him. The man fled with all his speed into the wood, and I called in vain on my interpreters to speak to him, but they were so agitated with fear as to have lost the power of utterance. It is impossible to describe the distress and alarm of these poor people, who believing that they were attacked by enemies, expected an immediate massacre, which, among themselves, never fails to follow such an event.

Our prisoners consisted of three women, and seven children, which apparently composed three families. At length, however, by our demeanor, and our presents, we contrived to dissipate their apprehensions. One of the women then informed us, that their people, with several others had left that place three nights before, on a trading journey to a tribe whom she called Annah, which is the name the Chepewyans give to the Knisteneaux, at the distance of three days. ["Annah" probably should read "Atnah," the Athapascan term for most other tribes.[21]] She added also, that from the mountains before us, which were covered with snow, the sea was visible; and accompanied her information with a present of a couple of dried fish. We now expressed our desire that the man might be induced to return, and conduct us in the road to the sea. Indeed, it was not long before he discovered himself in the wood, when he was assured, both by the women and our interpreters, that we had no hostile design against him; but these assurances had no effect in quieting his apprehensions. I then attempted to go to him alone, and shewed him a knife, beads, &c. to induce him to come to me, but he, in return, made an hostile display of his bow and arrows; and, having for a time exhibited a variety of strange antics, again disappeared. However, he soon presented himself in another quarter, and after a succession of parleys between us, he engaged to come and accompany us.

While these negotiations were proceeding, I proposed to visit the fishing machines, to which the women readily consented, and I found in them twenty small fish, such as trout, carp, and jub, for which I gave her a large knife; a present that appeared to be equally unexpected and gratifying to her. Another man now came towards 203 us, from a hill, talking aloud from the time he appeared till he reached us. The purport of his speech was, that he threw himself upon our mercy, and we might kill him, if it was our pleasure, but that from what he had heard, he looked rather for our friendship than our enmity. He was an elderly person, of a decent appearance, and I gave him some articles to conciliate him to us. The first man now followed with a lad along with him, both of whom were the sons of the old man, and, on his arrival, he gave me several half-dried fish, which I considered as a peace offering. After some conversation with these people, respecting the country, and our future progress through it, we retired to rest, with sensations very different from those with which we had risen in the morning. The weather had been generally cloudy throughout the day, and when the sun was obscured, extremely cold for the season. At noon I obtained a meridian altitude, which gave 52. 58. 53. North latitude. I likewise took time in the afternoon.

[July 14] This morning we had a bright sun, with an East wind. These people examined their fishing machines, when they found in them a great number of small fish, and we dressed as many of them as we could eat. Thus was our departure retarded until seven, when we proceeded on our journey, accompanied by the man and his two sons. As I did not want the younger, and should be obliged to feed him, I requested of his father to leave him, for the purpose of fishing for the women. He replied, that they were accustomed to fish for themselves, and that I need not be apprehensive of their encroaching upon my provisions, as they were used to sustain themselves in their journies on herbs, and the inner tegument of the bark of trees, for the stripping of which he had a thin piece of bone, then hanging by his side. The latter is of a glutinous quality, of a clammy, sweet taste, and is generally considered by the more interior Indians as a delicacy, rather than an article of common food. Our guide informed me that there is a short cut across the mountains, but as there was no trace of a road, and it would shorten our journey but one day, he should

prefer the beaten way.

We accordingly proceeded along a lake [Eliguk Lake], West five miles. We then crossed a small river [Ulgako Creek], and passed through a swamp, about South-West, when we began gradually to ascend for some time till we gained the summit of a hill, where we had an extensive view to the South-East, from which direction a considerable river appeared to flow, at the distance of about three miles: it was represented to me as being navigable for canoes. [This was the Dean River, which flows into the head of Dean Channel. The hill they were on separates the drainages of three rivers—the West Road and the Nechako, both flowing east into the Fraser, and the Dean, flowing west into the Pacific. They now descended into the Nechako drainage.] The descent of this hill was more steep than its ascent, and was succeeded by another, whose top, though not so elevated as the last, afforded a view of the range of mountains, covered with snow, which, according to the intelligence of our guide, terminates in the ocean. We now left a small lake [Malaput Lake] on our left, then crossed a creek running out of it, and at one in the afternoon came to a house, of the same construction and dimensions as have already been mentioned, but the materials were much better prepared and finished. The timber was squared on two sides, and the bark taken off the two others; the ridge pole was also shaped in the same manner, extending about eight or ten feet beyond the gable end, and supporting a shed over the door; the end of it was carved into the similitude of a snake's head. Several hieroglyphics and figures of a similar workmanship, and painted with red earth, decorated the interior of the building. The inhabitants had left the house but a short time, and there were several bags or bundles in it, which I did not suffer to be disturbed. Near it were two tombs, surrounded in a neat manner with boards, and covered with bark. Beside them several poles had been erected, one of which was squared, and all of them painted. From each of them were suspended several rolls or parcels of bark, and our guide gave the following account of them; which, as far as we could judge from our imperfect knowledge of the language, and the incidental errors of interpretation, appeared to involve two different modes of treating their dead; or it might be one and the same ceremony, which we did not distinctly comprehend: at all events, it is the practice of these people to burn the bodies of their dead, except the larger bones, which are rolled up in bark and suspended from poles, as I have already described. According to the other account, it appeared that they actually bury their dead; and when another of the family dies, the remains of the person who was last interred are taken from the grave and burned, as has been already mentioned; so that the members of a family are thus successively buried and burned, to make room for each other; and one tomb proves sufficient for a family through succeeding generations. There is no house in this country without a tomb in its vicinity. Our last course extended about ten miles.

We continued our journey along the lake [Gatcho Lake] before the house, and, crossing a river [Entiako River] that flowed out of it, came to a kind of bank, or weir, formed by the natives, for the purpose of placing their fishing machines, many of which, of different sizes, were lying on the side of the river. Our guide placed one of them, with the certain expectation that on his return he should find plenty of fish in it. We proceeded nine miles further, on a good road, West-South-West, when we came to a small lake [Lilie Lake, a tributary of the Dean River. They were now in the coastal drainage.]: we then crossed a river that ran out of it, and our guides were in continual expectation of meeting with some of the natives. To this place our course was a mile and an half, in the same direction as the last. At nine at night we crossed a river [Dean River] on rafts, our last distance being about four miles South-East, on a winding road, through a swampy country, and along a succession of small lakes. We were now quite exhausted, and it was absolutely necessary for us to stop for the night. The weather being clear throughout the day, we had no reason to complain of the cold. Our guides encouraged us with the hope, that in two days of similar exertion, we should arrive among the people of the other nation.

206   [July 15] At five this morning we were again in motion, and pass-

ing along a river [an unnamed tributary of the Dean River], we at length forded it. This stream was not more than knee deep, about thirty yards over, and with a stony bottom. The old man went onward by himself, in the hope of falling in with the people, whom he expected to meet in the course of the day. At eleven we came up with him, and the natives whom he expected, consisting of five men and part of their families. They received us with great kindness, and examined us with the most minute attention. They must, however, have been told that we were white, as our faces no longer indicated that distinguishing complexion. They called themselves Neguia Dinais [Carriers], and were come in a different direction from us, but were now going the same way, to the Anah-yoe Tesse or River [Bella Coola River?], and appeared to be very much satisfied with our having joined them. They presented us with some fish which they had just taken in the adjoining lake.

Here I expected that our guides, like their predecessors, would have quitted us, but, on the contrary, they expressed themselves to be so happy in our company, and that of their friends, that they voluntarily, and with great cheerfulness, proceeded to pass another night with us. Our new acquaintance were people of a very pleasing aspect. The hair of the women was tied in large loose knots over the ears, and plaited with great neatness from the division of the head, so as to be included in the knots. Some of them had adorned their tresses with beads, with a very pretty effect. The men were clothed in leather, their hair was nicely combed, and their complexion was, fairer, or perhaps it may be said, with more propriety, that they were more cleanly, than any of the natives whom we had yet seen. Their eyes, though keen and sharp, are not of that dark colour, so generally observable in the various tribes of Indians; they were, on the contrary, of a grey hue, with a tinge of red. There was one man amongst them of at least six feet four inches in height; his manners were affable, and he had a more prepossessing appearance than any Indian I had met with in my journey; he was about twenty-eight years of age, and was treated with particular respect by his party. Every man, 207 woman, and child, carried a proportionate burden, consisting of beaver coating and parchment, as well as skins of the otter, the marten, the bear, the lynx, and dressed moose-skins. The last they procure from the Rocky-Mountain Indians [Sekanis]. According to their account, the people of the sea coast prefer them to any other article. Several of their relations and friends, they said, were already gone, as well provided as themselves, to barter with the people of the coast; who barter them in their turn, except the dressed leather, with white people who, as they had been informed, arrive there in large canoes.

Such an escort was the most fortunate circumstance that could happen in our favour. They told us, that as the women and children could not travel fast, we should be three days in getting to the end of our journey; which must be supposed to have been very agreeable information to people in our exhausted condition.

In about half an hour after we had joined our new acquaintance, the signal for moving onwards was given by the leader of the party, who vociferated the words, Huy, Huy, when his people joined him and continued a clamorous conversation. We passed along a winding road over hills, and through swampy vallies, from South to West. We then crossed a deep, narrow river, which discharges itself into a lake [upper Tanya Lake], on whose side we stopped at five in the afternoon, for the night, though we had reposed several times since twelve at noon; so that our mode of travelling had undergone a very agreeable change. I compute the distance of this day's journey at about twenty miles. In the middle of the day the weather was clear and sultry.

We all sat down on a very pleasant green spot, and were no sooner seated than our guide and one of the party prepared to engage in play. They had each a bundle of about fifty small sticks, neatly polished, of the size of a quill, and five inches long: a certain number of these sticks had red lines round them; and as many of these as one of the players might find convenient were curiously rolled up in dry grass, and according to the judgment of his antagonist respecting their number and marks, he lost or won. Our friend was apparently the loser, as he parted with his bow and arrows, and several articles which I had given him.

[July 16] The weather of this morning was the same as yesterday; but our fellow-travellers were in no hurry to proceed, and I was under the necessity of pressing them into greater expedition, by representing the almost exhausted state of our provisions. They, however, assured us, that after the next night's sleep we should arrive at the river where they were going, and that we should there get fish in great abundance. My young men, from an act of imprudence, deprived themselves last night of that rest which was so necessary to them. One of the strangers asking them several questions respecting us, and concerning their own country, one of them gave such answers as were not credited by the audience; whereupon he demanded, in a very angry tone, if they thought he was disposed to tell lies, like the Rocky-Mountain Indians; and one of that tribe happening to be of the party, a quarrel ensued, which might have been attended with the most serious consequences, if it had not been fortunately prevented by the interference of those who were not interested in the dispute.

Though our stock of provisions was getting so low, I determined, nevertheless, to hide about twenty pounds of pemmican, by way of providing against our return. I therefore left two of the men behind, with directions to bury it, as usual, under the place where we had made our fire.

Our course was about West-South-West by the side of the lake [lower Tanya Lake], and in about two miles we came to the end of it. Here was a general halt, when my men overtook us. I was now informed, that some people of another tribe were sent for, who wished very much to see us, two of whom would accompany us over the mountains; that, as for themselves, they had changed their mind, and intended to follow a small river which issued out of the lake, and went in a direction very different from the line of our journey. [The guides had decided to follow the Takia River and Dean River 209 to the coast, instead of crossing the mountains to the Bella Coola River.] This was a disappointment, which, though not uncommon to us, might have been followed by considerable inconveniences. It was my wish to continue with them whatever way they went; but neither my promises or entreaties would avail: these people were not to be turned from their purpose; and when I represented the low state of our provisions, one of them answered, that if we would stay with them all night, he would boil a kettle of fish-roes for us. Accordingly, without receiving any answer, he began to make preparation to fulfil his engagement. He took the roes out of a bag, and having bruised them between two stones, put them in water to soak. His wife then took an handful of dry grass in her hand, with which she squeezed them through her fingers; in the mean time her husband was employed in gathering wood to make a fire, for the purpose of heating stones. When she had finished her operation, she filled a watape kettle nearly full of water, and poured the roes into it. When the stones were sufficiently heated, some of them were put into the kettle, and others were thrown in from time to time, till the water was in a state of boiling; the woman also continued stirring the contents of the kettle, till they were brought to a thick consistency; the stones were then taken out, and the whole was seasoned with about a pint of strong rancid oil. [The oil of the eulachen or candlefish was an important food for the coastal Indians, and they traded it to the Indians of the interior.] The smell of this curious dish was sufficient to sicken me without tasting it, but the hunger of my people surmounted the nauseous meal. When unadulterated by the stinking oil, these boiled roes are not unpalatable food.

In the mean time four of the people who had been expected arrived, and, according to the account given of them, were of two tribes whom I had not yet known. After some conversation, they proposed, that I should continue my route by their houses; but the old guide, who was now preparing to leave us, informed me that it would lengthen my journey; and by his advice I proposed to them to conduct us along the road which had been already marked out to us.

This they undertook without the least hesitation; and, at the same time, pointed out to me the pass in the mountain, bearing South by East by compass. Here I had a meridian altitude, and took time.

At four in the afternoon we parted with our late fellow-travellers in a very friendly manner, and immediately forded the river [Takia River]. The wild parsnep, which luxuriates on the borders of the lakes and rivers, is a favourite food of the natives: they roast the tops of this plant, in their tender state, over the fire, and taking off the outer rind, they are then a very palatable food.

We now entered the woods, and some time after arrived on the banks of another river [Taiataeszi Creek] that flowed from the mountain, which we also forded. The country soon after we left the river was swampy; and the fire having passed through it, the number of trees, which had fallen, added to the toil of our journey. In a short time we began to ascend, and continued ascending till nine at night. We walked upwards of fourteen miles, according to my computation, in the course of the day, though the straight line of distance might not be more than ten. Notwithstanding that we were surrounded by mountains covered with snow, we were very much tormented with musquitoes.

[July 17] Before the sun rose, our guides summoned us to proceed, when we descended into a beautiful valley, watered by a small river [Kohasganko River]. At eight we came to the termination of it, where we saw a great number of moles, and began again to ascend. We now perceived many ground-hogs, and heard them whistle in every direction. The Indians went in pursuit of them, and soon joined us with a female and her litter, almost grown to their full size. They stripped off their skins, and gave the carcases to my people. They also pulled up a root [claytonia], which appeared like a bunch of white berries of the size of a pea; its shape was that of a fig, while it had the colour and taste of a potatoe. [They were now in the Rainbow Range, one of the small but impressive ranges east of the main Coast Range, lying between the Dean River and Bella Coola River drainages.]

We now gained the summit of the mountain, and found ourselves surrounded by snow. But this circumstance is caused rather by the quantity of snow drifted in the pass, than the real height of the spot, as the surrounding mountains rise to a much higher degree of elevation. The snow had become so compact that our feet hardly made a perceptible impression on it. We observed, however, the tracks of a herd of small deer [woodland caribou] which must have passed a short time before us, and the Indians and my hunters went immediately in pursuit of them. Our way was now nearly level, without the least snow, and not a tree to be seen in any part of it. The grass is very short, and the soil a reddish clay, intermixed with small stones. The face of the hills, where they are not enlivened with verdure, appears at a distance as if fire had passed over them. It now began to hail, snow, and rain, nor could we find any shelter but the leeward side of an huge rock. The wind also rose into a tempest, and the weather was as distressing as any I had ever experienced. After an absence of an hour and an half, our hunters brought a small doe of the rein-deer species [caribou], which was all they had killed, though they fired twelve shots at a large herd of them. Their ill success they attributed to the weather. I proposed to leave half of the venison in the snow, but the men preferred carrying it, though their strength was very much exhausted. We had been so long shivering with cold in this situation that we were glad to renew our march. Here and there were scattered a few crowberry bushes and stinted willows; the former of which had not yet blossomed.

Before us appeared a stupendous mountain [Stupendous Mountain, 8790 feet, in the Coast Range, south of the Bella Coola River], whose snow-clad summit was lost in the clouds; between it and our immediate course flowed the river [Bella Coola River] to which we were going. The Indians informed us that it was at no great distance. As soon as we could gather a sufficient quantity of wood, we stopped to dress some of our venison; and it is almost superfluous to add, that we made a heartier meal than we had done for many a day before. To the comfort which I have just mentioned, I added that of taking off my beard, as well as changing my linen, and my people followed the humanising example. We then set forwards, and came to a large pond, on whose bank we found a tomb but lately made, with a pole as usual erected beside it, on which two figures of birds were painted, and by them the guides distinguished the tribe to which the deceased person belonged. One of them, very unceremoniously, opened the bark and shewed us the bones which it contained, while the other threw down the pole, and having possessed himself of the feathers that were tied to it, fixed them on his own head. I therefore conjectured, that these funeral memorials belonged to an individual of a tribe at enmity with them.

We continued our route with a considerable degree of expedition, and as we proceeded the mountains appeared to withdraw from us. The country between them soon opened to our view, which apparently added to their awful elevation. We continued to descend till we came to the brink of a precipice, from whence our guides discovered the river to us, and a village on its banks. This precipice, or rather succession of precipices, is covered with large timber, which consists of the pine, the spruce, the hemlock, the birch, and other trees. Our conductors informed us, that it abounded in animals, which, from their description, must be wild goats. In about two hours we arrived at the bottom, where there is a conflux of two rivers, that issue from the mountains. We crossed the one which was to the left. They are both very rapid, and continue so till they unite their currents, forming a stream of about twelve yards in breadth. [This was Burnt Bridge or Kahylskt Creek. The Indians led Mackenzie down the very steep and narrow valley of the creek, along the east bank.] Here the timber was also very large; but I could not learn from our conductors why the most considerable hemlock trees were stripped of their bark to the tops of them. I concluded, indeed, at that time that the inhabitants tanned their leather with it. Here were also the largest and loftiest elder [alder] and cedar trees that I had ever seen. We were now sensible of an entire change in the climate, and the berries were quite ripe.

The sun was about to set, when our conductors left us to follow them as well as we could. We were prevented, however, from going far astray, for we were hemmed in on both sides and behind by such a barrier as nature never before presented to my view. Our guides had the precaution to mark the road for us, by breaking the branches of trees as they passed. This small river must, at certain seasons, rise to an uncommon height and strength of current most probably on the melting of the snow; as we saw a large quantity of drift wood lying twelve feet above the immediate level of the river. This circumstance impeded our progress, and the protruding rocks frequently forced us to pass through the water. It was now dark, without the least appearance of houses, though it would be impossible to have seen them, if there had been any, at the distance of twenty yards, from the thickness of the woods. My men were anxious to stop for the night; indeed the fatigue they had suffered justified the proposal, and I left them to their choice; but as the anxiety of my mind impelled me forwards, they continued to follow me, till I found myself at the edge of the woods; and, notwithstanding the remonstrances that were made, I proceeded, feeling rather than seeing my way, till I arrived at a house, and soon discovered several fires, in small huts, with people busily employed in cooking their fish. I walked into one of them without the least ceremony, threw down my burden, and, after shaking hands with some of the people, sat down upon it. They received me without the least appearance of surprize, but soon made signs for me to go up to the large house, which was erected, on upright posts, at some distance from the ground. A broad piece of timber with steps cut in it, led to the scaffolding even with the floor, and by this curious kind of ladder I entered the house at one end; and having passed three fires, at equal distances in the middle of the building, I was received by several people, sitting upon a very wide board, at the upper end of it. I shook hands with them, and seated myself beside a man, the dignity of whose countenance induced me to give him that preference. I soon discovered one of my 214 guides seated a little above me, with a neat mat spread before him, which I supposed to be the place of honour, and appropriated to strangers. In a short time my people arrived, and placed themselves near me, when the man by whom I sat immediately rose, and fetched, from behind a plank of about four feet wide, a quantity of roasted salmon. He then directed a mat to be placed before me and Mr. Mackay, who was now sitting by me. When this ceremony was performed, he brought a salmon for each of us, and half an one to each of my men. The same plank served also as a screen for the beds, whither the women and children were already retired; but whether that circumstance took place on our arrival, or was the natural consequence of the late hour of the night, I did not discover. The signs of our protector seemed to denote that we might sleep in the house, but as we did not understand him with a sufficient degree of certainty, I thought it prudent, from the fear of giving offence, to order the men to make a fire without, that we might sleep by it. When he observed our design, he placed boards for us that we might not take our repose on the bare ground, and ordered a fire to be prepared for us. We had not been long seated round it, when we received a large dish of salmon roes, pounded fine and beat up with water so as to have the appearance of a cream. Nor was it without some kind of seasoning that gave it a bitter taste. Another dish soon followed, the principal article of which was also salmon-roes, with a large proportion of gooseberries, and an herb that appeared to be sorrel. Its acidity rendered it more agreeable to my taste than the former preparation. Having been regaled with these delicacies, for such they were considered by that hospitable spirit which provided them, we laid ourselves down to rest with no other canopy than the sky; but I never enjoyed a more sound and refreshing rest, though I had a board for my bed, and a billet [stick of wood] for my pillow.

These were the coast Indians he had been seeking so long. They were Bella Coolas, a Coast Salish tribe who occupied the Bella Coola valley and parts of the Bentinck Arm-Dean Channel area. They were a prosperous tribe, depending largely on salmon. They lived in large houses in permanent villages, and they had a well-developed social organization. This village was on the east side of Burnt Bridge Creek two hundred yards above its junction with the Bella Coola River. Mackenzie later named it Friendly Village, but the inhabitants called it Noot-layuch. It was thirty-one miles from the mouth of the river.[22]

[July 18] At five this morning I awoke, and found that the natives had lighted a fire for us, and were sitting by it. My hospitable friend immediately brought me some berries and roasted salmon, and his companions soon followed his example. The former, which consisted among many others of gooseberries, whirtleberries [huckleberries], and raspberries, were the finest I ever saw or tasted, of their respective kinds. They also brought the dried roes of fish to eat with the berries.

Salmon is so abundant in this river [Bella Coola River], that these people have a constant and plentiful supply of that excellent fish. To take them with more facility, they had, with great labour, formed an embankment or weir across the river for the purposes of placing their fishing machines, which they disposed both above and below it. I expressed my wish to visit this extraordinary work, but these people are so superstitious, that they would not allow me a nearer examination than I could obtain by viewing it from the bank. The river is about fifty yards in breadth, and by observing a man fish with a dipping net, I judged it to be about ten feet deep at the foot of the fall. The weir is a work of great labour, and contrived with considerable ingenuity. It was near four feet above the level of the water, at the time I saw it, and nearly the height of the bank on which I stood to examine it. The stream is stopped nearly two thirds by it. It is constructed by fixing small trees in the bed of the river in a slanting position (which could be practicable only when the water is much lower than I saw it) with the thick part downwards; over these is laid a bed of gravel, on which is placed a range of lesser

216 trees, and so on alternately till the work is brought to its proper

height. Beneath it the machines are placed, into which the salmon fall when they attempt to leap over. On either side there is a large frame of timber-work six feet above the level of the upper water, in which passages are left for the salmon leading directly into the machines, which are taken up at pleasure. At the foot of the fall dipping nets are also successfully employed.

The water of this river is of the colour of asses milk, which I attributed in part to the limestone that in many places forms the bed of the river, but principally to the rivulets which fall from mountains of the same material. [The mountains are of granite, not limestone, and the water was colored by glacial flour.]

These people indulge an extreme superstition respecting their fish, as it is apparently their only animal food. Flesh they never taste, and one of their dogs having picked and swallowed part of a bone which we had left, was beaten by his master till he disgorged it. One of my people also having thrown a bone of the deer into the river, a native, who had observed the circumstance, immediately dived and brought it up, and, having consigned it to the fire, instantly proceeded to wash his polluted hands.

As we were still at some distance from the sea, I made application to my friend to procure us a canoe or two, with people to conduct us thither. After he had made various excuses, I at length comprehended that his only objection was to the embarking venison in a canoe on their river, as the fish would instantly smell it and abandon them, so that he, his friends, and relations, must starve. I soon eased his apprehensions on that point, and desired to know what I must do with the venison that remained, when he told me to give it to one of the strangers whom he pointed out to me, as being of a tribe that eat flesh. I now requested him to furnish me with some fresh salmon in its raw state; but, instead of complying with my wish, he brought me a couple of them roasted, observing at the same time, that the current was very strong, and would bring us to the next village, where our wants would be abundantly supplied. In short, he requested that we would make haste to depart. This was rather unexpected after so 217 much kindness and hospitality, but our ignorance of the language prevented us from being able to discover the cause.

At eight this morning, fifteen men armed, the friends and relations of these people, arrived by land, in consequence of notice sent them in the night, immediately after the appearance of our guides. They are more corpulent and of a better appearance than the inhabitants of the interior. Their language is totally different from any I had heard; the Atnah or Chin tribe, as far as I can judge from the very little I saw of that people, bear the nearest resemblance to them. They appear to be of a quiet and peaceable character, and never make any hostile incursions into the lands of their neighbours. [The Shuswap (Mackenzie's "Atnah") and the Bella Coolas both are Salishan tribes, quite different from the Athapascan Carriers.]

Their dress consists of a single robe tied over the shoulders, falling down behind to the heels, and before a little below the knees, with a deep fringe round the bottom. It is generally made of the bark of the cedar tree, which they prepare as fine as hemp; though some of these garments are interwoven with strips of the sea-otter skin, which give them the appearance of a fur on one side. Others have stripes of red and yellow threads fancifully introduced toward the borders, which have a very agreeable effect. The men have no other covering than that which I have described, and they unceremoniously lay it aside when they find it convenient. In addition to this robe, the women wear a close fringe hanging down before them about two feet in length, and half as wide. When they sit down they draw this between their thighs. They wear their hair so short, that it requires little care or combing. The men have theirs in plaits, and being smeared with oil and red earth, instead of a comb they have a small stick hanging by a string from one of the locks, which they employ to alleviate any itching or irritation in the head. The colour of the eye is grey with a tinge of red. They have all high cheek-bones, but the women are more remarkable for that feature than the men. Their houses, arms, and utensils I shall describe hereafter.

218   I presented my friend with several articles, and also distributed

some among others of the natives who had been attentive to us. One of my guides had been very serviceable in procuring canoes for us to proceed on our expedition; he appeared also to be very desirous of giving these people a favourable impression of us; and I was very much concerned that he should leave me as he did, without giving me the least notice of his departure, or receiving the presents which I had prepared for him, and he so well deserved. At noon I had an observation which gave 52. 28. 11. North longitude.

At one in the afternoon we embarked with our small baggage, in two canoes, accompanied by seven of the natives. The stream was rapid, and ran upwards of six miles an hour. We came to a weir, such as I have already described, where the natives landed us, and shot over it without taking a drop of water. They then received us on board again and we continued our voyage, passing many canoes on the river, some with people in them and others empty. We proceeded at a very great rate for about two hours and an half, when we were informed that there we must land, as the village was only at a short distance. I had imagined that the Canadians who accompanied me were the most expert canoe-men in the world, but they are very inferior to these people, as they themselves acknowledged, in conducting those vessels.

Some of the Indians ran before us, to announce our approach, when we took our bundles and followed. We had walked along a well-beaten path, through a kind of coppice [thicket], when we were informed of the arrival of our couriers at the houses, by the loud and confused talking of the inhabitants. As we approached the edge of the wood, and were almost insight of the houses, the Indians who were before me made signs for me to take the lead, and that they would follow. The noise and confusion of the natives now seemed to increase, and when we came in sight of the village, we saw them running from house to house, some armed with bows and arrows, others with spears, and many with axes, as if in a state of great alarm. This very unpleasant and unexpected circumstance I attributed to our sudden arrival, and the very short notice of it which had been given them. At all events, I had but one line of conduct to pursue, which was to walk resolutely up to them, without manifesting any signs of apprehension at their hostile appearance. This resolution produced the desired effect, for as we approached the houses, the greater part of the people laid down their weapons, and came foward to meet us. I was, however, soon obliged to stop from the number of them that surrounded me. I shook hands, as usual with such as were the nearest to me, when an elderly man broke through the crowd, and took me in his arms; another then came, who turned him away without the least ceremony, and paid me the same compliment. The latter was followed by a young man, whom I understood to be his son. These embraces, which at first rather surprised me, I soon found to be marks of regard and friendship. The crowd pressed with so much violence and contention to get a view of us, that we could not move in any direction. An opening was at length made to allow a person to approach me, whom the old man made me understand was another of his sons. I instantly stepped forward to meet him, and presented my hand, whereupon he broke the string of a very handsome robe of sea-otter skin, which he had on, and covered me with it. This was as flattering a reception as I could possibly receive, especially as I considered him to be the eldest son of the chief. Indeed it appeared to me that we had been detained here for the purpose of giving him time to bring the robe with which he had presented me. [This village was Nooskulst, on the north side of the river at the mouth of the Tsatleanootz River.[23] Mackenzie later called it the Great Village.]

The chief now made signs for us to follow him, and he conducted us through a narrow coppice, for several hundred yards, till we came to a house built on the ground, which was of larger dimensions, and formed of better materials than any I had hitherto seen; it was his residence. We were no sooner arrived there than he directed mats to be spread before it, on which we were told to take our seats, when the men of the village, who came to indulge their curiosity, were ordered to keep behind us. In our front other mats were placed, where the chief and his counsellors took their seats. In the intervening space, mats, which were very clean, and of a much neater workmanship than those on which we sat were also spread, and a small roasted salmon placed before each of us. When we had satisfied ourselves with the fish, one of the people who came with us from the last village approached, with a kind of ladle in one hand, containing oil, and in the other something that resembled the inner rind of the cocoa-nut, but of a lighter colour; this he dipped in the oil, and, having eat it, indicated by his gestures how palatable he thought it. He then presented me with a small piece of it, which I chose to taste in its dry state, though the oil was free from any unpleasant smell. A square cake of this was next produced, when a man took it to the water near the house, and having thoroughly soaked it, he returned, and, after he had pulled it to pieces like oakum, put it into a well made trough, about three feet long, nine inches wide, and five deep; he then plentifully sprinkled it with salmon oil, and manifested by his own example that we were to eat of it. I just tasted it, and found the oil perfectly sweet, without which the other ingredient would have been very insipid. The chief partook of it with great avidity, after it had received an additional quantity of oil. This dish is considered by these people as a great delicacy; and on examination, I discovered it to consist of the inner rind of the hemlock tree, taken off early in summer, and put into a frame, which shapes it into cakes of fifteen inches long, ten broad, and half an inch thick; and in this form I should suppose it may be preserved for a great length of time. This discovery satisfied me respecting the many hemlock trees which I had observed stripped of their bark.

In this situation we remained for upwards of three hours, and not one of the curious natives left us during all that time, except a party of ten or twelve of them, whom the chief ordered to go and catch fish, which they did in great abundance, with dipping nets, at the foot of the Weir.

At length we were relieved from the gazing crowd, and got a lodge erected, and covered in for our reception during the night. I now presented the young chief with a blanket, in return for the robe with which he had favoured me, and several other articles, that appeared to be very gratifying to him. I also presented some to his father, and amongst them was a pair of scissars, whose use I explained to him, for clipping his beard, which was of great length; and to that purpose he immediately applied them. My distribution of similar articles was also extended to others, who had been attentive to us. The communication, however, between us was awkward and inconvenient, for it was carried on entirely by signs, as there was not a person with me who was qualified for the office of an interpreter.

We were all of us very desirous to get some fresh salmon, that we might dress them in our own way, but could not by any means obtain that gratification, though there were thousands of that fish strung on cords, which were fastened to stakes in the river. They were even averse to our approaching the spot where they clean and prepare them for their own eating. They had, indeed, taken our kettle from us, lest we should employ it in getting water from the river; and they assigned as the reason for this precaution, that the salmon dislike the smell of iron. At the same time they supplied us with wooden boxes, which were capable of holding any fluid. Two of the men that went to fish, in a canoe capable of containing ten people, returned with a full lading of salmon, that weighed from six to forty pounds, though the far greater part of them were under twenty. They immediately strung the whole of them, as I have already mentioned, in the river.

I now made the tour of the village, which consisted of four elevated houses, and seven built on the ground, besides a considerable number of other buildings or sheds, which are used only as kitchens, and places for curing their fish. The former are constructed by fixing a certain number of posts in the earth, on some of which are laid, and to others are fastened, the supporters of the floor, at about twelve feet above the surface of the ground: their length is from an hundred to an hundred and twenty feet, and they are about forty feet in breadth. Along the centre are built three, four, or five hearths, for the two-fold purpose of giving warmth, and dressing their fish. The whole length of the building on either side is divided by cedar planks, into partitions or apartments of seven feet square, in the front of which there are boards, about three feet wide, over which, though they are not immovably fixed, the inmates of these recesses generally pass, when they go to rest. The greater part of them are intended for that purpose, and such are covered with boards, at the height of the wall of the house, which is about seven or eight feet, and rest upon beams that stretch across the building. On those also are placed the chests which contain their provisions, utensils, and whatever they possess. The intermediate space is sufficient for domestic purposes. On poles that run along the beams, hang roasted fish, and the whole building is well covered with boards and bark, except within a few inches of the ridge pole; where open spaces are left on each side to let in light and emit the smoke. At the end of the house that fronts the river, is a narrow scaffolding, which is also ascended by a piece of timber, with steps cut in it; and at each corner of this erection there are openings, for the inhabitants to ease nature. As it does not appear to be a custom among them to remove these heaps of excremental filth, it may be supposed that the effluvia does not annoy them.

The houses which rest on the ground are built of the same materials, and on the same plan. A sloping stage that rises to a cross piece of timber, supported by two forks, joins also to the main building, for those purposes which need not be repeated.

When we were surrounded by the natives on our arrival, I counted sixty-five men, and several of them may be supposed to have been absent; I cannot, therefore, calculate the inhabitants of this village at less than two hundred souls.

The people who accompanied us hither from the other village, had given the chief a very particular account of everything they knew concerning us: I was, therefore, requested to produce my astronomical instruments; nor could I have any objection to afford them this satisfaction, as they would necessarily add to our importance in their opinion.

Near the house of the chief I observed several oblong squares, of about twenty feet by eight. They were made of thick cedar boards, which were joined with so much neatness, that I at first thought they were one piece. They were painted with hieroglyphics, and figures of different animals, and with a degree of correctness that was not to be expected from such an uncultivated people. I could not learn the use of them, but they appeared to be calculated for occasional acts of devotion or sacrifice, which all these tribes perform at least twice in the year, at the spring and fall. I was confirmed in this opinion by a large building in the middle of the village, which I at first took for the half finished frame of a house. The ground plot of it was fifty feet by forty-five; each end is formed by four stout posts, fixed perpendicularly in the ground. The corner ones are plain, and support a beam of the whole length, having three intermediate props on each side, but of a larger size, and eight or nine feet in height. The two centre posts at each end are two feet and an half in diameter, and carved into human figures, supporting two ridge poles on their heads, at twelve feet from the ground. The figures at the upper part of this square represent two persons, with their hands upon their knees, as if they supported the weight with pain and difficulty: the others opposite to them stand at their ease, with their hands resting on their hips. In the area of the building there were the remains of several fires. The posts, poles, and figures, were painted red and black; but the sculpture of these people is superior to their painting.

[July 19] Soon after I had retired to rest last night, the chief paid me a visit to insist on my going to his bed-companion, and taking my place himself; but, notwithstanding his repeated entreaties, I resisted this offering of his hospitality.

At an early hour this morning I was again visited by the chief, in company with his son. The former complained of a pain in his breast; to relieve his suffering, I gave him a few drops of Turlington's balsam on a piece of sugar; and I was rather surprised to see him take it without the least hesitation. When he had taken my medicine, he requested me to follow him, and conducted me to a shed, where several people were assembled round a sick man, who was another of his sons. They immediately uncovered him, and showed me a violent ulcer in the small of his back, in the foulest state that can be imagined. One of his knees was also afflicted in the same manner. This unhappy man was reduced to a skeleton, and, from his appearance, was drawing near to an end of his pains. They requested that I would touch him, and his father was very urgent with me to administer medicine; but he was in such a dangerous state, that I thought it prudent to yield no further to the importunities than to give the sick person a few drops of Turlington's balsam in some water. I therefore left them, but was soon called back by the loud lamentations of the women, and was rather apprehensive that some inconvenience might result from my compliance with the chief's request. On my return I found the native physicians busy in practicing their skill and art on the patient. They blew on him, and then whistled; at times they pressed their extended fingers with all their strength on his stomach; they also put their fore fingers doubled into his mouth, and spouted water from their own with great violence into his face. To support these operations the wretched sufferer was held up in a sitting posture; and when they were concluded, he was laid down and covered with a new robe made of the skins of the lynx. I had observed that his belly and breast were covered with scars, and I understood that they were caused by a custom prevalent among them, of applying pieces of lighted touch wood [punk] to their flesh, in order to relieve pain or demonstrate their courage. He was now placed on a broad plank, and carried by six men into the woods, where I was invited to accompany them. I could not conjecture what would be the end of this ceremony, particularly as I saw one man carry fire, another an axe, and a third dry wood. I was, indeed, disposed to suspect that, as it was their custom to burn the dead, they intended to relieve the poor man from his pain, and perform the last sad duty of surviving affection. When they had advanced a short distance into the wood, they laid him upon a clear spot, and kindled a fire against his back, when the physician began to scarify the ulcer 225 with a very blunt instrument, the cruel pain of which operation the patient bore with incredible resolution. The scene afflicted me and I left it.

On my return to our lodge, I observed before the door of the chief's residence, four heaps of salmon, each of which consisted of between three and four hundred fish. Sixteen women were employed in cleaning and preparing them. They first separate the head from the body, the former of which they boil; they then cut the latter down the back on each side of the bone, leaving one third of the fish adhering to it, and afterwards take out the guts. The bone is roasted for immediate use, and the other parts are dressed in the same manner, but with more attention, for future provision. While they are before the fire, troughs are placed under them to receive the oil. The roes are also carefully preserved, and form a favourite article of their food.

After I had observed these culinary preparations, I paid a visit to the chief, who presented me with a roasted salmon; he then opened one of his chests, and took out of it a garment of blue cloth, decorated with brass buttons; and another of a flowered cotton, which I supposed were Spanish; it had been trimmed with leather fringe, after the fashion of their own cloaks. Copper and brass are in great estimation among them, and of the former they have great plenty: they point their arrows and spears with it, and work it up into personal ornaments; such as collars, ear-rings, and bracelets, which they wear on their wrists, arms, and legs. I presume they find it the most advantageous article of trade with the more inland tribes. They also abound in iron: I saw some of their twisted collars of that metal which weighed upwards of twelve pounds. It is generally in bars of fourteen inches in length, and one inch three quarters wide. The brass is in thin squares: their copper is in larger pieces, and some of it appeared to be old stills cut up. They have various trinkets; but their manufactured iron consists only of poniards and daggers. Some of the former have very neat handles, with a silver coin of a quarter

or eighth of a dollar fixed on the end of them. The blades of the latter are from ten to twelve inches in length, and about four inches broad at the top, from which they gradually lessen into a point.

When I produced my instruments to take an altitude, I was desired not to make use of them. I could not then discover the cause of this request, but I experienced the good effect of the apprehension which they occasioned, as it was very effectual in hastening my departure. I had applied several times to the chief to prepare canoes and people to take me and my party to the sea, but very little attention had been paid to my application till noon; when I was informed that a canoe was properly equipped for my voyage, and that the young chief would accompany me. I now discovered that they had entertained no personal fear of the instruments, but were apprehensive that the operation of them might frighten the salmon from that part of the river. The observation taken in this village gave me 52. 25. 52. North latitude.

In compliance with the chief's request I desired my people to take their bundles, and lay them down on the bank of the river. In the meantime I went to take the dimensions of his large canoe, in which, it was signified to me, that about ten winters ago he went a considerable distance towards the mid-day sun, with forty of his people, when he saw two large vessels full of such men as myself, by whom he was kindly received: they were probably the ships commanded by Captain Cook [Captain James Cook, the first explorer of this coast]. This canoe was built of cedar, forty-five feet long, four feet wide, and three feet and a half in depth. It was painted black and decorated with white figures of fish of different kinds. The gunwale, fore and aft, was inlaid with the teeth of the sea-otter.*

When I returned to the river, the natives who were to accompany us, and my people, were already in the canoe. The latter, however,

---

* As Captain Cook has mentioned, that the people of the sea-coast adorned their canoes with human teeth, I was more particular in my inquiries; the result of which was, the most satisfactory proof, that he was mistaken: but his mistake arose from the very great resemblance there is between human teeth and those of the sea-otter.

informed me, that one of our axes was missing. I immediately applied to the chief, and requested its restoration; but he would not understand me till I sat myself down on a stone, with my arms in a state of preparation, and made it appear to him that I should not depart till the stolen article was restored. The village was immediately in a state of uproar, and some danger was apprehended from the confusion that prevailed in it. The axe, however, which had been hidden under the chief's canoe, was soon returned. Though this instrument was not in itself of sufficient value to justify a dispute with these people, I apprehended that the suffering them to keep it, after we had declared its loss, might have occasioned the loss of every thing we carried with us, and of our lives also. My people were dissatisfied with me at the moment; but I thought myself right then, and I think now, that the circumstances in which we were involved, justified the measure which I adopted.

At one in the afternoon we renewed our voyage in a large canoe with four of the natives. We found the river almost one continued rapid, and in half an hour we came to a house, where, however, we did not land, though invited by the inhabitants. In about an hour we arrived at two houses, where we were, in some degree, obliged to go on shore, as we were informed that the owner of them was a person of consideration. He indeed received and regaled us in the same manner as at the last village; and to increase his consequence, he produced many European articles, and amongst them were at least forty pounds weight of old copper stills. We made our stay as short as possible, and our host embarked with us. In a very short time we were carried by the rapidity of the current to another house of very large dimensions, which was partitioned into different apartments, and whose doors were on the side. The inhabitants received us with great kindness; but instead of fish, they placed a long, clean, and well made trough before us full of berries. In addition to those which we had already seen, there were some black, that were larger than the huckle berry, and of a richer flavour; and others white, which re-

228 sembled the black-berry in every thing but colour. Here we saw a

woman with two pieces of copper in her under lip, as described by Captain Cook. I continued my usual practice of making these people presents in return for their friendly reception and entertainment.

The navigation of the river now became more difficult, from the numerous channels into which it was divided, without any sensible diminution in the velocity of its current. We soon reached another house of the common size, where we were well received; but whether our guides had informed them that we were not in want of any thing, or that they were deficient in inclination, or perhaps the means, of being hospitable to us, they did not offer us any refreshment. They were in a state of busy preparation. Some of the women were employed in beating and preparing the inner rind of the cedar bark, to which they gave the appearance of flax. Others were spinning with a distaff and spindle. One of them was weaving a robe of it, intermixed with stripes of the sea-otter skin, on a frame of adequate contrivance that was placed against the side of the house. The men were fishing on the river with drag-nets between two canoes. These nets are forced by poles to the bottom, the current driving them before it; by which means the salmon coming up the river are intercepted, and give notice of their being taken by the struggles they make in the bag or sleeve of the net. There are no weirs in this part of the river, as I suppose, from the numerous channels into which it is divided. The machines, therefore, are placed along the banks, and consequently these people are not so well supplied with fish as the village which has been already described, nor do they appear to possess the same industry. The inhabitants of the last house accompanied us in a large canoe. They recommended us to leave ours here, as the next village was but at a small distance from us, and the water more rapid than that which we had passed. They informed us also that we were approaching a cascade. I directed them to shoot it, and proceeded myself to the foot thereof, where I re-embarked, and we went on with great velocity, till we came to a fall, where we left our canoe, and carried our luggage along a road through a wood for some hundred yards, when we came to a village, 229 consisting of six very large houses, erected on palisades, rising twenty-five feet from the ground, which differed in no one circumstance from those already described, but the height of their elevation. They contained only four men and their families. The rest of the inhabitants were with us and in the small houses which we passed higher up the river.* These people do not seem to enjoy the abundance of their neighbours, as the men who returned from fishing had no more than five salmons; they refused to sell them, but gave me one roasted, of a very indifferent kind. In the house there were several chests or boxes containing different articles that belonged to the people whom we had lately passed. If I were to judge by the heaps of filth beneath these buildings, they must have been erected at a more distant period than any which we had passed. From these houses I could perceive the termination of the river, and its discharge into a narrow arm of the sea. [This village was on the south side of the river, near its mouth, approximately where the present town of Bella Coola is located. Mackenzie later named it Rascal's Village.]

As it was now half past six in the evening, and the weather cloudy, I determined to remain here for the night, and for that purpose we possessed ourselves of one of the unoccupied houses. The remains of our last meal, which we brought with us, served for our supper, as we could not procure a single fish from the natives. The course of the river is about West, and the distance from the great village upwards of thirty-six miles. There we had lost our dog, a circumstance of no small regret to me.

[July 20] We rose at a very early hour this morning, when I proposed to the Indians to run down our canoe, or procure another at this place. To both these proposals they turned a deaf ear, as they imagined that I should be satisfied with having come in sight of the sea. Two of them peremptorily refused to proceed; but the other two having consented to continue with us, we obtained a larger

---

* Mr. Johnstone [Captain George Vancouver's lieutenant] came to these houses the first day of the preceding month.

canoe than our former one, and though it was in a leaky state we were glad to possess it.

He had made up his mind years earlier to reach the Pacific, and now he was there. He had overcome just about every difficulty that man and nature could impose, but he still was not through. He was many miles from the open sea, at the head of one of the inlets that jut deep into the Northwest coast. He wanted to reach the sea if possible, and he was determined to establish his position before turning back. This was necessary for his discoveries to have their full meaning. The importance of his earlier exploration had been somewhat reduced by the fact that he did not know where he had been, that is, he did not know his longitude and was uncertain of his latitude. Now he had to make the necessary observations, and for this he needed a long stretch of open water to provide a natural horizon, and he needed a clear sky at the right time for making observations of the sun and of Jupiter. On that coast either patience or good luck is necessary to get both of these requirements together.

His route on salt water cannot be traced satisfactorily from his account. One difficulty is the footnotes. They must have been written after Vancouver's *Voyages* was published in 1798, when Mackenzie's memory of the scene had faded, and some of them are clearly incorrect. In addition, there are the usual difficulties with his courses, and he seems to have omitted one course altogether. Considering the conditions he did very well, but it was not until this century that his route was traced.[24]

At about eight we got out of the river, which discharges itself by various channels into an arm of the sea [North Bentinck Arm]. The tide was out, and had left a large space covered with sea-weed. The surrounding hills were involved in fog. The wind was at West, which was ahead of us, and very strong; the bay appearing to be   231 from one to three miles in breadth. As we advanced along the land we saw a great number of sea-otters. We fired several shots at them, but without any success, from the rapidity with which they plunge under the water. We also saw many small porpoises or divers. The white-headed eagle, which is common in the interior parts; some small gulls, a dark bird which is inferior in size to the gull, and a few small ducks, were all the birds which presented themselves to our view.

At two in the afternoon the swell was so high, and the wind, which was against us, so boisterous, that we could not proceed with our leaky vessel; we therefore landed in a small cove on the right side of the bay. Opposite to us appeared another small bay, in the mouth of which is an island, and where, according to the information of the Indians, a river discharges itself that abounds in salmon. [The cove was Green Bay, Mackenzie's Porcupine Cove, on the north side of North Bentinck Arm. The other small bay was actually the large South Bentinck Arm, and Kinkilst Island is deep in the arm, not in the mouth. The river that abounds in salmon is the Noeick River.]

Our young Indians now discovered a very evident disposition to leave us; and, in the evening, one of them made his escape. Mr. Mackay, however, with the other, pursued and brought him back; but as it was by no means necessary to detain him, particularly as provisions did not abound with us, I gave him a small portion, with a pair of shoes, which were necessary for his journey, and a silk handkerchief, telling him at the same time, that he might go and inform his friends, that we should also return in three nights. He accordingly left us, and his companion, the young chief [from the Great Village], went with him.

When we landed, the tide was going out, and at a quarter past four it was ebb, the water having fallen in that short period eleven feet and an half. Since we left the river, not a quarter of an hour had passed in which we did not see porpoises and sea-otters. Soon after ten it was high water, which rendered it necessary that our baggage should be shifted several times, though not till some of the things had been wetted.

We were now reduced to the necessity of looking out for fresh water, with which we were plentifully supplied by the rills that ran down from the mountains.

When it was dark the young chief returned to us, bearing a large porcupine on his back. He first cut the animal open, and having disencumbered it of the entrails, threw them into the sea; he then singed its skin, and boiled it in separate pieces, as our kettle was not sufficiently capacious to contain the whole: nor did he go to rest, till, with the assistance of two of my people who happened to be awake, every morsel of it was devoured.

I had flattered myself with the hope of getting a distance of the moon and stars, but the cloudy weather continually disappointed me, and I began to fear that I should fail in this important object; particularly as our provisions were at a very low ebb, and we had as yet no reason to expect any assistance from the natives. Our stock was, at this time, reduced to twenty pounds weight of pemmican, fifteen pounds of rice, and six pounds of flour, among ten half-starved men, in a leaky vessel, and on a barbarous coast. Our course from the river was about West-South-West, distance ten miles.

[July 21] At forty minutes past four this morning it was low water, which made fifteen feet perpendicular height below the high-water mark of last night. Mr. Mackay collected a quantity of small muscles [mussels] which we boiled. Our people did not partake of this regale, as they are wholly unacquainted with sea shell-fish. Our young chief being missing, we imagined that he had taken his flight; but, as we were preparing to depart, he fortunately made his appearance from the woods, where he had been to take his rest after his feast of last night. At six we were upon the water, when we cleared the small bay, which we named Porcupine Cove, and steered West-South-West for seven miles; we then opened a channel [Burke Channel] about two miles and an half wide at South-South-West, and had a view of ten or twelve miles into it. As I could not ascertain the 233 distance from the open sea, and being uncertain whether we were in a bay or among inlets and channels of islands, I confined my search to a proper place for taking an observation. We steered, therefore, along the land on the left, West-North-West a mile and an half [probably around Mesachie Nose into Labouchere Channel]; then North-West one fourth of a mile [probably four miles], and North three miles to an island [probably the peninsula at the northeast corner of Labouchere Channel]; the land continuing to run North-North-West, then along the island, South-South-West half a mile, West a mile and an half, and from thence directly across to the land on the left, (where I had an altitude,) South-West three miles.* From this position a channel [Dean Channel], of which the island we left appeared to make a cheek, bears North by East.

Under the land we met with three canoes, with fifteen men in them, and laden with their moveables, as if proceeding to a new situation, or returning to a former one. They manifested no kind of mistrust or fear of us, but entered into conversation with our young man, as I supposed, to obtain some information concerning us. It did not appear that they were the same people as those we lately seen, as they spoke the language of our young chief, with a different accent. They then examined every thing we had in our canoe, with an air of indifference and disdain. One of them in particular made me understand, with an air of insolence, that a large canoe had lately been in this bay, with people in her like me, and that one them, whom he called Macubah, had fired on him and his friends, and that Bensins had struck him on the back, with the flat part of his sword. He also mentioned another name, the articulation of which I could not determine. At the same time he illustrated these circumstances by the assistance of my gun and sword; and I do not doubt but he well deserved the treatment which he described. He also produced several European articles, which could not have been long in his possession. From his conduct and appearance, I wished very much to be rid of

---

234   * The Cape or Point Menzies of Vancouver [Edward Point].

him, and flattered myself that he would prosecute his voyage, which appeared to be in an opposite direction to our course. However, when I prepared to part from them, they turned their canoes about, and persuaded my young man to leave me, which I could not prevent.

"Macubah" and "Bensins" apparently were Vancouver and his naturalist Menzies, but Vancouver does not mention any such incident in his *Voyage*.[25] Mackenzie had thought that because the coast Indians were used to dealing with white traders they would receive him well, but he misjudged the character of both the traders and the Indians. The traders were unscrupulous, the Indians fierce and sullen, and the result was frequent bloodshed.

These new Indians were Bella Bellas, who lived at Elcho Harbour and near the mouth of Dean Channel. Culturally they were similar to the Bella Coola, but linguistically they were quite distinct, being related to the Kwakiutl of Vancouver Island. They had many contacts with the Bella Coola and intermarriage was common, so that many individuals from the two tribes could understand each other. These Bella Bellas were speaking the Bella Coola language with the chief's son.

We coasted along the land * at about West-South-West for six miles [actually much more than this], and met a canoe with two boys in it, who were dispatched to summon the people on that part of the coast to join them. The troublesome fellow now forced himself into my canoe, and pointed out a narrow channel [Elcho Harbour] on the opposite shore, that led to his village, and requested us to steer towards it, which I accordingly ordered. His importunities now became very irksome, and he wanted to see every thing we had, particularly my instruments, concerning which he must have re-

---

* Named by Vancouver King's Island [King Island].   235

ceived information from my young man. He asked for my hat, my handkerchief, and, in short, every thing that he saw about me. At the same time he frequently repeated the unpleasant intelligence that he had been shot at by people of my colour. At some distance from the land a channel [Dean Channel] opened to us, at South-West by West, and pointing that way, he made me understand that Macubah came there with his large canoe. When we were in mid-channel, I perceived some sheds, or the remains of old buildings, on the shore; and as, from that circumstance, I thought it probable that some Europeans might have been there, I directed my steersman to make for that spot. The traverse is upwards of three miles North-West.

We landed, and found the ruins of a village, in a situation calculated for defence. The place itself was over grown with weeds, and in the centre of the houses there was a temple, of the same form and construction as that which I described at the large village. We were soon followed by ten canoes, each of which contained from three to six men. They informed us that we were expected at the village, where we should see many of them. From their general deportment I was very apprehensive that some hostile design was meditated against us, and for the first time I acknowledged my apprehensions to my people. I accordingly desired them to be very much upon their guard, and to be prepared if any violence was offered to defend themselves to the last.

> He had landed at the mouth of Elcho Harbour, on the east side. Just south of the abandoned village was a large rock that apparently had been used as a defensive position by the villagers. Its sides are steep or overhanging in most places, and in other places had been built up with rocks or logs to make it less accessible.[26] The Indians were Bella Bellas from the village of Atko, at the head of Elcho Harbour.

We had no sooner landed, than we took possession of a rock, where there was not space for more than twice our number, and which admitted of our defending ourselves with advantage, in case we should be attacked. The people in the three first canoes were the most troublesome, but, after doing their utmost to irritate us, they went away. They were, however, no sooner gone, than a hat, a handkerchief, and several other articles, were missing. The rest of our visitors continued their pressing invitations to accompany them to their village, but finding our resolution to decline them was not to be shaken, they about sun-set relieved us from all further importunities, by their departure.

Another canoe, however soon arrived, with seven stout well-looking men. They brought a box, which contained a very fine sea-otter skin, and a goat skin, that was beautifully white. For the former they demanded my hanger [a short sword], which, as may well be supposed, could not be spared in our present situation, and they actually refused to take a yard and an half of common broad cloth, with some articles, for the skin, which proves the unreflecting improvidence of our European traders. The goat-skin was so bulky that I did not offer to purchase it. These men also told me that Macubah had been there, and left his ship behind a point of land in the channel, South-West from us; from whence he had come to their village in boats, which these people represented by imitating our manner of rowing. When I offered them what they did not choose to accept for the otter-skin, they shook their heads, and very distinctly answered "No, no." And to mark their refusal of any thing we asked from them, they emphatically employed the same British monosyllable. In one of the canoes which had left us, there was a seal, that I wished to purchase, but could not persuade the natives to part with it. They had also a fish, which I now saw for the first time. It was about eighteen inches in length, of the shape and appearance of a trout, with strong, sharp teeth. We saw great numbers of the animals which we had taken for sea otters, but I was now disposed to think that a great part of them at least must have been seals.

The natives having left us, we made a fire to warm ourselves, and as for supper, there was but little of that, for our whole daily allow- 237 ance did not amount to what was sufficient for a single meal. The weather was clear throughout the day, which was succeeded by a fine moon-light night. I directed the people to keep watch by two in turn, and laid myself down in my cloak.

[July 22] This morning the weather was clear and pleasant; nor had any thing occurred to disturb us throughout the night. One solitary Indian, indeed, came to us with about half a pound of boiled seal's flesh, and the head of a small salmon, for which he asked a handkerchief, but afterwards accepted a few beads. As this man came alone, I concluded that no general plan had been formed among the natives to annoy us, but this opinion did not altogether calm the apprehensions of my people.

Soon after eight in the morning, I took five altitudes for time, and the mean of them was 36. 48. at six in the afternoon, 58. 34. time, by the watch, which makes the achrometer slow apparent time 1. 21. 44.

Two canoes now arrived from the same quarter [Elcho Harbour] as the rest, with several men, and our young Indian along with them. They brought a very few small sea-otter skins, out of season, with some pieces of raw seal's flesh. The former were of no value, but hunger compelled some of my people to take the latter, at an extravagant price. Mr. Mackay lighted a bit of touch wood with a burning-glass, in the cover of his tobacco-box, which so surprised the natives, that they exchanged the best of their otter skins for it. [The thing that impressed the Bella Coolas most about Mackenzie was his ability to make fire quickly. They still remember this.[27]] The young man was now very anxious to persuade our people to depart, as the natives, he said, were as numerous as musquitoes, and of very malignant character. This information produced some very earnest remonstrances to me to hasten our departure, but as I was determined not to leave this place, except I was absolutely compelled to it, till I had ascertained its situation, these solicitations were not repeated.

While I was taking a meridian, two canoes, of a larger size, and well manned, appeared from the main South-West channel [Dean Channel]. They seemed to be the fore-runners of others, who were coming to co-operate with the people of the village, in consequence of the message sent by the two boys, which has been already mentioned; and our young Indian [the chief's son from the Great Village], who understood them, renewed his entreaties for our departure, as they would soon come to shoot their arrows, and hurl their spears at us. In relating our danger, his agitation was so violent that he foamed at the mouth. Though I was not altogether free from apprehensions on the occasion, it was necessary for me to disguise them, as my people were panic struck, and some of them asked if it was my determination to remain there to be sacrificed. My reply was the same as their former importunities had received, that I would not stir till I had accomplished my object; at the same time, to humour their fears, I consented that they should put every thing into the canoe, that we might be in a state of preparation to depart. The two canoes now approached the shore, and in a short time five men, with their families, landed very quietly from them. My instruments being exposed, they examined them with much apparent admiration and astonishment. My altitude, by an artificial horizon, gave 52. 21. 33; that by the natural horizon was 52. 20. 48. North latitude.*

These Indians were of a different tribe from those which I had already seen, as our guide did not understand their language. [Actually these Indians were Bella Bellas too, but they were speaking their own language.] I now mixed up some vermilion in melted grease, and inscribed, in large characters, on the South-East face of the rock on which we had slept last night, this brief memorial—"Alexander Mackenzie, from Canada, by land, the twenty-second of July, one thousand seven hundred and ninety-three."

As I thought that we were too near the village, I consented to leave this place, and accordingly proceeded North-East three miles, when we landed on a point, in a small cove, where we should not be readily seen, and could not be attacked except in our front. [This cove is on the Dean Channel just southwest of the mouth of Cascade Inlet.]

---

* This I found to be the cheek of Vancouver's Cascade Canal [actually Elcho Harbour, west of Cascade Inlet].

Among other articles that had been stolen from us, at our last station, was a sounding-line, which I intended to have employed in this bay, though I should not probably have found the bottom, at any distance from the shore, as the appearance both of the water and land indicated a great depth. The latter displayed a solid rock, rising, as it appeared to me, from three to seven hundred feet above high water mark. Where any soil was scattered about, there were cedars, spruce-firs, white birch, and other trees of large growth. From its precipices issued streams of fine water, as cold as ice.

The two canoes, which we had left at our last station, followed us hither, and when they were preparing to depart, our young chief embarked with them. I was determined, however, to prevent his escape, and compelled him, by actual force, to come on shore; for I thought it much better to incur his displeasure, than to suffer him to expose himself to any untoward accident among strangers, or to return to his father before us. The men in the canoe made signs for him to go over the hill [Cape McKay], and that they would take him on board at the other side of it. As I was necessarily engaged in other matters, I desired my people to take care that he should not run away; but they peremptorily refused to be employed in keeping him against his will. I was, therefore, reduced to the necessity of watching him myself.

I took five altitudes, and the mean of them was 29. 23. 48 at 3. 5. 53. in the afternoon, by the watch, which makes it

slow apparent time	$1^{m[h]}$	$22^{h[m]}$	38^s		
In the forenoon it was	1	21	44	2	44	22
		Mean of both .	1	22	11
Difference nine hours going of the time-piece slow					8
			1	22	19

I observed an emersion of Jupiter's third satellite, which gave 8. 32. 21. difference of longitude. I then observed an emersion of Jupiter's first satellite, which gave 8. 31. 48. The mean of these observations is 8. 32. 2. which is equal to 128. 2. West of Greenwich.

I had now determined my situation, which is the most fortunate circumstance of my long, painful, and perilous journey, as a few cloudy days would have prevented me from ascertaining the final longitude of it.*

THE RETURN TRIP

At twelve it was high water, but the tide did not come within a foot and an half of the high water mark of last night. As soon as I had completed my observations, we left this place: it was then ten o'clock in the afternoon. We returned the same way that we came, and though the tide was running out very strong, by keeping close in with the rocks, we proceeded at a considerable rate, as my people were very anxious to get out of the reach of the inhabitants of this coast.

[July 23] During our course we saw several fires on the land to the Southward, and after the day dawned, their smokes were visible. At half past four this morning we arrived at our encampment of the night of the 21st [20th], which had been named Porcupine Cove. The tide was out, and considerably lower than we found it when we were here before; the high-water mark being above the place where we had made our fire. This fluctuation must be occasioned by the action of the wind upon the water, in those narrow channels.

---

* Mr. Meares was undoubtedly wrong in the idea, so earnestly insisted on by him in his voyage, that there was a North-West practicable passage to the Southward of sixty-nine degrees and an half of latitude, as I flatter myself has been proved by my former voyage. Nor can I refrain from expressing my surprise at his assertion, that there was an inland sea or archipelago of great extent between the islands of Nootka [Vancouver Island and others] and the main, about the latitude where I was at this time. Indeed I have been informed that Captain Grey [Robert Gray, discoverer of the Columbia River], who commanded an American vessel, and on whose authority he ventured this opinion, denies that he had given Mr. Meares any such information. Besides, the contrary is indubitably proved by Captain Vancouver's survey, from which no appeal can be made.

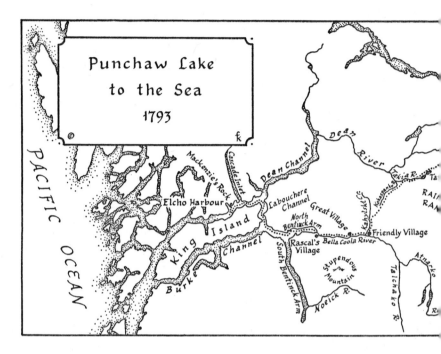

As we continued onwards, towards the river [Bella Coola River], we saw a canoe, well manned, which at first made from us with great expedition, but afterwards waited, as if to reconnoitre us; however, it kept out of our way, and allowed us to pass. The tide being much lower than when we were here before, we were under the necessity of landing a mile below the village. We observed that stakes were fixed in the ground along the bay, and in some places machines were fastened to them, as I afterwards learned, to intercept the seals and otters. These works are very extensive, and must have been erected with no common labour. The only bird we saw to-day was the white-headed eagle.*

Our guide directed us to draw the canoe out of the reach of the tide and to leave it. He would not wait, however, till this operation was performed, and I did not wish to let him go alone. I therefore

---

* This bay was now named Mackenzie's Outlet [North Bentinck Arm].

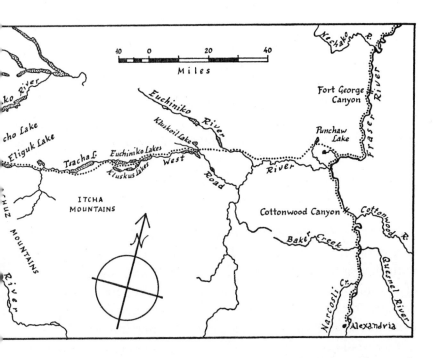

followed him through a bad road encumbered with underwood. When we had quitted the wood, and were in sight of the houses, the young man being about fifteen or twenty paces before me, I was surprised to see two men running down towards me from one of the houses, with daggers in their hands and fury in their aspect. From their hostile appearance, I could not doubt of their purpose. I therefore stopped short, threw down my cloak, and put myself in a posture of defence, with my gun presented towards them. Fortunately for me, they knew the effect of fire-arms, and instantly dropped their daggers, which were fastened by a string to their wrists, and had before been held in a menacing attitude. I let my gun also fall into my left hand, and drew my hanger. Several others soon joined them, who were armed in the same manner; and among them I recognised the man whom I have already mentioned as being so troublesome to us, and who now repeated the names of Macubah and Bensin, signifying at the same time by his action, as on a former occasion, that he 243 had been shot at by them. Until I saw him my mind was undisturbed; but the moment he appeared, conceiving that he was the cause of my present perilous situation, my resentment predominated, and, if he had come within my reach, I verily believe, that I should have terminated his insolence for ever.

The rest now approached so near, that one of them contrived to get behind me, and grasped me in his arms. I soon disengaged myself from him; and, why he did not avail himself of the opportunity which he had of plunging his dagger into me, I cannot conjecture. They certainly might have overpowered me, and though I should probably have killed one or two of them, I must have fallen at last.

One of my people now came out of the wood. On his appearance they instantly took to flight, and with the utmost speed sought shelter in the houses from whence they had issued. It was, however, upwards of ten minutes before all my people joined me; and as they came one after the other, these people might have successively dispatched every one of us. If they had killed me in the first instance, this consequence would certainly have followed, and not one of us would have returned home to tell the horrid fate of his companions.

After having stated the danger I had encountered, I told my people that I was determined to make these natives feel the impropriety of their conduct toward us, and compel them to return my hat and cloak, which they had taken in the scuffle, as well as the articles previously purloined from us; for most of the men who were in the three canoes that we first saw, were now in the village. I therefore told my men to prime their pieces afresh, and prepare themselves for an active use of them, if the occasion should require it.

We now drew up before the house, and made signs for some one to come down to us. At length our young chief appeared, and told us that the men belonging to the canoes had not only informed his friends that we had treated him very ill, but that we had killed four of their companions whom we had met in the bay. When I had explained to them, as well as it was in my power, the falsehood of such a story, I insisted on the restoration of every thing that had

244

been taken from us, as well as a necessary supply of fish, as the conditions of my departure; accordingly the things were restored, and a few dried fish along with them. A reconciliation now took place, but our guide or young chief was so much terrified that he would remain no longer with us, and requested us to follow with his father's canoe, or mischief would follow. I determined, however, before my departure, to take an observation, and at noon got a meridian altitude, making this place, which I named Rascal's Village [Bella Coola], 52. 23. 43. North latitude.

On my informing the natives that we wanted something more to eat, they brought us two salmons; and when we signified that we had no poles to set the canoe against the current, they were furnished with equal alacrity, so anxious were they for our departure. I paid, however, for every thing which we had received, and did not forget the loan of the canoe.

The current of the river was so strong, that I should have complied with the wishes of my people, and gone by land, but one of my Indians was so weak, that it was impossible for him to perform the journey. He had been ill some time; and, indeed, we had been all of us more or less afflicted with colds on the sea coast. Four of the people therefore set off with the canoe, and it employed them an hour to get half a mile. In the mean time the native, who has been already mentioned as having treated us with so much insolence, and four of his companions, went up the river in a canoe, which they had above the rapid, with as many boxes as men in her. This circumstance was the cause of fresh alarm, as it was generally concluded that they would produce the same mischief and danger in the villages above, as they had in that below. Nor was it forgotten that the young chief had left us in a manner which would not be interpreted in our favour by his father and friends.

At length the canoe arrived, and the people declared in the most unreserved terms, that they would proceed no further in her; but when they were made acquainted with the circumstances which have just been described, their violence increased, and the greater 245 part of the men announced their determination to attempt the mountains, and endeavour, by passing over them, to gain the road by which we came to the first village. So resolved were they to pursue this plan, that they threw every thing which they had into the river, except their blankets. I was all this time sitting patiently on a stone, and indulging the hope that, when their frantic terror had subsided, their returning reason would have disposed them to perceive the rashness of their project; but when I observed that they persisted in it, I no longer remained a silent listener to their passionate declarations, but proceeded to employ such arguments as I trusted would turn them from their senseless and impracticable purpose. After reproving my young Indian in very severe terms, for encouraging the rest to follow their mad design of passing the mountains, I addressed myself generally to them, stating the difficulty of ascending the mountains, the eternal snows with which they were covered, our small stock of provisions, which two days would exhaust, and the consequent probability that we should perish with cold and hunger. I urged the folly of being affected by the alarm of danger which might not exist, and if it did, I encouraged them with the means we possessed of surmounting it. Nor did I forget to urge the inhumanity and injustice of leaving the poor sick Indian to languish and die. I also added, that as my particular object had been accomplished, I had now no other but our common safety; that the sole wish of my heart was to employ the best means in my power, and to pursue the best method which my understanding could suggest, to secure them and myself from every danger that might impede our return.

My steersman, who had been with me for five years in that capacity, instantly replied that he was ready to follow me wherever I should go, but that he would never again enter that canoe, as he had solemnly sworn he would not, while he was in the rapid. His example was followed by all the rest, except two, who embarked with Mr. Mackay,* myself, and the sick Indian. The current, however,

---

* It is but common justice to him to mention in this place, that I had every reason to be satisfied with his conduct.

was so strong that we dragged up the greatest part of the way, by the branches of trees. Our progress, as may be imagined, was very tedious, and attended with uncommon labour; the party who went by land being continually obliged to wait for us. Mr. Mackay's gun was carried out of the canoe and lost, at a time when we appeared to stand in very great need of it, as two canoes, with sixteen or eighteen men, were coming down the stream; and the apprehensions which they occasioned did not subside till they shot by us with great rapidity.

At length we came in sight of the house, when we saw our young Indian with six others, in a canoe coming to meet us. This was a very encouraging circumstance, as it satisfied us that the natives who had preceded, and whose malignant designs we had every reason to suspect, had not been able to prejudice the people against us. We, therefore, landed at the house, where we were received in a friendly manner, and having procured some fish, we proceeded on our journey.

It was almost dark when we arrived at the next house, and the first persons who presented themselves to our observation were the turbulent Indian and his four companions. They were not very agreeable objects; but we were nevertheless well received by the inhabitants, who presented us with fish and berries. The Indians who had caused us so much alarm, we now discovered to be inhabitants of the islands, and traders in various articles, such as cedar-bark, prepared to be wove into mats, fishspawn, copper, iron, and beads, the latter of which they get on their own coast. For these they receive in exchange roasted salmon, hemlock-bark cakes, and the other kind made of salmon roes, sorrel, and bitter berries. Having procured as much fish as would serve us for our supper, and the meals of the next day, all my people went to rest except one, with whom I kept the first watch.

[July 24] After twelve last night, I called up Mr. Mackay, and one of the men, to relieve us, but as a general tranquillity appeared to prevail in the place, I recommended them to return to their rest. I was the first awake in the morning, and sent Mr. Mackay to see if our 247 canoe remained where we left it; but he returned to inform me that the Islanders had loaded it with their articles of traffic, and were ready to depart. On this intelligence I hurried to the water side, and seizing the canoe by the stem, I should certainly have overset it, and turned the three men that were in it, with all their merchandise, into the river, had not one of the people in the house, who had been very kind to us, informed me that this was their own canoe, and that my guide had gone off with ours. At the same moment the other two Indians who belonged to the party, jumped nimbly into it, and pushed off with all the haste and hurry that their fears may be supposed to dictate.

We now found ourselves once more without a guide or a canoe. We were, however, so fortunate as to engage, without much difficulty, two of these people to accompany us; as, from the strength of the current, it would not have been possible for us to have proceeded by water without their assistance. As the house was upon an island, we ferried over the pedestrian party to the main bank of the river, and continued our course till our conductors came to their fishing ground, when they proposed to land us, and our small portion of baggage; but as our companions were on the opposite shore, we could not acquiesce, and after some time persuaded them to proceed further with us. Soon after we met the chief, who had regaled us in our voyage down the river. He was seining between two canoes, and had taken a considerable quantity of salmon. He took us on board with him, and proceeded upwards with great expedition. These people are surprisingly skilful and active in setting against a strong current. In the roughest part they almost filled the canoe with water, by way of a sportive alarm to us.

We landed at the house of the chief, and he immediately placed a fish before me. Our people now appeared on the opposite bank, when a canoe was sent for them. As soon as they had made their meal of fish, they proceeded on their route, and we followed them, the chief and one of the natives having undertaken to conduct us.

248   At five in the afternoon we came to two houses, which we had not

seen in going down. They were upon an island, and I was obliged to send for the walking party, as our conductors, from the lateness of the hour, refused to proceed any further with us till the next day. One of our men, being at a small distance before the others, had been attacked by a female bear, with two cubs, but another of them arrived to his rescue, and shot her. Their fears probably prevented them from killing the two young ones. They brought a part of the meat, but it was very indifferent. We were informed that our former guide, or young chief, had passed this place, at a very early hour of the morning, on foot.

These people take plenty of another fish, besides salmon, which weigh from fifteen to forty pounds. This fish is broader than the salmon, of a greyish colour, and with a hunch on its back; the flesh is white, but neither rich nor well flavoured. Its jaw and teeth are like those of a dog, and the latter are larger and stronger than any I had ever seen in a fish of equal size: those in front bend inwards, like the claws of a bird of prey. It delights in shallow water, and its native name is Dilly. [This was either chum or humpback salmon].

We received as many fish and berries from these people as completely satisfied our appetites. The latter excelled any of the kind that we had seen. I saw also three kinds of gooseberries, which, as we passed through the woods, we found in great abundance.

[July 25] I arose before the sun, and the weather was very fine. The men who were to accompany us went to visit their machines, and brought back plenty of fish, which they strung on a rope, and left them in the river. We now embarked thirteen in a canoe, and landed my men on the South bank, as it would have been impracticable to have stemmed the tide with such a load. The under-wood was so thick that it was with great difficulty they could pass through it. At nine we were under the necessity of waiting to ferry them over a river from the South, which is not fordable. After some time we came to two deserted houses, at the foot of a rapid, beyond which our boatmen absolutely refused to conduct us by water. Here was a road which led opposite to the village. We had, however, the curiosity to 249 visit the houses, which were erected upon posts; and we suffered very severely for the indulgence of it; for the floors were covered with fleas, and we were immediately in the same condition, for which we had no remedy but to take to the water. There was not a spot round the houses, free from grass, that was not alive, as it were, with this vermin.

Our guides proposed to conduct us on our way, and we followed them on a well-beaten track. They, however, went so fast, that we could not all of us keep up with them, particularly our sick Indian, whose situation was very embarrassing to us, and at length they contrived to escape. I very much wished for these men to have accompanied us to the village, in order to do away any ill impressions which might have arisen from the young chief's report to his father, which we were naturally led to expect would not be in our favour.

This road conducted us through the finest wood of cedar trees that I had ever seen. I measured several of them that were twenty-four feet in the girth, and of a proportionate height. The alder trees are also of an uncommon size; several of them were seven feet and an half in circumference, and rose to forty feet without a branch; but my men declared that they had, in their progress, seen much larger of both kinds. The other wood was hemlock, white birch, two species of spruce-firs, willows, &c. Many of the large cedars appeared to have been examined, as I supposed, by the natives, for the purpose of making canoes, but finding them hollow at heart, they were suffered to stand. There was but little underwood, and the soil was a black rich mould, which would well reward the trouble of cultivation. From the remains of bones on certain spots, it is probable that the natives may have occasionally burned their dead in this wood.

As it was uncertain what our reception might be at the village [the Great Village], I examined every man's arms and ammunition, and gave Mr. Mackay, who had unfortunately lost his gun, one of my pistols. Our late conductors had informed us that the man whom we 250 left in a dying state, and to whom I had administered some Turlington's balsam, was dead; and it was by no means improbable that I might be suspected of hastening his end.

At one in the afternoon we came to the bank of the river, which was opposite to the village, which appeared to be in a state of perfect tranquillity. Several of the natives were fishing above and below the weir, and they very readily took us over in their canoes. The people now hurried down to the water side, but I perceived none of the chief's family among them. They made signs to me to go to his house; I signified to them not to crowd about us, and indeed drew a line, beyond which I made them understand they must not pass. I now directed Mr. Mackay and the men to remain there, with their arms in readiness, and to keep the natives at a distance, as I was determined to go alone to the chief's house; and if they should hear the report of my pistols, they were ordered to make the best of their way from these people, as it would then be equally fruitless and dangerous to attempt the giving me any assistance, as it would be only in the last extremity, and when I was certain of their intention to destroy me, that I should discharge my pistols. My gun I gave to Mr. Mackay, when, with my loaded pistols in my belt, and a poniard [dagger] in my hand, I proceeded to the abode of the chief. I had a wood to pass in my way thither, which was intersected by various paths, and I took one that led to the back instead of the front of the house; and as the whole had been very much altered since I was here before, I concluded that I had lost my way. But I continued to proceed, and soon met with the chief's wife, who informed me, that he was at the next house. On my going round it, I perceived that they had thrown open the gable ends, and added two wings, nearly as long as the body, both of which were hung round with salmon as close as they could be placed. As I could discover none of the men, I sat down upon a large stone near some women who were supping on salmon roes and berries. They invited me to partake of their fare, and I was about to accept their invitation, when Mr. Mackay joined me, as both himself and all my party were alarmed at my being alone. Nor was his alarm lessened by an old man whom he met in   251 the wood, and who made use of signs to persuade him to return. As he came without his gun, I gave him one of my pistols. When I saw the women continue their employment without paying the least attention to us, I could not imagine that any hostile design was preparing against us: though the non-appearance of the men awakened some degree of suspicion that I should not be received with the same welcome as on my former visit. At length the chief appeared, and his son, who had been our guide, following him: displeasure was painted in the old man's countenance, and he held in his hand a bead tobacco pouch which belonged to Mr. Mackay, and which the young chief had purloined from him. When he had approached within three or four yards of me, he threw it at me with great indignation, and walked away. I followed him, however, until he had passed his son, whom I took by the hand, but he did not make any very cordial return to my salutation; at the same time he made signs for me to discharge my pistol, and give him my hanger which Mr. Mackay had brought me, but I did not pay the least attention to either of his demands.

We now joined the chief, who explained to me that he was in a state of deep distress for the loss of his son, and made me understand that he had cut off his hair and blackened his face on the melancholy occasion. He also represented the alarm which he had suffered respecting his son who had accompanied us; as he apprehended we had killed him, or had all of us perished together. When he had finished his narrative, I took him and his son by their hands, and requested them to come with me to the place where I had left my people, who were rejoiced to see us return, having been in a state of great anxiety from our long absence. I immediately remunerated the young chief for his company and assistance in our voyage to the sea, as well as his father, for his former attentions. I gave them cloth and knives, and, indeed, a portion of every thing which now remained to us. The presents had the desired effect of restoring us to their favour; but these people are of so changeable a nature, that there is no security with them. I procured three robes and two otter-skins, and if I could have given such articles in exchange as they preferred, I should probably have obtained more. I now represented the length of the way which I had to go, and requested some fish to support us on our journey, when he desired us to follow him to the house, where mats were immediately arranged and a fish placed before each of us.

We were now informed, that our dog, whom we had lost, had been howling about the village ever since we left it, and that they had reason to believe he left the woods at night to eat the fish he could find about the houses. I immediately dispatched Mr. Mackay and a man in search of the animal, but they returned without him.

When I manifested my intention to proceed on my journey, the chief voluntarily sent for ten roasted salmon, and having attended us with his son, and a great number of his people, to the last house in the village, we took our leave. It was then half past three in the afternoon.

I directed Mr. Mackay to take the lead, and the others to follow him in Indian files, at a long and steady pace, as I determined to bring up the rear. I adopted this measure from a confusion that was observable among the natives which I did not comprehend. I was not without my suspicions that some mischief was in agitation, and they were increased from the confused noise we heard in the village. At the same time a considerable number came running after us; some of them making signs for us to stop, and others rushing by me. I perceived also, that those who followed us were the strangers who live among these people, and are kept by them in a state of awe and subjection; and one of them made signs to me that we were taking a wrong road. I immediately called out to Mr. Mackay to stop. This was naturally enough taken for an alarm, and threw my people into great disorder. When, however, I was understood, and we had mustered again, our Indian informed us, that the noise we heard was occasioned by a debate among the natives, whether they should stop us or not. When, therefore, we had got into the right road, I made such arrangements as might be necessary for our defence, if we 253 should have an experimental proof that our late and fickle friends were converted into enemies.

Our way was through a forest of stately cedars, beneath a range of lofty hills, covered with rocks, and without any view of the river. The path was well beaten, but rendered incommodious by the large stones which lay along it.

As we were continuing our route, we all felt the sensation of having found a lost friend at the sight of our dog; but he appeared, in a great degree, to have lost his former sagacity. He ran in a wild way backwards and forwards; and though he kept our road, I could not induce him to acknowledge his master. Sometimes he seemed disposed to approach as if he knew us; and then, on a sudden, he would turn away, as if alarmed at our appearance. The poor animal was reduced almost to a skeleton, and we occasionally dropped something to support him, until by degrees he recovered his former sagacity.

When the night came on we stopped at a small distance from the river, but did not venture to make a fire. Every man took his tree, and laid down in his clothes, and with his arms, beneath the shade of its branches. We had removed to a short distance from the path; no centinel was now appointed, and every one was left to watch for his own safety.

[July 26] After a very restless, though undisturbed night, we set forward as soon as day appeared, and walked on with all possible expedition, till we got to the upper, which we now called Friendly Village, and was the first we visited on our outward journey.

It was eight in the morning of a very fine day when we arrived, and found a very material alteration in the place since we left it. Five additional houses had been erected and were filled with salmon: the increase of inhabitants was in the same proportion. We were received with great kindness, and a messenger was dispatched to inform the chief, whose name was Soocomlick, and who was then at his fishing weir, of our arrival. He immediately returned to the village to confirm the cordial reception of his people; and having conducted us to his house, entertained us with the most respectful hospitality. In short, he behaved to us with so much attention and kindness, that I did not withhold any thing in my power to give, which might afford him satisfaction. I presented him with two yards of blue cloth, an axe, knives, and various other articles. He gave me in return a large shell which resembled the under shell of a Guernsey oyster, but somewhat larger. Where they procure them I could not discover, but they cut and polish them for bracelets, ear-rings, and other personal ornaments. He regretted that he had no sea otter skins to give me, but engaged to provide abundance of them whenever either my friends or myself should return by sea; an expectation which I thought it right to encourage among these people. He also earnestly requested me to bring him a gun and ammunition. I might have procured many curious articles at this place, but was prevented by the consideration that we must have carried them on our backs upwards of three hundred miles through a mountainous country. The young chief, to his other acts of kindness, added as large a supply of fish as we chose to take.

Our visit did not occasion any particular interruption of the ordinary occupation of the people; especially of the women, who were employed in boiling sorrel, and different kinds of berries, with salmon-roes, in large square kettles of cedar wood. This pottage, when it attained a certain consistency, they took out with ladles, and poured it into frames of about twelve inches square and one deep, the bottom being covered with a large leaf, which were then exposed to the sun till their contents became so many dried cakes. The roes that are mixed up with the bitter berries, are prepared in the same way. From the quantity of this kind of provision, it must be a principal article of food, and probably of traffic. These people have also portable chests of cedar, in which they pack them, as well as their salmon, both dried and roasted. It appeared to me, that they eat no flesh, except such as the sea may afford them, as that of the sea-otter and the seal. The only instance we observed to the contrary, was in the young Indian who accompanied us among the islands, and has been already mentioned as feasting on the flesh of a porcupine: whether this be their custom throughout the year, or only during the season of the salmon fishery; or, whether there were any casts of them, as in India, I cannot pretend to determine. It is certain, however, that they are not hunters; and I have already mentioned the abhorrence they expressed at some venison which we brought to their village. During our former visit to these people, they requested us not to discharge our fire-arms, lest the report should frighten away the salmon, but now they expressed a wish that I should explain the use and management of them. Though their demeanour to us was of the most friendly nature, and they appeared without any arms, except a few who accidentally had their daggers, I did not think it altogether prudent to discharge our pieces; I therefore fired one of my pistols at a tree marked for the purpose, when I put four out of five buck-shot, with which it was loaded, into the circle, to their extreme astonishment and admiration.

These people were in general of the middle stature, well-set, and better clothed with flesh than any of the natives of the interior country. Their faces are round, with high cheek bones, and their complexion between the olive and the copper. They have small grey eyes with a tinge of red; they have wedge heads [deliberately distorted in infancy by a special cradle board], and their hair is of a dark brown colour, inclining to black. Some wear it long, keep it well combed, and let it hang loose over their shoulders, while they divide and tie it in knots over the temples. Others arrange its plaits, and bedawb it with brown earth, so as to render it impervious to the comb; they, therefore, carry a bodkin about them to ease the frequent irritation, which may be supposed to proceed from such a state of the head. The women are inclined to be fat, wear their hair short, and appear to be very subject to swelled legs, a malady that probably proceeds from the posture in which they are always sitting; as they are chiefly employed in the domestic engagements of spinning, weaving, preparing the fish, and nursing their children, who did not appear to be numerous. Their cradle differed from any that I had seen; it consisted of a frame fixed round a board of sufficient length, in which the child, after it has been swathed, is placed on a bed of moss, and a conductor contrived to carry off the urinary discharge. They are slung over one shoulder by means of a cord fastened under the other, so that the infant is always in a position to be readily applied to the breast, when it requires nourishment. I saw several whose heads were inclosed in boards covered with leather, till they attain the form of a wedge. The women wear no clothing but the robe, either loose or tied round the middle with a girdle, as the occasion may require, with the addition of a fringed apron, already mentioned, and a cap, in the form of an inverted bowl or dish. To the robe and cap, the men add, when it rains, a circular mat with an opening in the middle sufficient to admit the head, which, extending over the shoulders, throws off the wet. They also occasionally wear shoes of dressed moose-skin, for which they are indebted to their neighbours. Those parts, which among all civilized nations are covered from familiar view, are here openly exposed.

They are altogether dependant on the sea and rivers for their sustenance, so that they may be considered as a stationary people; hence it is that the men engage in those toilsome employments, which the tribes who support themselves by the chase leave entirely to the women. Polygamy is permitted among them, though, according to my observation, most of the men were satisfied with one wife, with whom, however, chastity is not considered as a necessary virtue. I saw but one woman whose under lip was split and disfigured with an appendant ornament. The men frequently bathe, and the boys are continually in the water. They have nets and lines of various kinds and sizes, which are made of cedar bark, and would not be known from those made of hemp. Their hooks consist of two pieces of wood or bone, forming, when fixed together, an obtuse [acute?] angle.

Their spears or darts are from four to sixteen feet in length, the barb or point being fixed in a socket, which, when the animal is struck, slips from it; thus the barb being fastened by a string to the 257 handle, remains as a buoy; or enables the aquatic hunter to tire and take his prey. They are employed against sea otters, seals, and large fish.

Their hatchets are made principally of about fourteen inches of bar-iron, fixed into a wooden handle, as I have already described them; though they have some of bone or horn: with these, a mallet and wooden wedge, they hew their timbers and form their planks. They must also have other tools with which they complete and polish their work, but my stay was so short, my anxiety so great, and my situation so critical, that many circumstances may be supposed to have escaped me.

Their canoes are made out of the cedar tree, and will carry from eight to fifty persons.

Their warlike weapons, which, as far as I could judge, they very seldom have occasion to employ, are bows and arrows, spears, and daggers. The arrows are such as have been already described, but rather of a slighter make. The bows are not more than two feet and an half in length; they are formed of a slip of red cedar; the grain being on one side untouched with any tool, while the other is secured with sinews attached to it by a kind of glue. Though this weapon has a very slender appearance, it throws an arrow with great force, and to a considerable distance. Their spears are about ten feet long, and pointed with iron. Their daggers are of various kinds, being of British, Spanish, and American manufacture.

Their household furniture consists of boxes, troughs, and dishes formed of wood, with different vessels made of watape. These are employed, according to their several applications, to contain their valuables and provisions, as well as for culinary purposes, and to carry water. The women make use of muscle-shells to split and clean their fish, and which are very well adapted to that purpose.

Their ornaments are necklaces, collars, bracelets for the arms, wrists, and legs, with ear-rings, &c.

They burn their dead, and display their mourning, by cutting their hair short, and blackening their faces. Though I saw several places where bodies had been burned, I was surprised at not seeing any tomb or memorial of the dead, particularly when their neighbours are so superstitiously attentive of the erection and preservation of them.

From the number of their canoes, as well as the quantity of their chests and boxes, to contain their moveables, as well as the insufficiency of their houses to guard against the rigours of a severe winter, and the appearance of the ground around their habitations, it is evident that these people reside here only during the summer or salmon season, which does not probably last more than three months. It may be reasonably inferred, therefore, that they have villages on the sea-coast, which they inhabit during the rest of the year. There it may be supposed they leave the sick, the infirm, and the aged; and thither they may bear the ashes of those who die at the place of their summer residence.

Of their religion I can say but little, as my means of observation were very contracted. I could discover, however, that they believed in a good and an evil spirit: and that they have some forms of worship to conciliate the protection of one, and perhaps to avert the enmity of the other, is apparent from the temples which I have described; and where, at stated periods, it may be presumed they hold the feasts, and perform the sacrifices, which their religion, whatever it may be, has instituted as the ceremonials of their public worship.

From the very little I could discover of their government, it is altogether different from any political regulation which had been remarked by me among the savage tribes. It is on this river alone that one man appears to have an exclusive and hereditary right to what was necessary to the existence of those who are associated with him. I allude to the salmon weir, or fishing place, the sole right to which confers on the chief an arbitrary power. Those embankments could not have been formed without a very great and associated labour; and, as might be supposed, on the condition that those who assisted in constructing it should enjoy a participating right in the advantages to be derived from it. Nevertheless, it evidently appeared 259 to me, that the chief's power over it and the people, was unlimited and without control. No one could fish without his permission, or carry home a larger portion of what he had caught, than was set apart for him. No one could build a house without his consent; and all his commands appeared to be followed with implicit obedience. The people at large seemed to be on a perfect equality, while the strangers among them were obliged to obey the commands of the natives in general, or quit the village. They appear to be of a friendly disposition, but they are subject to sudden gusts of passion, which are as quickly composed; and the transition is instantaneous, from violent irritation to the most tranquil demeanor. Of the many tribes of savage people whom I have seen, these appear to be the most susceptible of civilization. They might soon be brought to cultivate the little ground about them which is capable of it. There is a narrow border of a rich black soil, on either side of the river, over a bed of gravel, which would yield any grain or fruit, that are common to similar latitudes in Europe.

The very few words which I collected of their language, are as follow:

Zimilk,	Salmon.
Dilly,	A fish of the size of a salmon, with canine teeth.
Sepnas,	Hair of the head.
Kietis,	An axe.
Clougus,	Eyes.
Itzas,	Teeth.
Ma-acza,	Nose.
Ich-yeh,	Leg.
Shous-shey,	Hand.
Watts,	Dog.
Zla-achle,	House.
Zimnez,	Bark mat robe.
Couloun,	Beaver or otter ditto.
Dichts,	Stone.

Neach,	Fire.
Ulkan,	Water.
Gits com,	A mat.
Shiggimia,	Thread.
Till-kewan,	Chest or box.
Thlogatt,	Cedar bark.
Achimoul,	Beads got upon their coast.
Il-caiette,	A bonnet.
Couny,	A clam shell.
Nochasky,	A dish composed of berries and salmon roes.
Caiffre,	What?

At eleven in the morning we left this place, which I called Friendly Village, accompanied by every man belonging to it, who attended us about a mile, when we took a cordial leave of them; and if we might judge from appearances, they parted from us with regret.

In a short time we halted, to make a division of our fish, and each man had about twenty pounds weight of it, except Mr. Mackay and myself, who were content with shorter allowance, that we might have less weight to carry. We had also a little flour, and some pemmican. Having completed this arrangement with all possible expedition, we proceeded onwards, the ground rising gradually, as we continued our route. When we were clear of the wood, we saw the mountain towering above, and apparently of impracticable ascent. We soon came to the fork of the river [Burnt Bridge Creek], which was at the foot of the precipice, where the ford was three feet deep, and very rapid. Our young Indian, though much recovered, was still too weak to cross the water, and with some difficulty I carried him over on my back.

It was now one in the afternoon, and we had to ascend the summit of the first mountain before night came on, in order to look for water. I left the sick Indian, with his companion and one of my men, to follow us, as his strength would permit him. The fatigue of ascending 261 these precipices [a climb of about 3,800 feet] I shall not attempt to describe, and it was past five when we arrived at a spot where we could get water, and in such an extremity of weariness, that it was with great pain any of us could crawl about to gather wood for the necessary purpose of making a fire. To relieve our anxiety, which began to increase every moment for the situation of the Indian, about seven he and his companions arrived; when we consoled ourselves by sitting round a blazing fire, talking of past dangers, and indulging the delightful reflection that we were thus far advanced on our homeward journey. Nor was it possible to be in this situation without contemplating the wonders of it. Such was the depth of the precipices below, and the height of the mountains above, with the rude and wild magnificence of the scenery around, that I shall not attempt to describe such an astonishing and awful combination of objects; of which, indeed, no description can convey an adequate idea. Even at this place, which is only, as it were, the first step towards gaining the summit of the mountains, the climate was very sensibly changed. The air that fanned the village which we left at noon, was mild and cheering; the grass was verdant, and the wild fruits ripe around it. But here the snow was not yet dissolved, the ground was still bound by the frost, the herbage had scarce begun to spring, and the crowberry bushes were just beginning to blossom.

[July 27] So great was our fatigue of yesterday, that it was late before we proceeded to return over the mountains, by the same route which we had followed in our outward journey. There was little or no change in the appearance of the mountains since we passed them, though the weather was very fine.

[July 28] At nine this morning we arrived at a spot, where we slept with the natives on the 16th instant, and found our pemmican in good condition where we had buried it.

The latitude of this place, by observation, when I passed, I found to be 52. 46. 32. I now took time, and the distance between sun and moon. I had also an azimuth, to ascertain the variation.

We continued our route with fine weather, and without meeting

a single person on our way, the natives being all gone, as we supposed, to the Great River [Fraser River]. We recovered all our hidden stores of provisions, and arrived about two in the afternoon of
Sunday, August the 4th, at the place which we had left a month
before [Fraser River].

A considerable number of Indians were encamped on the opposite
side of the small river [a creek flowing into the Fraser], and in consequence of the weather, confined to their lodges: as they must have
heard of, if not seen, us, and our arms being out of order from the
rain, I was not satisfied with our situation; but did not wish to create
an alarm. We, therefore, kept in the edge of the wood, and called to
them, when they turned out like so many furies, with their arms in
their hands, and threatening destruction if we dared to approach
their habitations. We remained in our station till their passion and
apprehensions had subsided, when our interpreter gave them the
necessary information respecting us. They proved to be strangers to
us, but were the relations of those whom we had already seen here,
and who, as they told us, were upon an island at some distance up the
river. A messenger was accordingly sent to inform them of our
arrival.

[August 5] On examining the canoe, and our property, which we
had left behind, we found in it perfect safety; nor was there the print
of a foot near the spot. We now pitched our tent, and made a blazing
fire, and I treated myself, as well as the people, with a dram; but we
had been so long without tasting any spirituous liquor, that we had
lost all relish for it. The Indians now arrived from above, and were
rewarded for the care they had taken of our property with such articles as were acceptable to them.

At nine this morning I sent five men in the canoe, for the various articles we had left below, and they soon returned with them,
and except some bale goods, which had got wet, they were in good
order, particularly the provisions, of which we were now in great
need.

Many of the natives arrived both from the upper and lower parts 263 of the river, each of whom was dressed in a beaver robe. I purchased fifteen of them, and they preferred large knives in exchange. It is an extraordinary circumstance, that these people, who might have taken all the property we left behind us, without the least fear of detection, should leave that untouched, and purloin any of our utensils, which our confidence in their honesty gave them a ready opportunity of taking. In fact, several articles were missing, and as I was very anxious to avoid a quarrel with the natives, in this stage of our journey, I told those who remained near us, without any appearance of anger, that their relations who were gone, had no idea of the mischief that would result to them from taking our property. I gravely added, that the salmon, which was not only their favorite food, but absolutely necessary to their existence, came from the sea which belonged to us white men; and that as, at the entrance of the river, we could prevent those fish from coming up it, we possessed the power to starve them and their children. To avert our anger, therefore, they must return all the articles that had been stolen from us. This finesse succeeded. Messengers were dispatched to order the restoration of every thing that had been taken. We purchased several large salmon of them and enjoyed the delicious meal which they afforded.

At noon this day, which I allotted for repose, I got a meridian altitude, which gave 53. 24. 10. I also took time. The weather had been cloudy at intervals.

[August 6] Every necessary preparation had been made yesterday for us to continue our route to-day; but before our departure, some of the natives arrived with part of the stolen articles; the rest, they said, had been taken by people down the river, who would be here in the course of the morning, and recommended their children to our commiseration, and themselves to our forgiveness.

The morning was cloudy, with small rain; nevertheless I ordered the men to load the canoe, and we proceeded in high spirits on finding ourselves once more so comfortably together in it. We landed at a house on the first island, where we procured a few salmon, and four fine beaver skins. There had been much more rain in these parts than in the country above, as the water was pouring down the hills in torrents. The river consequently rose with great rapidity, and very much impeded our progress.

The people [Carrier Indians] on this river are generally of the middle size, though I saw many tall men among them. In the cleanliness of their persons they resemble rather the Beaver Indians than the Chepewyans. They are ignorant of the use of fire arms, and their only weapons are bows and arrows, and spears. They catch the larger animals in snares; but though their country abounds in them, and the rivers and lakes produce plenty of fish, they find a difficulty in supporting themselves, and are never to be seen but in small bands of two or three families. There is no regular government among them; nor do they appear to have a sufficient communication or understanding with each other, to defend themselves against an invading enemy, to whom they fall an easy prey. They have all the animals common on the West side of the mountains, except the buffalo and the wolf; at least we saw none of the latter, and there being none of the former, it is evident that their progress is from the South-East.

> Wolves occurred throughout British Columbia, even though Mackenzie did not see them on the Fraser. Buffalo did not occur in that area, but it is not clear what Mackenzie means by "their progress is from the South-East." They were abundant in the Peace River country east of Peace River Canyon, and Mackenzie's party later shot one near the west end of the Canyon.[28]

The same language, is spoken, with very little exception, from the extent of my travels down this river, and in a direct line from the North-East head of it in the latitude 53° or 54° to Hudson's Bay; so that a Chepewyan, from which tribe they have all sprung, might leave Churchill River, and proceeding in every direction to the North-

West of this line without knowing any language except his own, would understand them all [All these tribes spoke Athapascan languages.]: I except the natives of the sea coast, who are altogether a different people. As to the people to the Eastward of this river, I am not qualified to speak of them.

At twelve we ran our canoe upon a rock, so that we were obliged to land in order to repair the injury she had received; and as the rain came on with great violence, we remained here for the night. The salmon were now driving up the current in such large shoals, that the water seemed, as it were, to be covered with the fins of them.

[August 7] About nine this morning the weather cleared and we embarked. The shoals of salmon continued as yesterday. There were frequent showers throughout the day, and every brook was deluged into a river. The water had risen at least one foot and an half perpendicular in the last twenty-four hours. In the dusk of the evening we landed for the night.

[August 8] The water continued rising during the night; so that we were disturbed twice in the course of it, to remove our baggage. At six in the morning we were on our way, and proceeded with continual and laborious exertion, from the increased rapidity of the current. After having passed the two carrying places of Rocky Point, and the Long Portage [both at Fort George Canyon], we encamped for the night.

[August 9] We set off at five, after a rainy night, and in a foggy morning. The water still retained its height. The sun, however, soon beamed upon us; and our clothes and baggage were in such a state that we landed to dry them. After some time we re-embarked, and arrived at our first encampment on this river about seven in the evening. The water fell considerably in the course of the day.

[August 10] The weather was cloudy with slight showers, and at five this morning we embarked, the water falling as fast as it had risen. This circumstance arises from the mountainous state of the country on either side of the river, from whence the water rushes

down almost as fast as it falls from the heavens, with the addition of the snow it melts in its way. At eight in the evening we stopped for the night.

[August 11] At five this morning we proceeded with clear weather. At ten we came to the foot of the long rapid [Giscome Canyon], which we ascended with poles much easier than we expected. The rapids that were so strong and violent in our passage downwards, were now so reduced, that we could hardly believe them to be the same. At sun-set we landed and encamped.

[August 12] The weather was the same as yesterday, and we were on the water at a very early hour. At nine we came to a part of the river where there was little or no current. At noon we landed to gum the canoe, when I took a meridian altitude, which gave 54. 11. 36. North latitude. We continued our route nearly East, and at three in the afternoon approached the fork [McGregor River], when I took time, and the distance between the sun and moon. At four in the afternoon we left the main branch [Fraser River]. The current was quite slack, as the water had fallen six feet, which must have been in the course of three days. At sun-set we landed and took our station for the night.

[August 13] There was a very heavy rain in the night, and the morning was cloudy; we renewed our voyage, however, at a very early hour, and came to the narrow gut [channel] between the mountains of rock, which was a passage of some risk; but fortunately the state of the water was such, that we got up without any difficulty, and had more time to examine these extraordinary rocks than in our outward passage. They are as perpendicular as a wall, and give the idea of a succession of enormous Gothic churches. We were now closely hemmed in by the mountains, which have lost much of their snow since our former passage by them. We encamped at a late hour, cold, wet, and hungry: for such was the state of our provisions, that our necessary allowance did not answer to the active cravings of our appetites.

[August 14] The weather was cold and raw, with small rain, but our necessities would not suffer us to wait for a favourable change of 267 it, and at half past five we arrived at the swampy carrying-place between this branch [Herrick Creek?] and the small river [James Creek?]. At three in the afternoon the cold was extreme, and the men could not keep themselves warm even by their violent exertions, which our situation required; and I now gave them the remainder of our rum to fortify and support them. The canoe was so heavy that the lives of two of them were endangered in this horrible carrying place. At the same time it must be observed, that from the fatiguing circumstances of our journey, and the inadequate state of our provisions, the natural strength of the men had been greatly diminished. We encamped on the banks of the bad river [James Creek?].

[August 15] The weather was now clear, and the sun shone upon us. The water was much lower than in the downward passage, but as cold as ice, and, unfortunately, the men were obliged to be continually in it to drag on the canoe. There were many embarras, through which a passage might have been made, but we were under the necessity of carrying both the canoe and baggage.

About sun-set we arrived at our encampment of the 13th of June, where some of us had nearly taken our eternal voyage. The legs and feet of the men were so benumbed, that I was very apprehensive of the consequences. The water being low, we made a search for our bag of ball, but without success. The river was full of salmon, and another fish like the black bass.

[August 16] The weather continued to be the same as yesterday, and at two in the afternoon we came to the carrying-place which leads to the first small lake [Arctic Lake]; but it was so filled with drift wood, that a considerable portion of time was employed in making our way through it. We now reached the high land [the Continental Divide] which separates the source of the Tacoutche Tesse, or Columbia River, and Unjigah, or Peace River: the latter of which, after receiving many tributary streams, passes through the great Slave Lake, and disembogues itself in the Frozen [Arctic] Ocean, in latitude 69½ North, longitude 135. West from Greenwich;

268 while the former, confined by the immense mountains that run

nearly parallel with the Pacific Ocean, and keep it in a Southern course, empties itself in 46. 20. North latitude, and longitude 124. West from Greenwich. [The Tacoutche Tesse was actually the Fraser River. It enters the sea at about 49° N.]

If I could have spared the time, and had been able to exert myself, for I was now afflicted with a swelling in my ankles, so that I could not even walk, but with great pain and difficulty, it was my intention to have taken some salmon alive, and colonised them in the Peace River [Parsnip River]; though it is very doubtful whether that fish would live in waters that have not a communication with the sea. [The swelling of his ankles could have had many causes and there is no way of telling which was responsible. An attempt to colonize the Parsnip River with salmon would certainly have been unsuccessful though of course it does have a communication with the sea.]

Some of the inhabitants had been here since we passed; and I apprehended, that on seeing our road through their country, they mistook us for enemies, and had therefore deserted the place, which is a most convenient station; as on one side, there is great plenty of white fish, and trout, jub, carp, &c. and on the other, abundance of salmon, and probably other fish. Several things that I had left here in exchange for articles of which I had possessed myself, as objects of curiosity, were taken away. The whirtle berries were now ripe, and very fine of their kind.

[August 17] The morning was cloudy, and at five we renewed our progress. We were compelled to carry from the lake to the Peace River [Parsnip River], the passage, from the falling of the water, being wholly obstructed by drift-wood. The meadow through which we passed was entirely inundated; and from the state of my foot and ancle, I was obliged, though with great reluctance, to submit to be carried over it.

At half past seven we began to glide along with the current of the Peace River; and almost at every canoe's length we perceived beaver roads to and from the river. At two in the afternoon, an object at- 269 tracted our notice at the entrance of a small river, which proved to be the four beaver skins, already mentioned to have been presented to me by a native, and left in his possession to receive them on my return. I imagine, therefore, that being under the necessity of leaving the river, or, perhaps, fearing to meet us again, he had taken this method to restore them to me; and to reward his honesty, I left three times the value of the skins in their place. The snow appeared in patches on the mountains. At four in the afternoon we passed the place where we found the first natives, and landed for the night at a late hour. In the course of the day we caught nine outardes, or Canada geese, but they were as yet without their feathers.

[August 18] As soon as it was light we proceeded on our voyage, and drove on before the current, which was very much diminished in its strength, since we came up it. The water indeed was so low, that in many parts it exposed a gravelly beach. At eleven we landed at our encampment of the seventh of June, to gum the canoe and dry our clothes: we then re-embarked, and at half past five arrived at the place, where I lost my book of memorandums, on the fourth of June, in which were certain courses and distances between that day and twenty sixth of May, which I had now an opportunity to supply. They were as follow:

North-North-West half a mile, East by North half a mile, North by East a quarter of a mile, North-West by West a quarter of a mile, West-South-West half a mile, North-West a mile and a quarter, North-North-West three quarters of a mile, North by East half a mile, North-West three quarters of a mile, West half a mile, North-West three quarters of a mile, West-North-West one mile and a quarter, North three quarters of a mile, West by North one quarter of a mile, North-West one mile and an half, West-North-West half a mile, North-North-West three quarters of a mile, West one quarter of a mile, North-North-East half a mile, North-North-West two miles, and North-West four miles.

We were seven days in going up that part of the river which we came down to-day; and it now swarmed, as it were, with beavers and wild fowl. There was rain in the afternoon, and about sun-set we took our station for the night.

[August 19] We had some small rain throughout the night.

Our course to-day was South-South-West three quarters of a mile, West-North-West half a mile, North half a mile, North-West by West three quarters of a mile, North by West half a mile; a small river to the left, South-West by West three quarters of a mile, West-North-West a mile and an half, North-West by North four miles, a rivulet on the right; West-North-West three quarters of a mile; a considerable river from the left, North-North-West two miles, North half a mile, West-North-West one mile and an half; a rivulet on the right, North-West by West one mile and a quarter, West-North-West one mile, West-South-West a quarter of a mile, North-North-West half a mile, North-West half a mile, West-South-West three quarters of a mile, North-West by West three miles, West-South-West three quarters of a mile, North-West by West one mile; a small river on the right, South-West a quarter of a mile, West-North-West, islands, four miles and an half, a river on the left; North half a mile, West a quarter of a mile, North a quarter of a mile, North-West by West three quarters of a mile, North-North-East three quarters of a mile, North-West by North half a mile, West-North-West a mile and an half, and North-West by North half a mile.

The mountains were covered with fresh snow, whose showers had dissolved in rain before they reached us.

North-West three quarters of a mile, South-West a quarter of a mile, North a mile and three quarters, West-North-West a mile and a quarter, North-West a mile and an half, North-North-West half a mile, West-North-West a quarter of a mile, North half a mile; here the current was slack: North-West by North half a mile, North-West by West a quarter of a mile, North-North-West a quarter of a mile, North-West by West one mile and a quarter, North half a mile, North-East by North one mile and three quarters, South-West one mile and a quarter, with an island, North by East one mile, North-West.

Here the other branch [Finlay River] opened to us, at the distance of three quarters of a mile.   271

I expected from the slackness of the current in this branch, that the Western one would be high, but I found it equally low. I had every reason to believe that from the upper part of this branch [Finlay River], the distance could not be great to the country through which I passed when I left the Great River; but it has since been determined otherwise by Mr. J. Finlay, who was sent to explore it [in 1797], and found its navigation soon terminated by falls and rapids.

The branches are about two hundred yards in breadth, and the water was six feet lower than on our upward passage.

Our course, after the junction [on the Peace], was North-North-West one mile, the rapid [Finlay Rapids] North-East down it three quarters of a mile, North by West one mile and a quarter, North by East one mile and an half, East by South one mile, North-East two miles and an half, East-North-East a quarter of a mile; a rivulet; East by South one mile and an half, North-East two miles, East-North-East one mile, North-North-East a quarter of a mile, North-East by East half a mile, East-South-East a quarter of a mile, East-North-East half a mile, North-East two miles, North-East by East two miles and a quarter, South-East by East a quarter of a mile; a rivulet from the left; East by North a mile and an half, East by South one mile, East-North-East one mile and three quarters; a river on the right [Eauclaire Creek]; North-North-East three quarters of a mile, North-East a mile and an half, North-East by East a mile and a quarter, East-North-East half a mile, and North-East by North half a mile.

Here we landed at our encampment of the 27th of June [actually May 28 and 29], from whence I dispatched a letter in an empty keg, as was mentioned in that period of my journal, which set forth our existing state, progress, and expectation.

[August 20] Though the weather was clear, we could not embark this morning before five, as there was a rapid [Ne-parle-pas Rapids] near us, which required day-light to run it, that we might not break our canoe on the rocks. The baggage we were obliged to carry. Our course was North by East a mile and an half, North-North East a mile and an half down another rapid on the West side; it requires great care to keep directly between the eddy current, and that which was driving down with so much impetuosity. We then proceeded North-North-West, a river from the right; a mile and a quarter, North-North-East a mile and an half, a river [Nabesche River?] from the left; North one mile and three quarters, North-East two miles, North-East by East two miles and a quarter, East by North one mile, North-East by East four miles, a river from the left, and East by South a mile and an half. Here was our encampment on the 26th of May, beyond which it would be altogether superfluous for me to take the courses, as they are inserted in their proper places.

As we continued our voyage, our attention was attracted by the appearance of an Indian encampment. We accordingly landed, and found there had been five fires, and within that number of days; so that there must have been some inhabitants in the neighbourhood, though we were not so fortunate as to see them. It appeared that they had killed a number of animals, and fled in a state of alarm, as three of their canoes were left carelessly on the beach, and their paddles laying about in disorder. We soon after came to the carrying-place called Portage de la Montagne de Roche. Here I had a meridian altitude, which made the latitude 56. 3. 51. North. [This was Rocky Mountain Portage around Peace River Canyon. For some reason he followed his own trail back around the canyon, rather than the Indian portage.]

The water, as I have already observed, was much lower than when we came up it, though at the same time, the current appeared to be stronger from this place to the forks; the navigation, however, would now be attended with greater facility, as there is a stony beech all the way; so that poles, or the towing line, may be employed with the best effect, where the current overpowers the use of paddles.

We were now reduced to a very short allowance; the disappointment, therefore, at not seeing any animals was proportioned to our exigences, as we did not possess at this time more than was sufficient to serve us for two meals. I now dispatched Mr. Mackay and the Indians to proceed to the foot of the rapids, and endeavour in their

way to procure some provisions, while I prepared to employ the utmost expedition in getting there; having determined, notwithstanding the disinclination of my people, from the recollection of what
they had suffered in coming that way, to return by the same route. I
had observed, indeed, that the water which had fallen fifteen feet
perpendicular, at the narrow pass below us, had lost much of its
former turbulence.

As dispatch was essential in procuring a supply of provisions, we
did not delay a moment in making preparation to renew our progress. Five of the men began to carry the baggage, while the sixth and
myself took the canoe asunder, to cleanse her of the dirt, and expose
her lining and timbers to the air, which would render her much
lighter. About sun-set Mr. Mackay and our hunters returned with
heavy burdens of the flesh of a buffalo: though not very tender, it was
very acceptable, and was the only animal that they had seen, though
the country was covered with tracks of them, as well as of the moose-
deer and the elk. The former had done rutting, and the latter were
beginning to run. Our people returned, having left their loads midway on the carrying-place. My companion and myself completed our
undertaking, and the canoe was ready to be carried in the morning.
A hearty meal concluded the day, and every fear of future want was
removed.

[August 21] When the morning dawned we set forwards, but as a
fire had passed through the portage, it was with difficulty we could
trace our road in many parts; and with all the exertion of which we
were capable, we did not arrive at the river till four in the afternoon.
We found almost as much difficulty in carrying our canoe down the
mountain as we had in getting it up; the men being not so strong as
on the former occasion, though they were in better spirits; and I was
now enabled to assist them, my ankle being almost well. We could
not, however, proceed any further till the following day, as we had
the canoe to gum, with several great and small poles to prepare;
those we had left here having been carried away by the water,
though we had left them in a position from fifteen to twenty feet

above the water-mark, at that time. These occupations employed us till a very late hour.

[August 22] The night was cold, and though the morning was fine and clear, it was seven before we were in a state of preparation to leave this place, sometimes driving with the current, and at other times shooting the rapids. The latter had lost much of their former strength; but we, nevertheless, thought it necessary to land very frequently, in order to examine the rapids before we could venture to run them. However, the canoe being light, we very fortunately passed them all, and at noon arrived at the place where I appointed to meet Mr. Mackay and the hunters: there we found them, with plenty of excellent fat meat, ready roasted, as they had killed two elks within a few hundred yards of the spot where we then were. When the men had satisfied their appetites, I sent them for as much of the meat as they could carry. In coming hither, Mr. Mackay informed me, that he and the hunters kept along the high land, and did not see or cross the Indian path. At the same time, there can be no doubt but the road from this place [the Indian portage from near Hudson Hope] to the upper part of the rapids is to be preferred to that which we came, both for expedition and safety.

After staying here about an hour and a half, we proceeded with the stream, and landed where I had forgotten my pipe-tomahawk and seal, on the eighteenth of May. The former of them I now recovered.

On leaving the mountains we saw animals grazing in every direction. In passing along an island, we fired at an elk, and broke its leg; and, as it was now time to encamp, we landed; when the hunters pursued the wounded animal, which had crossed over to the main land, but could not get up the bank. We went after it, therefore, in the canoe, and killed it. To give some idea of our appetites, I shall state the elk, or at least the carcase of it, which we brought away, to have weighed two hundred and fifty pounds; and as we had taken a very hearty meal at one o'clock, it might naturally be supposed that we should not be very voracious at supper; nevertheless, a kettle full 275 of the elk flesh was boiled and eaten, and that vessel replenished and put on the fire. All that remained, with the bones, &c. was placed, after the Indian fashion, round the fire to roast; and at ten next morning the whole was consumed by ten persons and a large dog, who was allowed his share of the banquet. This is no exaggeration; nor did any inconvenience result from what may be considered as an inordinate indulgence.

[August 23] We were on the water before day-light; and when the sun rose a beautiful country appeared around us, enriched and animated by large herds of wild cattle [buffalo]. The weather was now so warm, that to us, who had not of late been accustomed to heat, it was overwhelming and oppressive. In the course of this day we killed a buffalo and a bear; but we were now in the midst of abundance, and they were not sufficiently fat to satisfy our fastidious appetites; so we left them where they fell. We landed for the night, and prepared ourselves for arriving at the Fort [Fort Fork] on the following day.

[August 24] The weather was the same as yesterday, and the country increasing in beauty; though as we approached the Fort, the cattle appeared proportionably to diminish. We now landed at two lodges of [Beaver] Indians, who were as astonished to see us, as if we had been the first white men whom they had ever beheld. When we had passed these people not an animal was to be seen on the borders of the river.

At length, as we rounded a point, and came in view of the Fort, we threw out our flag, and accompanied it with a general discharge of our fire-arms; while the men were in such spirits, and made such an active use of their paddles, that we arrived before the two men whom we left here in the spring, could recover their senses to answer us. Thus we landed at four in the afternoon, at the place which we left on the ninth of May.——Here my voyages of discovery terminate. Their toils and their dangers, their solicitudes and sufferings, have not been exaggerated in my description. On the contrary, in many instances, language has failed me in the attempt to describe them. I received, however, the reward of my labours, for they were crowned with success.

As I have now resumed the character of a trader, I shall not trouble my readers with any subsequent concern, but content myself with the closing information, that after an absence of eleven months, I arrived at Fort Chepewyan, where I remained, for the purposes of trade, during the succeeding winter.

Epilogue

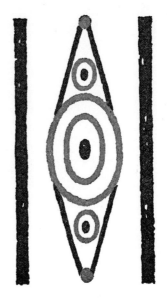

EPILOGUE

THAT WINTER was a bad one for him. The confined life of the trading post must have been made worse by the let-down from the physical and mental strain of the summer. Years later he was to write in his *Voyages* that his labors were crowned with success, but that may not have been apparent at the time. His trip of 1793 was his second attempt to find a practical route to the Pacific, and it was at least in part a failure. He had reached the Pacific, but he knew that his route could not be used for trade.

The state of his mind during this winter is shown by letters to his cousin Roderick. In January he wrote:

We may expect him [Simon McTavish] at the Portage where it will be necessary for every person concerned to meet. I am fully bent on going down. I am more anxious now than ever. For I think it unpardonable in any man to remain in this country who can afford to leave it. What a pretty Situation I am in this winter—starving & alone—without the power of doing myself or any body else any Service [?] The Boy at Lac La Loche [undecipherable] or even my own Servant is equal to the performance of my Winter Employment.[1]

Many of the men in the fur trade either liked the life or found in it a refuge from something even worse, but not Mackenzie. He was too active and intelligent to be able to accept the confinement, and too fond of the pleasures of life to accept willingly the hardships. The previous winter, at Fort Fork, he had written of his desire to leave the Northwest, and the events of the summer had only strengthened his determination.

In addition to the routine duties of the post, he was trying to write up his journal for publication, but it did not go well. In March he wrote to Roderick:

It is now the season in which I promised to write you—and would wish that I could fulfil another promise I made you last fall and this winter— I need not say that I mean my Journal—which I wished you to peruse at your leisure in order to correct the calculations & other errors with that freedom due from one friend to another. Last fall I was to begin copying it—but the greatest part of my time was taken up in vain speculations— I got into such a habit of thinking that I was often lost in thoughts nor could I ever write to the purpose—what I was thinking of—would often occur to me instead of what which I ought to do—I never passed so much of my time so insignificantly—nor so uneasy—Although I am not super-stitious—dreams amongst other things—caused me much annoyance I could not close my eyes without finding myself in company with the Dead—I had visions of late which almost convince me that I lost a near relation or a friend—

It was the latter end of January when I began my work—thinking then I had time enough—though the reverse is the fact—and I will be satis-fied & so must you, if I can finish the copy to give you reading of it in the Spring—I find it a work that will require more time than I was aware of —for it is not a quarter finished.[2]

This is a terrible confession. The rigid self-discipline of the sum-mer had been replaced by a near paralysis of the will. Perhaps it can be understood by those who know the difficulty of doing any kind of creative work when deprived of the stimulus of intellectual com-panionship.

In the spring of 1794 he left Athabasca for the last time, and Roderick took charge of the department. Mackenzie was never to go west of Grand Portage again. His explorations were over, but he had not accomplished his main purpose—finding a way to reduce the transportation costs of the North West Company and bringing the 282 Company into the trade of the North Pacific and China. For more than a decade he was to continue to search for a solution to this problem, but he was to do it in Montreal and London, rather than in the field.

He began his efforts at once. In the summer he attended the meeting of the partners at Grand Portage and reported to them on his discoveries. The partners were enthusiastic and awarded him another share in the company, although this trip had cost the company about £1,500 and produced no immediate results.[3] At this meeting he probably also urged on the partners the plan of expansion for which he was to fight for so long. After the meeting he went to Montreal, but on the way he stopped off at Niagara to visit Lieutenant-Colonel Simcoe, the lieutenant governor of Upper Canada. He told Simcoe of his discoveries and of his plans for extending the trade to the Pacific coast, seeking to enlist Simcoe's support. Simcoe must have been impressed, because he wrote that Mackenzie was "as intelligent as he is adventurous."[4] From Montreal Mackenzie went to London through the United States, but there is no record of what he did there.[5]

The next year he returned to Montreal and entered the firm of McTavish and Frobisher, the Montreal agents of the North West Company.[6] He was now one of the most powerful members of the Company, and he went to the annual meeting at Grand Portage each summer. It is not clear what took place during this period, but apparently Mackenzie continued to press for extending the trade onto the Pacific slope and for the other parts of his vigorous plan of expansion. Most of the wintering partners supported Mackenzie, but he was opposed by Simon McTavish, who controlled enough votes to have his own way.[7]

McTavish was unpopular with the other partners, and he usually is made the conservative villain, opposing Mackenzie's progressive plans. That may be unjust, because he took progressive steps on his own initiative.[8] He rented the military posts on the Great Lakes for the exclusive use of the North West Company, and he sent a trading expedition to Hudson Bay, carrying the competition to the very home of the Hudson's Bay Company. He had also found ways of getting North West Company furs to China, circumventing the monopoly of the East India Company by using American ships. Mackenzie's failure to find a practical route to the Pacific had caused McTavish to withdraw his support for further expansion in that direction—if furs from west of the Rockies had to be brought out by the canoe route to Montreal they would cost more than they could be sold for. At any rate, during this period no trading was done on the Pacific coast. The Mackenzie River trade was extended, though, and new posts were built far down the river.

The plans for expansion now received a serious blow—renewed competition. If the North West Company was to expand farther, it needed to be able to devote all its resources to the effort, but now it became necessary to waste much of them in maintaining its position in the established departments. It had faced no serious competition since the merger of 1787, because it had been able to ruin the few independent traders who tried to enter the Northwest. Now it was faced with competition too powerful to be destroyed so easily.

At the time of the first merger, the Southwest trade via Lake Michigan into the United States was twice as important as the Northwest trade. In the years that followed, the Southwest trade became less important while the Northwest trade grew rapidly, but there was still a large trade from the Southwest. This trade depended on British control of the military posts on the south side of the Great Lakes, especially the post at Michilimackinac. The Treaty of Versailles that ended the American Revolution in 1783 had placed the International Boundary along the Great Lakes and the canoe route from Grand Portage to Lake of the Woods, which meant that the British were to give up their posts on the south side of the lakes. Both parties had seen fit to ignore certain provisions of the treaty, and this was one that Britain chose to ignore, so that she retained control of these posts and Canadian traders were able to continue in the Southwest trade.

Finally in 1796 Detroit, Michilimackinac, and other posts were 284 turned over to the United States, and that government excluded the

Canadian traders from the trade in the American territories. This left powerful companies with much capital and nowhere to invest it. The obvious solution was to enter the Northwest trade. The North West Company had tripled its profits in ten years, and there should be plenty to go around. Late in the decade two of the largest companies from the Southwest had entered the Northwest trade. In 1798 some of the North West Company partners left that firm and joined the competition, apparently because they were dissatisfied with McTavish's rule. The new companies sent traders out to the principal departments of the Northwest, including the vital Athabasca department. The fight was on.

Mackenzie probably sympathized with the new companies from the start. He was under contract to the old company and was not free to leave, but he may have had a hand in organizing one of the competing companies.[9] His contract expired in 1799, and because of his disagreement with his associates it was not renewed although the wintering partners tried to get him to stay.[10] It is not known whether he left of his own accord or was forced out. This was a time of intrigue, of plot and counterplot, and for the most part the people concerned were careful not to put their thoughts or actions on paper. As a result, the history of the period will never be fully known. One trader wrote "Who should be the first—McTavish or [Mackenzie]—and as there could not be two Caesars in Rome one must remove."[11] In the struggle for power, Mackenzie lost.

Mackenzie's vision extended beyond mere bickering between rival companies, and he had become convinced that under the existing conditions he could do nothing more in Canada. After the summer meeting at Grand Portage, where he ended his connection with the Company, he returned to Montreal and from there sailed for London. He wanted to enlist the support of the British government for the plans that he had not been able to put into effect in Montreal. When he left the Company his cousin Roderick McKenzie took his place. Mackenzie resented this and it caused a temporary break in their friendship.

That meeting at Grand Portage was one of the last ever held there. Grand Portage was south of the Pigeon River, and hence in the United States. That country had no love for the British, and it was beginning to enforce its prerogatives. The Canadian traders had to find another route from Lake Superior to Rainy Lake. The North West Company had foreseen this and had tried to find an alternative route, but had failed to find a satisfactory one. The old Kaministiquia route of the French had been totally forgotten. In 1797 Roderick McKenzie learned of this route from some Indians. He explored it and reported that it was a good route and lay entirely within Canada. Beginning in 1801 the rival companies moved their headquarters from Grand Portage to Kaministiquia. The North West Company post there was named Fort William.[12]

The fur trade had made Mackenzie wealthy, and he was able to live the best life that London had to offer. In Canada he had become a friend of Edward, Duke of Kent, who was stationed there in the army. Edward was a son of the king, George III, and father of the future Queen Victoria. In London Mackenzie renewed this friendship, which gave him access to high places. Presumably he used every opportunity to press his plans on men of influence.

The next spring (1800) he returned to Montreal and apparently was influential in the merger of the two largest competitors of the North West Company. The united company was called the New North West Company and was organized on the lines of the old company. Sometimes it was known as the XY Company, after the North West Company's old competitor. It had as much capital as the old company, but a much smaller organization. Its chief handicap was that it had few men who were experienced in the Northwest.

Mackenzie returned to London that fall. He may have spent the summer of 1801 in Montreal,[13] but in the fall he was in London again. Here he arranged to publish the journals of his explorations in a further attempt to get support for his plans. In the preface to the

Voyages he denied rumors that the long delay in their publication was caused by "a misunderstanding between a person high in office and myself" or "by that precaution which the policy of commerce will sometimes suggest."

The delay actually arose from the very active and busy mode of life in which I was engaged since the voyages have been completed; and when, at length, the opportunity arrived, the apprehension of presenting myself to the Public in the character of an Author, for which the course and occupations of my life have by no means qualified me, made me hesitate in committing my papers to the Press; being much better calculated to perform the voyages, arduous as they might be, than to write an account of them.[14]

As a prelude he told the history of the fur trade in Canada and something of the Indians. At the end he described the geography of British North America and outlined his plans for expansion.

The *Voyages* was published in November 1801, and two months later he presented a detailed outline of his plans to the government. This outline, entitled "Preliminaries to the Establishment of a Permanent British Fishery and Trade in Furs etc. on the Continent and West Coast of North America," [15] is the best statement of his views.

There were four points. The first was to form a civil and military establishment at Nootka Sound, on the west coast of Vancouver Island. Nootka had originally been occupied by Spain, but she had been forced to give up her exclusive rights to it. It was the only settlement between the Russians in Alaska and the Spanish in California. An official British post there would go a long way toward establishing British possession of the Northwest coast and would serve the British traders in the area. In addition to Nootka, subordinate posts were to be established at the mouth of the Columbia River to the south and at Sea Otter Harbour to the north. Britain later acquired Nootka, but the other areas now belong to the United States.

The second point was that the East India Company and the South Seas Company should be deprived of their monopolies or that they should be required to grant licenses to other British traders. These 287 companies, like the Hudson's Bay Company, had royal charters which gave them exclusive rights to the trade in certain areas. The East India Company had a monopoly of the China trade and the South Seas Company had a monopoly of the trade on the Northwest coast, though it did not actually trade there. These companies were more eager to defend their monopolies than to use them, and as a result British trade lagged.

The North Pacific trade was expensive, and a single trip required years. To be profitable it had to follow a triangular route—manufactured goods were carried from the home country to the North Pacific and traded there for furs, especially sea otter. These were taken to Canton and traded for spices and other Chinese goods, which were then taken back to the home country and sold. A good profit could be had on each of these transactions. Because of the monopolies the British traders were unable to do this, and although they had been the first to follow the Russians to the North Pacific they had now been largely displaced by the Americans. American traders were not restricted by monopolies, they had faster ships, and their business methods were less conservative (and less respectable). In addition to the fur trade there was a large whale fishery. Mackenzie was confident that a properly organized company with the necessary privileges would be able to reëstablish Britain's leadership in the trade.

His third point was a familiar one—require the Hudson's Bay Company to permit transit through its territories from Hudson Bay. The North West Company had been trying for years to get government support for this, but had always failed. The west side of Hudson Bay was hundreds of miles closer to the fur country of the Northwest than was Montreal, and if goods could be taken that far by ship, transportation costs would be much less.

The fourth point was the establishment of "the Fishery and Fur Company" in London, to combine the whale fishery of the Pacific with the fur trade of North America. The fur traders of Montreal were the people best qualified to carry out this plan (of course), and if such a plan were offered them the North West Company and the New North West Company would unite voluntarily.

This was political and commercial strategy on a grand scale. The plan was an achievement equal to his great explorations. If carried out it would open up new fields for British commerce, give Britain large new territories, and give British North America an outlet to the Pacific. Unfortunately it was not carried out. The government probably listened sympathetically to Mackenzie's plans, but it had more pressing matters to attend to. War with Napoleon was imminent and there were no men or arms to spare for garrisoning Nootka. The chartered companies, of course, opposed any infringement of their privileges. And the Montreal traders were in no position to embark on such a venture—they were too busy quarreling among themselves. Also, they were opposed to any plan that would reduce the importance of Montreal as a fur trading center. If the furs were shipped out via Hudson Bay there would be no business for Montreal traders.[16] Lord Hobart, the colonial secretary, suggested to Mackenzie that the first step in carrying out his plan should be to unite the two rival Montreal companies. Mackenzie accordingly returned to Canada to try to do this.

In the meantime George III recognized Mackenzie's services by knighting him, on February 10, 1802. After this, Mackenzie took time to visit his sisters in Scotland, and a grand ball was held for him there. He was a native son and he had become a famous explorer and a wealthy merchant, and had been knighted by the king. His people were proud of him.

He returned to Canada later in 1802, and presumably approached the leaders of both fur companies with his plan. The plan was good but old hatreds were too great, and McTavish especially would not have agreed to any plan that Mackenzie might have offered. In short, it was no go, and in October Mackenzie had to write the government that he had failed. In his letter he continued to urge his plan, suggesting that a merger be forced by granting a license to one of the companies with provision that the other could join it. He again

289

urged establishing posts on the Pacific coast, "so as to prevent other nations anticipating us in an object the importance of which cannot at present be foreseen in all its consequences." [17]

Sir Alexander Mackenzie was more welcome in Montreal than mere Alexander Mackenzie had ever been. He was lionized by local society, and he began to take an active interest in the Beaver Club. This was an organization of fur traders, French and British, who had spent at least one winter in the Northwest. The meetings began early and ended late, and consisted of heavy eating, heavier drinking, and loud singing of the voyageurs' songs. Life in the Northwest was never as pleasant or as exhausting as this.

In 1804 Mackenzie was elected to the Legislative Assembly of Quebec, but he did not like the political life and soon retired. During his first session he wrote to Roderick:

The Society is certainly very agreeable and I feel myself much obliged by the attention I universally receive and this the stronger as it is from Strangers—persons with whom I am but slightly acquainted—I am heartily tired of Lagislation. I sincerely wish that those who thought themselves my friends in being the means of getting me to so honorable a Situation, had been otherwise employed." [18]

He was also a powerful figure in the fur trade. After he realized in 1802 that he would not be able to persuade the two companies to unite, he joined the New North West Company and became one of the most powerful members. The next summer he went to the Company's meeting on Lake Superior, and in the fall he went to London on Company business.

The rivalry between the old and new companies grew even worse and the fur trade experienced all the familiar evils of cutthroat competition—both companies lost money, the Indians were debauched, the beaver populations were seriously depleted, and the trade was on the way to ruin. It was saved by the unexpected death of Simon McTavish in 1804. With McTavish out of the way the two companies quickly merged, Mackenzie's company getting one-quarter of the shares of the united company.[19] Mackenzie himself was excluded from any active participation in the trade, but he reorganized the new company under the name "Sir Alexander Mackenzie and Company." [20] Early the next year he returned to Scotland, leaving Canada for the last time.

The united North West Company was now in a position to exploit the area that Mackenzie had discovered beyond the Rockies. Mackenzie himself could have no part in it, but Duncan McGillivray, the Montreal agent, shared his ideas. In 1797 James Finlay, who had not been strong enough to go with Mackenzie in 1793, went up the Peace River to the forks, explored the Finlay River for some distance, and retraced Mackenzie's route up the Parsnip River. He was the first man to follow Mackenzie beyond the Rockies and the first trader on the Finlay, but nothing came of his trip. Soon after, Rocky Mountain Fort was established on the Peace at the east end of Rocky Mountain Portage, the Indian route around the Peace River Canyon that had given Mackenzie's party such difficulty.[21]

The first attempt to establish the trade permanently on the west side of the mountains was made in 1800, when some men were sent across the Rockies far south of Mackenzie's route to build a fort there, in preparation for a trading venture the next year by Duncan McGillivray and David Thompson. Apparently this plan was not carried out; at any rate nothing came of it.

In 1804, after the death of McTavish but before the union of the two companies, the North West Company decided to make another attempt, this time following Mackenzie's route up the Peace River.[22] This had been in the air for a long time; it was the obvious next step for expansion, and now there was a new incentive—the threat of competition from the south. The ever-present danger of commercial and territorial expansion by the United States had become very real. The year before, the Louisiana Purchase had added to the United States a vast region from the Mississippi to the Rockies, and in the same year President Jefferson had made plans to send a military expedition under Lewis and Clark to the Columbia by way of the

Missouri. The announced purpose of the expedition was scientific, but no one was fooled—Jefferson's main aims were to secure the Oregon country for the United States and to capture the Canadian fur trade.

The man chosen to lead the Company's thrust beyond the Rockies was Simon Fraser.[23] He was born in Vermont, in 1766, but like Mackenzie he had been taken to Canada by his Loyalist family because of the Revolution. He entered the North West Company in 1792 and became a partner in 1801. He probably was chosen to head the new department largely because he had been stationed at Athabasca for years and knew the country.

Fraser made his first move in 1805, when he sent one of his men up the Parsnip River to look for a suitable site for a trading post. The man found the Pack River, which Mackenzie had missed, and went up it to Lake McLeod. Later in the year Fraser went to Lake McLeod and built Fort McLeod there.[24] It was the first British settlement on the mainland west of the Rockies. Fraser left some men there and returned to Rocky Mountain Fort for the winter.

The next spring he went back to Fort McLeod. In the meantime he had sent a man overland to explore the country to the west. The man reached Stuart Lake and reported that it would be a good place for a post and that it drained into a branch of the "Columbia." Fraser decided to go there by way of this river. He descended the Pack to the Parsnip and went up the Parsnip, retracing Mackenzie's route across the divide and down James Creek. En route he learned from Indians that there was a much better route via Giscome Portage direct from Lake McLeod, and this route was used thereafter. He went down the "Columbia" to the Nechaco River, another one that Mackenzie had missed. In his journal Fraser was careful to point out all of Mackenzie's mistakes, and to complain that Mackenzie had exaggerated the difficulties he faced.

Up the Nechako to Stuart River and up that to Stuart Lake, and there they met the local Indians and established a post. Fraser called it Nakazlen, but now it is called Fort St. James. Later that year Fort

Epilogue

Fraser was established on Fraser Lake, and the next year Fort George, at the junction of the Fraser and the Nechako.

Fraser named this region New Caledonia—it was essentially what is now central British Columbia. The furs were plentiful and of high quality. The local race of beaver is very dark, and these "black" pelts brought higher prices than others. The Indians there were already supplied with manufactured goods, obtained from the marine traders on the coast via Indian middlemen, but they were glad to buy from the Canadian traders instead, to avoid the unholy prices charged by the other tribes. It was a good region, but Fraser deserves much credit for the success of the fur trade there. Establishing four posts in a virgin territory in three years, with limited men and supplies (sometimes they almost starved) and with terrible transportation problems, was quite a feat. They chose their sites well, and all of them are still occupied.

The most important part of Fraser's work was still before him. New Caledonia could bring little profit as long as goods had to be carried by the long canoe route to and from Montreal. The sea was a short distance away, and Fraser had to find a practical route to it. Mackenzie had gone a long way down the great river, but had decided that it was not practical and turned back to follow an overland route to the sea. This route was of no value for trade, and Mackenzie became convinced that the great river would be navigable. In 1808 Fraser set out to descend the river that he and everyone else thought was the Columbia, hoping that he would be able to send his furs out by this route. His voyage beyond the point where Mackenzie turned back was one of the great physical feats of exploration. In places the river is too rough to run in canoes, and the banks are too high and steep for portaging. Somehow they made it, but when they reached the mouth of the river Fraser determined his latitude and realized that he was too far north to be on the Columbia. This not only was not the right river but it was not even navigable. It was useless to Fraser, and he regretted that he had bothered to come down it. The river was later named for him, and he well deserved it.

Like everyone before him, he had failed to find a navigable route to the Pacific, and the furs had to continue to go out by way of the Peace. Some years later, after the Columbia River country had been opened up, the furs were taken down the Fraser by boat to Alexandria, the point where Mackenzie had turned back, from there by horse to Lake Okanagan, then by boat again to the Columbia and down it to meet the ships which carried them around Cape Horn to Britain. This was a difficult journey, certainly, but better than the canoe route across Canada.

The year before Fraser explored his river a greater explorer had crossed the Rockies for the first time. David Thompson was born in England in 1770. When only fourteen he entered the service of the Hudson's Bay Company and came to Canada. Later he learned surveying and carried out some worthwhile explorations. The Hudson's Bay Company of that period had little interest in exploration, and Thompson was told to pay attention to the business of trading. He was a born explorer, though, and he left the Hudson's Bay Company to join the North West Company. His primary duties now were surveys and exploration. In 1804 he became a partner, and later he was assigned to develop a route from the upper Saskatchewan River across the Rockies to the Pacific. This route required going over the mountains instead of through them, but it was much more direct than the route via Athabasca.

Thompson's first step was to send a man across Howse Pass to cut a road and build canoes on the other side, in 1806. The next year Thompson followed this road to the Columbia River. When he had determined his longitude he knew that he was too far east to be on Mackenzie's great river, which was still thought to be the Columbia. Thompson named his river the Kootanae. The name Kootenay is now applied to a nearby tributary of the Columbia.

Thompson opened up the fur trade on the Columbia but he still was more interested in exploring, and in the next few years he made extensive surveys of the Columbia and its tributaries in southeastern British Columbia and adjacent parts of the United States. It is a mystery why he did not descend the Columbia to its mouth and set up a post there, to establish British claims to the area. The upper Columbia was merely another fur district, but the lower Columbia offered a practical route to the sea. Thompson must have known by 1809 that he was on the Columbia, but it was not until two years later that he went all the way down it. He intended to build a fort near the mouth, but when he got there he found an American fort—the Astorians had beaten him by four months. He retired from the trade the following year. The Astorians held their fort only a short time. In 1813 Britain was at war with the United States and the Astorians were forced to sell the post to the North West Company. The Canadian company developed an extensive trade in the Oregon country,[25] but the United States still could claim prior possession and this was one of the things that finally gave the region to the United States.

The North West Company was now at the height of its expansion and power. It had a great number of posts, extending west to the Pacific, north to the Arctic, and south into what is now the United States. In much of that area it had a complete monopoly of the trade. It had vast capital, good connections in Britain and the United States, and much influence with the government and courts of Canada. Yet it was nearing its downfall. The Company had been badly hurt by the severe competition of the New North West Company. Its organization, which had proved so successful during the decades of active expansion, now proved unsatisfactory when the frontier had been pushed to the Pacific, and there was nowhere left to expand. Most serious of all was increased competition from the Hudson's Bay Company.[26]

The English company had always been a thorn in the side of the Canadian traders, but for the most part the Canadians had gotten the better of the competition, even after the English had begun to establish posts away from Hudson Bay. The Canadians had an organization and methods better adapted to the nature of the country 295 and the trade, and their tactics were more aggressive. Around the turn of the century the opposition of the North West Company and the loss of the European market during the Napoleonic wars had caused the Hudson's Bay Company to operate at a loss at times.

The Hudson's Bay Company always had the advantage of relatively cheap transportation, thanks to the strategic location of the Bay. The North West Company had tried every means to get this advantage for itself. It tried to persuade the British government to cancel the other company's charter, or to require that company to grant or lease transit rights to the North West Company. It tried to get control of the other company by buying up its stock. All of these efforts failed, and the North West Company was never able to use the Hudson Bay route to the Northwest.

The situation became more serious when the Hudson's Bay Company was revitalized by new leadership. Colin Robertson, a former North West Company man now employed by the Hudson's Bay Company, advised on reorganization, and the reforms he suggested did much to improve the competitive position of the Company. It was reorganized on lines similar to those of the North West Company, giving the men in the field a stronger personal interest in the success of their efforts than they had had as mere employees. Personnel and supply policies were improved in various ways, and larger boats were substituted for canoes to reduce transportation costs.

With its new vitality, the Company tried to extend its activities into new areas. Legally it was limited to the waters draining into Hudson Bay, but the North West Company had never respected the Hudson's Bay Company charter and that company saw no reason to be limited by it either. All the Lake Winnipeg-Saskatchewan-Churchill River country was Hudson's Bay Company territory, but Methye Portage marked the divide between Hudson Bay waters and those of the Arctic drainage, and the North West Company considered everything north of there to be its own property. In 1802 the Hudson's Bay Company sent a trader to Athabasca, in its first attempt to enter the trade in this region. By acts of violence against

Hudson's Bay men and by bribing and threatening the Indians the North West Company turned this attempt into a fiasco, and the Hudson's Bay men were withdrawn after several years. Athabasca was crucial, because by then the fur-bearer populations in the other departments had been so depleted that most of the North West Company's profits came from that one department. The Hudson's Bay Company made another attempt at Athabasca in 1815, with equally disastrous results. Three years later a third attempt was made, which lasted until the two companies united.[27]

In an effort to gain control of the Hudson's Bay Company, Alexander Mackenzie had bought some of its stock himself and had persuaded one of his countrymen, the wealthy Lord Selkirk, to buy much more stock. In interesting Selkirk in the Company Mackenzie made a serious mistake, because Selkirk had a mind of his own. He was of philanthropic nature, and he had taken an interest in resettling Highlanders who had been forced off their lands by changing agricultural practices. His first such venture, to Prince Edward Island in eastern Canada, had been fairly successful, and now he was looking for larger territories suitable for farming.[28] On reading Mackenzie's description of the Red River country in his *Voyages* he decided that this was the region he wanted. It was in the Hudson Bay drainage, so belonged to that Company. By 1811 he had enough power in the Company to get the partners to make a grant of 116,000 square miles in the Red River Valley for establishing an agricultural colony, to be known as Assiniboia. The project was bitterly opposed by the Company's wintering partners and by the North West Company. All fur traders were opposed, because settlement meant the end of the trade. The North West Company was inalterably opposed because the grant lay directly across its communication lines, and it would be at the mercy of the colony.

In spite of opposition Selkirk was able to assemble a group of colonists in Scotland. They were to embark at Stornoway, Mackenzie's birthplace. The collector of customs there was a relative of Mackenzie and did everything he could to keep the colonists from sailing. He spread dissent among them and he claimed that some were deserters from the King's service. Most colonists finally sailed for Hudson Bay, and after great delay and hardships arrived in the new colony. For several years the colony, supported by the local Hudson's Bay Company posts, was in active opposition to the North West Company. Both sides interfered with each other whenever they could, and both resorted to violence at times.

Matters came to a head when North West Company agents stirred up the local half-breeds and led them against the settlers' fort at Seven Oaks, near the present site of Winnipeg. Many of the settlers and the governor of the colony were killed. Shortly afterward Selkirk himself reached the Red River with a small army of his own and the colony was reëstablished. Open warfare between the two companies followed. Canoe brigades were stopped and turned back or the goods were seized. There were a few murders. Selkirk and some of the officers of both companies were justices of the peace, and they used their authority to further their own partisan ends. Warrants were issued for the arrest of members of the opposing company, and sometimes men were held captive for long periods of time. Many men were tried in the Canadian courts on charges ranging up to murder. The North West Company won most of the trials, partly because of its influence with the Canadian government. Selkirk and a few North Westers were fined, and one North West Company man was sentenced to hang for murder.

The North West Company won in court, but legal costs and bribes had cut into its capital. The Company itself had no reserve fund, because all profits were distributed every year, and in this fight the individual partners had to go deeply into debt. The disruption of the trade had cut off all profits, and the Company faced ruin. In 1820 Mackenzie and Selkirk died, and the wintering partners forced the Montreal agents to seek a merger with the Hudson's Bay Company. In the following year the rival companies merged, on terms very favorable to the English company. In the long run the unification of the trade probably was beneficial, but the immediate results were disastrous for Canada. Its principal business was diverted to Hudson Bay, and some of its wealthiest citizens were bankrupt. Montreal especially was hurt, because York Factory replaced it as the center of the fur trade.[29]

All during the bitterest part of the struggle between the two companies Mackenzie was in Britain. He had no active part in the fur trade but he still had a strong interest in it and he opposed Selkirk's plans as well as he could, both legally and extra-legally. He had left Canada for the last time in 1805, writing to Roderick, "Never mind the folly of the times for my own part I am determined to make myself as comfortable as circumstances will allow. I have a large field before me — I do not leave Canada without regret." [30]

The next year he wrote to Roderick that he had heard of Roderick's plan to write a history of the fur trade and offered his help.

I must however take the liberty of reminding you that the difficulties you have already experienced are trivial in comparison to those you have still to encounter before you get through your undertaking. Your object must be to relate matters as they occurred which may make more enemies than friends. Besides you will have to advance at least two thousand pounds before you receive a shilling for the work.

I wish you would give instruction to collect from the English Chief and other Chippeweans the fullest account they possibly can give of Hearnes journey with them to the North sea where according to what I learn he never went.[31]

Samuel Hearne had gone with the Indians from Hudson Bay to the Coppermine River and down it to the Arctic coast in 1771. This made him, rather than Mackenzie, the first overland explorer in the Arctic. Besides, he was a member of the Hudson's Bay Company and not to be trusted.

For several years Mackenzie lived a leisurely life and traveled occasionally with the Duke of Kent. In 1812, at the age of forty-eight, he married a member of the same clan, Geddes Mackenzie, and bought Avoch, the estate of his wife's father. At Avoch he played the part of the benevolent squire, taking an interest in the affairs of the area and spending money for various public causes. He built a sea wall to protect a road from the sea, and he had an oyster bed laid down. The Mackenzies had a town house in London and spent part of each year there. They had several children.

In 1819 Mackenzie wrote apparently his last letter to Roderick. It is a moving picture of domestic happiness and approaching death:

Occurrences with Lord Selkirk and the HB Company are so various and numerous that it would require a volume to detail and comment upon them. Most of the prominent events I learn from the public prints. Upon the whole they have not turned out so disastrous to the NW Company as might naturally have be[en] apprehended. The losses sustained in the country though severe and serious have been in a considerable degree recompensed by the high prices obtained for the furs, the sales of which were certainly managed with great judgment in London.

The North West Company agreement is drawing to a close and he expects a serious change in its direction. It is of no matter to him, but he will be happy to see the business continued and carried on with vigor.

They will have a large amount to account to me, the present agents do not seem disposed to reduce it as they have not paid me a shilling of principal or interest since I became a partner under the firm of "Sir Alexander McKenzie & Co."

I hope that before now you have discovered the annual income of your estate to exceed your expectations. Whatever it may be now it certainly must increase. I should not be sorry to hear of your having disposed of it advantageously; perhaps then you might think of investing it in your own native land. Follow the example of our old friend M W MacGillivray who I find has bought an estate in Argylshire for £20,000.

I trust Mrs. Mackenzie and your young family are continuing in their usual good health. Margaret must now be a stout lady; My namesake about finishing his education for college; had you sent him to this country it might have been as well. What do you think of sending Roderic Charles

300

here when he is fit. we have two good academies in this country, at Thain and Fortrose. I shall have a little fellow, if God spare him, this day eleven months old that would accompany him. Our little girl is very thriving. Her mother has not recovered her usual health since her last confinement and I have at last been overtaken with the consequences of my sufferings in the North West. I think it is of the same nature with M. MacGillivrays complaint, but it has not yet arrived at a severe crisis. I have in obedience of orders become a water drinker and milk sop. I have not tasted wine, spirituous or malt liquor for several months which I think has been of service to me.

The symptoms of the disorder are very disagreeable and most uncomfortable. The exercise of walking, particularly uphill, brings on a headache, stupor or dead pain which at once pervades the whole frame, attended with listlessness and apathy which I cannot well describe. Exercise in a carriage, if not violent, has a beneficial effect. The great doctor Hamilton of Edinburg calls it a shake of the constitution and I am acting now under his guidance. The only medicine he has prescribed is pills of his own which I take every evening.

He had heard that Roderick's brother Donald is representing the North West Company on the Columbia River.

It is now believed there are plenty beaver in that country, and it will be very hard if it is wrested from us through the ignorance of our negotiators. That crafty, cunning statesman Gallatin (Astor's friend) was the principal negotiator on the part of the americans. He would be too many for our people who are governed more by theory than practice. . . .

Lady MacKenzie is sitting by me and the children are playing on the floor. the former joins me most cordially in kind regards to you Mrs. Mackenzie and your young family.[32]

It is not certain what his illness was, perhaps Bright's disease or cirrhosis of the liver. It probably was caused or at least aggravated by the hard life of the Northwest, and it may have been foreshadowed by the crippling swelling of the ankles that he suffered when returning from the coast in 1793. A year after writing this letter he was well enough to go with his family to Edinburgh, but on the way back he was taken ill and died in a country inn.

Mrs. Mackenzie lived for another forty years, and reared all her children to maturity. She continued to divide her time between Avoch and London. Apparently she took legal action against the Hudson's Bay Company to recover her husband's interest in the North West Company, and in 1830 was awarded £10,000. In 1832 fire destroyed Avoch, including most of Mackenzie's manuscripts.

It is always difficult to assess the importance of a person in history. Our efforts to relate cause and effect may not be very reliable, and it may be that certain things will necessarily be done at certain times and that the persons who do them are merely the agents of historical necessity. If Mackenzie had not crossed the continent in 1793 some other member of the North West Company surely would have done so before very long, but this seems to be begging the issue. History is often a race between opposing interests, and the man who gets there first wins the prize. This was surely true of the history of the Northwest. By 1793 Spain and Russia had passed the summit of their power in that region, but the United States was just beginning to become interested in it. The final territorial settlement was a result of the cumulative effects of many individual actions by Britons and Americans. Vancouver missed the Columbia, but Gray entered it a few weeks later, giving the United States a claim to the area. Thompson intended to build a post near the mouth of the Columbia, but the Astorians got there four months earlier, strengthening the American claim. Similarly, Mackenzie's exploration of the Pacific slope in 1793 gave Britain a claim to the area he traversed, and his plans for extending the trade to the coast strengthened that claim. If the British government had acted on his full plan, it is possible that the Oregon country and southeastern Alaska would be British today.

Aside from their political importance, his discoveries added much to geographic knowledge. His first journey proved, again, that there

was no Northwest Passage far enough south to be navigable and that there was no Strait of Anian connecting Hudson Bay with the Pacific. These hardy myths had been disproved repeatedly before, but until Mackenzie's journey there still were a stubborn few who continued to believe in them. On this journey he explored the entire length of one of North America's largest rivers and learned that it did not lead to the Pacific as had been thought. He also learned that the mountains extend north almost to the Arctic coast. On his second journey he discovered one of the major rivers of the Pacific coast, but he cannot be said to have added it to human knowledge because he mistakenly reported that it was a river already known. More important than this was what he learned about the nature of the land beyond the Rockies. Instead of a single chain of mountains there was a great jumble of them—he was never able to figure it all out, but he knew that it was more formidable than had been supposed. He brought back reports of rivers worse than any the traders had seen before, and of Indian tribes with strange languages and ways. Most important of all, he replaced myth and rumor with solid facts —not very many facts, and some of them wrong, but he brought the area into the realm of human knowledge and thus made it easier for those who would follow him.

He had sought a practical route to the Pacific, but he did not find it. What did he really accomplish as a trailblazer? On his first voyage he explored the Mackenzie River. This was a bad choice, from his point of view, but it seemed reasonable at the time. It was a well-marked route and required few decisions. Today it is the principal access to a vast part of northwestern Canada. He made his next attempt up the Peace River. This was an obvious route—the valley of the Peace is almost the only gap in the great chain of mountains that forms the backbone of the continent. It was the route followed by the fur trade for years, and even after it was abandoned for transport it was still used for communications. It is not in use today, having been replaced by a railroad and a highway which follow other routes. He made a mistake in not taking the Indian portage around the Canyon, but he soon realized that himself.

His first major decision was at the forks of the Peace. He rightly decided to ignore the Finlay River, which leads into a big country of difficult transportation and few furs. It is almost uninhabited even today. The Parsnip continued in use as long as the Peace was used, but Mackenzie's route over the Continental Divide was not a good one and it has seldom been used since. His next major decision was to turn back on the Fraser. This may have been unfortunate, because he possibly could have reached the sea. If he had he would have found that he was not on the Columbia and that his river was not navigable. If the Canadian traders had known this before they settled New Caledonia they might have directed their efforts farther south and established possession of the Oregon country before the Americans got there. The Great West Road which Mackenzie followed from the Fraser to the sea was long a major Indian route, but it was seldom followed by Europeans. It is long since obliterated, but a similar route is still used at times by the Indians. Most of the route that he followed in 1793 is almost inaccessible today. There are a few isolated trading posts along it, and several small towns. In places it is paralleled by highways.

Mackenzie's most spectacular achievements were geographic and political, but he also played an important role in building Canada's largest business. His explorations led to expansion to the north and the west, and his administrative abilities strengthened the whole operation of the North West Company. By treating the Indians in the regions he explored in a decent manner he smoothed the way for the traders who followed him.

It is ironical that his efforts to further his plans for unification and expansion of the fur trade often had results quite different from what he intended. Twice he contributed to the ruinous competition which split the North West Company, and later he played an indirect role in the struggle between that Company and the Hudson's Bay Company.

He published his *Voyages* largely to win support for his plans, but they were read by people whose interests were contrary to his. One of these readers was Napoleon, who had dreams of reconquering Canada by way of the Mississippi River. He was going to use Mackenzie's book as the best available description of the interior of Canada. Reverses elsewhere forced him to cancel this plan, and perhaps saved Canada from invasion.

Lord Selkirk was another reader of the *Voyages*. It was here that he got the idea of colonizing the Red River Valley, and it was Mackenzie himself who started his interest in the Hudson's Bay Company.

Perhaps the most important opponent who read the *Voyages* was President Thomas Jefferson of the United States. The idea of western exploration was not new to Jefferson. He had been an advocate of territorial expansion all his life, and in 1793, the very year of Mackenzie's voyage, he had sent André Michaux to ascend the Missouri River. Michaux got nowhere, but Jefferson did not give up the plan. The knowledge that Mackenzie had reached the Pacific first was additional incentive; when he became president he sent Lewis and Clark to establish an American claim to the Oregon country. They carried a copy of Mackenzie's *Voyages* with them to Oregon.[33]

It is interesting to compare the first two transcontinental crossings. Mackenzie of course was first, by twelve years. The Lewis and Clark expedition, though, was more substantial and added more to our knowledge. Mackenzie's trip was a quick thrust, lasting less than a year, while the American expedition was more leisurely, lasting more than two years. Mackenzie spent only three months west of the Rockies and only a few days on the coast, while Lewis and Clark spent almost a year west of the Rockies and a whole winter on the coast. Mackenzie apologized for the paucity of information on the country and its natural history in his report, but Lewis and Clark had no need to apologize—they took voluminous notes on geography, natural history, and Indians, and they sent large scientific collections back to Jefferson. Most of these differences resulted largely from the different nature of the two expeditions. Mackenzie's was a bold individual venture, carried out with the men and supplies available and on a tight schedule, while Lewis and Clark were on a well-organized government mission, with disciplined soldiers to support them.

In spite of these differences there were similarities between the expeditions which were imposed by the nature of the country and its inhabitants. First of all, neither could have been successful without the help of the Indians. The Indians guided the explorers in critical places, and they fed them when they had run low on food. Both parties made fast friends of important tribes, but both had trouble with the Indians on the coast. Both parties started out believing that the route would be much easier than it was, that there would be one portage between watersheds and then clear sailing to the sea. Both learned that the rivers were worse than any they had seen before, and that there was not one range of mountains but several. Both parties came to deceptive river forks, and the leaders of both decided correctly, against the judgment of their men. Both parties found game abundant east of the mountains but found little on the coast. And lastly, both explorations were of prime geopolitical importance.

What sort of man was Mackenzie? That has to be inferred from his actions and his writings, as there are almost no contemporary comments on him. Certainly he was strong and active, intelligent, and ambitious. He could plan and carry out wilderness exploration, and he could also plan commercial ventures on a world-wide scale. He made many friends and was noted for his public spirit. So far all right, but he was a man of contradictions, or seems to have been from the little that we know of his character. Some of his letters to Roderick show that he was by no means as strong-willed as his actions would suggest, and at times he suffered from serious unrest. Many of the traders liked or at least respected him, but he also had bitter enemies and was capable of being a bitter enemy himself. His contempt for Peter Pond, to whom he owed so much, shows that he was not above personal prejudices, and his treatment of opponents shows that he could be ruthless. He was in a dirty trade and his business ethics did not rise above those of the trade. Although he spent years in the Northwest he was not a frontiersman by choice, and he seems to have greatly preferred the life of Montreal and London. In the *Voyages* he often tells of how his men enjoyed the hospitality of the Indian women. He does not say that he did so himself, but apparently, like most of the traders, he had an Indian wife. Their son Andrew became a clerk in the North West Company.[34] And today there are Indian families from the St. Lawrence to the Pacific that claim descent from him.

A telling indication of his character as a leader is the fact that though he twice led men on long and dangerous explorations none of his men was killed and none deserted him. Furthermore, no native was killed or even fired at by Mackenzie's parties.

Eight Europeans and two Indians left Fort Forks in May, 1793, headed west. All of them returned a few months later and the party broke up. They had shared a memorable experience, risked death together many times, and seen things that they could not have imagined before. They seem to have had no ties of sentiment or affection, though, and they went separate ways. Most of them continued in the fur trade for years. Jacques Beauchamp, who had the character of a simple fellow, was with a North West Company party on the lower Mackenzie River in 1802 when he was killed by Eskimos. Alexander McKay became a partner in the North West Company, but later left that Company and joined John Jacob Astor's Pacific Fur Company.[34] He was killed by Indians near Nootka in 1811. François Beaulieux was more fortunate. He eventually retired from the trade and settled in Quebec. He was baptized at the age of seventy and lived for almost thirty years after that. He died seventy-nine years after the most exciting voyage of his life.[35]

And so it went. They had had their moment of greatness. Did they really understand what they had done?

Appendixes

Mackenzie Chronology

1764?	Born in Stornoway, Scotland.
1774.	His father brings him to New York.
1778.	Goes to Montreal.
1779.	Enters fur trade in Montreal.
1784.	Goes to Detroit for his company.
1785–1787.	Is in Churchill district.
1787.	Goes to Athabasca.
January, 1788.	Visits Small and McKenzie at Lake Ile à la Crosse; later returns to Athabasca.
Summer, 1788.	Goes out to Rainy Lake depot; returns to Athabasca.
June 3– September 12, 1789.	Goes down Mackenzie River to Arctic Ocean; returns to Fort Chipewyan.
1789–90.	Winters at Fort Chipewyan.
Summer, 1790.	Goes to meeting of the partners at Grant Portage; returns to Fort Chipewyan.
1790–91.	Winters at Fort Chipewyan.
Summer, 1791.	Goes to Grand Portage and London, to study navigation.
1792.	Returns to Fort Chipewyan. Leaves for Pacific coast on October 10. Arrives at Fort Fork on November 1.
May 9, 1793.	Leaves Fort Fork for coast.
July 19, 1793.	Reaches the sea at Bella Coola.
August 24, 1793.	Arrives back at Fort Fork.
Fall, 1793.	Returns to Fort Chipewyan.
1794.	Leaves Athabasca for the last time; goes to Montreal and London.

1795.	Returns to Montreal.
1795–1799.	Is active in North West Comany in Montreal; probably helps organize New North West Company.
1799.	Goes to partners' meeting at Grand Portage for the last time. Leaves North West Company. Goes to London.
1800.	Goes to Montreal; later returns to London.
Summer, 1801.	Goes to Montreal (?), but soon returns to London.
November, 1801.	Publishes his *Voyages*.
1802.	Presents his "Preliminaries" to the government. Is knighted. Returns to Montreal and joins the New North West Company.
1804.	Is elected to legislature of Quebec.
1805.	Returns to Great Britain, leaving Canada for the last time.
1812.	Marries Geddes Mackenzie.
1816.	Daughter Margaret born.
1818.	Son Alexander born.
1819.	Son George born.
March 11, 1820.	Dies while traveling in Scotland.

PART OF THE MAP FROM THE FIRST EDITION
OF MACKENZIE'S *Voyages*

APPENDIX TWO

Mackenzie's Route

ELEVATIONS AND DISTANCES

	ELEVATION (in feet)	DISTANCE (in miles)	
Old Fort Chipewyan	695	——	
Fort Fork	1,030	500+	
Finlay Forks	1,952	309	
Continental Divide	2,650	171	
Point where Mackenzie left Fraser	1,680	133	
Alexandria	1,500	67	
Bella Coola	0	218	(from Fraser)
Mackenzie's Rock	0	41	
Outbound		1,506+	
Return		1,305+	
TOTAL		2,811+	

Data mostly from Surveys and Mapping Branch, British Columbia Department of Lands and Forests; elevation of Continental Divide from T. H. Taylor in Woollacott.

Swannell, 1959, says that Mackenzie traveled about 1,200 miles going westward, 940 by water and 260 by land, and 1,120 miles on the return trip, 860 by water and 260 by land.

ITINERARY

October 10, 1792.	Left Fort Chipewyan.
12.	Entered Peace River.
13.	Passed Peace Point.

17.	Passed Vermilion Falls and camped at upper end.
18.	Camped on Grande Isle.
19.	Camped below Fort Liard.
20.–23.	At Fort Liard.
23.–31.	On Peace River below Smoky River.
November 1, 1792, to May 9, 1793.	At Fort Fork.
May 9.	Left Fort Fork, camped on Peace River three miles above the fort.
13.	Crossed 119th meridian, camped six to eight miles below Pouce Coupé River.
14.	Camped near Rolla Landing, B. C., a mile below Kiskatinaw River.
15.	Camped midway between Beatton River and Pine River.
16.	Camped at Bear Flat.
17.	Camped about six miles above Halfway River.
18.	Camped just below Hudson Hope.
19.	Passed Flowerpot Island, camped between Box Canyon and Grant Flat.
20.–21.	Camped at Grant Flat.
22.–23.	Camped on the portage around Peace River Canyon.
24.	Camped at head of Peace River Canyon.
25.	Camped five miles above Peace River Canyon.
26.	Camped near Carbon River.
27.	Camped between previous camp and Ne-parle-pas Rapids.
28.–29.	Camped three miles above Ne-parle-pas Rapids.
30.	Camped between Eauclaire Creek and Bernard Creek.
31.	Entered Parsnip River, camped several miles above mouth.
June 1–10.	Camped on Parsnip River.
11.	Left Parsnip River, camped on Arctic Lake.
12.	Crossed Continental Divide, camped on James Creek.
13.–16.	Camped on James Creek.
17.	Camped on Herrick Creek (?).

315

18.	Entered Fraser River, camped two miles below Salmon River.
19.	Camped near Woodpecker.
20.	Camped a few miles above Quesnel.
21.	Camped just below Narcosli Creek.
22.	Camped at Alexandria.
23.	Headed upriver, camped a little south of Narcosli Creek.
24.–25.	At Narcosli Creek.
26.	Camped above Quesnel.
June 27 to July 1.	On Canoe Island, between Quesnel and Cottonwood Canyon.
July 2.	Camped between Cottonwood Canyon and West Road River.
3.	Camped ten miles above West Road River.
4.	Left the Fraser River and headed overland, camped east of Punchaw Lake.
5.	Camped between Punchaw Lake and Blackwater.
6.	Camped on Euchiniko River.
7.	Camped on West Road River.
8.	Camped between Kluskoil and Euchiniko lakes.
9.	Camped on West Road River near Kluskus River.
10.	Camped near Kluskus lakes.
11.	Camped on Tsacha Lake.
12.	Camped on north side of West Road River.
13.	Camped on Ulgako Creek or a tributary.
14.	Camped south of Dean River.
15.	Camped on Tanya Lake.
16.	Camped on the divide between Taiataeszi Creek and Kohasganko River.
17.	Camped near mouth of Burnt Bridge Creek (Friendly Village).
18.	Camped at Great Village.
19.	Camped at Bella Coola (Rascal's Village).
20.	Camped at Green Bay
21.	Camped at Mackenzie's Rock.
22.	Began return journey. Did not camp.

23. Entered Bella Coola River, camped above Bella Coola.
24. Camped below Great Village.
25. Camped below Burnt Bridge Creek.
26. Passed Friendly Village, began overland trek, camped in Rainbow Range.
27. Camped in Rainbow Range.
28. Crossed divide between Taiataeszi Creek and Kohasganko River.

August 4. Reached Fraser River, camped there.
5. Stayed at same camp.
6. Began return journey up Fraser River.
7. Camped on Fraser River.
8. Camped at head of Fort George Canyon.
9. Camped two miles below Salmon River.
10. Camped between Salmon River and Giscome Canyon.
11. Camped between Giscome Canyon and McGregor River.
12. Camped on McGregor River.
13. Camped on McGregor River above the canyon.
14.–15. Camped on James Creek.
16. Camped on Arctic Lake.
17.–18. On Parsnip River.
19. Entered Peace River, camped three miles above Ne-parle-pas Rapids.
20. Camped at head of Peace River Canyon.
21. Crossed portage, camped at Grant Flat.
22.–23. On Peace River.
24. Arrived at Fort Fork.

COÖRDINATES

	THE *Voyages*		CORRECT	
Fort Fork [1]	56° 09′,	117° 35′ 15″	56° 08′,	117° 28′
Arctic Lake [2]	54° 24′,	121°	54° 21′,	121° 41′
Canoe Island [3]	53° 02′ 32″,	——	53° 09′,	122° 43′
	53° 03′ 07″,	122° 48′		
	53° 03′ 17″,	——		
	53° 03′ 32″,	——		
Great Village	52° 25′ 52″,	——		
Mackenzie Rock	52° 20′ 48″,	——	52° 23′,	127° 28′
Cove SW of Cascade Inlet	——,	128° 02′	52° 24.5′,	127° 26′
Bella Coola	52° 23′ 43″,	——	52° 22′,	126° 45.5′
Head of Peace River Can-yon	56° 03′ 51″,	——	56° 02′,	122° 11′

MAPS OF MACKENZIE'S ROUTE

The best single map of Mackenzie's route is the 1940 edition of the pre-emption map of central British Columbia, scale 1:1,000,000, published by the British Columbia Department of Lands. It is no longer in print, but can be found in some libraries. Mackenzie's route from Fort Fork to the sea is marked on it, but it may not be entirely correct.

All the area traversed by Mackenzie will eventually be covered by the maps of the National Topographic Series. The 1:1,000,000 series is complete and the 1:250,000 series is almost complete, but only a few sheets of the 1:50,000 series have appeared for this area. An intermediate series on a scale of approximately 1:500,000 is also complete. The following sheets cover Mackenzie's route from Fort Chipewyan to the sea:

74L/10, 11, 14, 13; 84I/16; 84P/1; 74M/4; 84P/2; 84I/15, 14, 11, 12; 84J/9, 8, 7, 6, 5; 84K/8, 1, 7, 2, 3; 84F/14, 15, 10, 11, 6, 3; 84C/14, 11, 6,

[1] Information from Provincial Secretary of Alberta, in letter from Donald Tannas, September 28, 1960.

[2] Information on British Columbia locations from Surveys and Mapping Branch, British Columbia Department of Lands and Forests, in letter from W. R. Young, August 10, 1960.

[3] Canoe Island could not be located exactly, and it probably does not now exist. The position given is that of a small island six miles above Cottonwood.

3, 4; 83N/13; 83M/16, 15; 84D/2, 7, 6, 3, 4; 94A/1, 2, 3, 6, 4; 93P/13; 93O/16; 94B/1 east, 1 west, 2, 3; 93O/14; 94B/4; 93O/13, 12, 11, 6, 3, 2; 93J/15, 16, 9; 93I/12, 5, 4; 93J/1, 2; 93G/15, 10, 7, 2; 93B/15, 16, 9; 93G/6, 5, 4; 93F/1, 2; 93C/15, 14, 13; 93D/16, 9, 8, 7, 6.

74—1:1,000,000

74L—1:250,000

74L/10—1:50,000

Indexes to sheets that are currently available may be obtained from either the Surveys and Mapping Branch, Department of Mines and Technical Surveys, Ottawa, or the Surveys and Mapping Branch, Department of Lands and Forests, Victoria, B. C.

RETRACING MACKENZIE'S ROUTE

I started at Montreal, where the Lachine Rapids marked the end of navigation in Mackenzie's day and the beginning of the canoe route into the interior. At the Chateau Ramezay historical museum I met Louis Carrier, the curator, who told me much about Mackenzie and the fur trade and grieved over the rapid disappearance of historic sites in Montreal. He took me to his home in Ste. Anne de Bellevue and showed me the beach from which the fur traders began their voyages.

Leaving Montreal, I followed the traders up the Ottawa River. In Ottawa I talked with Dr. W. Kaye Lamb, Dominion Archivist, about Mackenzie, and Dr. Lamb let me examine the Mackenzie papers from the Masson collection. Here I found the versions of Mackenzie's letters used in this edition.

The fur traders left the Ottawa River for Lake Nipissing, and from there followed the French River down to Georgian Bay. I met them where the highway crosses the French River, and again on Mackinac Island, between Lake Huron and Lake Michigan, the famous Michilimackinac of the fur traders. The fort built by the British army in 1780 is still standing, maintained by the state of Michigan as a historical park, but there is little evidence of the traders.

At Sault Ste. Marie I saw the remnants of St. Mary's Falls, at the outlet of Lake Superior. The traders bound for the Northwest portaged around the falls and followed the north shore of the lake to Grand Portage, now in Minnesota. I met them again there. Grand Portage was the entrance to the Northwest, one of the most important posts in the fur trade. The original log fort has long since decayed, but it has been partly reconstructed by the WPA. It is on the Chippewa reservation and is in poor condition. Fortunately it has since come under the control of the National Park Service.

At Grand Portage the traders left their canoes behind and carried their goods over a nine-mile portage to Fort Charlotte on the Pigeon River. The river empties into Lake Superior, but the portage was made to avoid the long stretch of bad water below Fort Charlotte. A trail now follows the approximate route of the portage, but I did not take it. The site of Fort Charlotte is marked by a plaque.

In the city of Fort William, Ontario, I looked for the site of the original Fort William, the trading post built to replace Grand Portage, but was told that the site was not even marked.

From Fort Charlotte the fur route went west up a series of lakes and rivers along what is now the International Boundary. I crossed the route at Kenora, where the canoes left Lake of the Woods on their way to Lake Winnipeg. Later I saw Lake Winnipeg itself from Winnipeg Beach. This is one of the largest lakes on the continent, and formerly was the hub of the fur-trade routes in the Northwest.

At Hudson's Bay House in Winnipeg I visited Miss Malvina Bolus, the editor of the Hudson's Bay Company's magazine, *The Beaver*. She gave me much information on early trading posts, and allowed me to examine her files on some of them.

From Lake Winnipeg the trade route went far north and west through a maze of lakes and rivers that still can be reached only by canoe or plane. I did not touch the route again until Waterways, on the Clearwater River in northern Alberta. To get there I took the Northern Alberta Railway north from Edmondton. This was a three-hundred-mile trip, at an average speed of twenty-two miles per hour, and the train was made up of some of the oldest equipment on the continent. Waterways is the end of the railroad, and the beginning of river transportation. This is the base of operations for the Northern Transportation Company, whose barges carry freight into the enormous Mackenzie Basin, as far as the Arctic Ocean.

320   The next day—and from now on I will mostly let my own diary speak

—"I went for a short run on the Radium Scout to take a barge to the pickup point on the Athabasca at Mile 7, four miles below the Clearwater. On the Athabasca the left bank is low, the right bank steep and high, and the channel is close to the right bank. Even at high water it would be possible to walk across much of the river. The right bank is of sloping rock that appears to be limestone, for perhaps five feet, and above that gentler wooded slope. In places there are high cliffs of oil sand above the rock. When we entered the Clearwater the difference in the water of the two rivers was marked. The Athabasca is high now and its water enters the mouth of the Clearwater. There is a sharp but crooked line between the dark brown, relatively clear waters of the Clearwater and the lighter, muddier waters of the Athabasca. The Athabasca may be muddier because it runs through farmland part of the way."

July 2. "We took my things down to the boat, and at 3:00 P.M. we sailed. Our boat is the *Peace,* which was brought from the U.S. during the war. We had one tug and picked up two more on the Athabasca. Our skipper is Bill Goodlad, from the Shetland Islands."

July 3. "I don't think it got dark last night—there was some light every time I looked out, and we did not tie up at all. Early this morning there was mist on the river and I got up at 4:30 to photograph it. We were at about Mile 88. Most of this country is quite flat, with low banks, densely wooded with aspen and conifers. In places the trees may be as much as twelve inches in diameter. The mosquitoes are annoying now, even in the middle of the river. The crew say there is little game in this country— few deer, few moose, not much of anything else.

"Our first stop today was the government airfield and radio station at Embarras, Mile 118. We had a small load for there. It is on a flat sand deposit twenty-five feet above the river—different from most of the area. Later we passed more of this, all on the right bank; and at Reed's trading post, Mile 135, the hands had to carry the freight up a loose sand trail to a flat bank above. According to one account Pond's fort probably was just below here, but that would be fifty miles above the lake, while contemporary accounts say thirty or forty miles. This is where the Embarras River begins—actually a branch of the Athabasca. Below here is the Athabasca delta. There are the usual islands in this stretch, of varying size, flat, maybe a foot and a half above water, with low dense willow growth. The larger islands have trees similar to the mainland.

"The last high ground is just below Reed's. One map shows Reed's as 'Old Fort,' which may refer to Pond's. There are scattered cabins on the delta, but it seems a poor area for a fort. We followed mostly the easternmost channel through the delta. The ground is about two feet above water level, flat, vertical banks, vegetation mostly willow three to fifteen feet high and fairly dense. In places there are marshes and open water. At the Devil's Elbow is a sharp **S** Bend and we ran aground there, but got off without trouble. Near the mouth of the river the willows give way to marsh, and the marsh breaks up into smaller and smaller islands. Finally there are a few stranded tree trunks in the water and beyond that the open lake. From here Old Fort Point (site of Fort Chipewyan in Mackenzie's day) is the most conspicuous projection to the east, but its tip is hidden by Little Goose Island.

"There is a string of rocky islands surrounding new Fort Chipewyan harbor, some very small, Potato Island the largest. The town itself is on rock, spread out for maybe a mile along the shore. The south side of the lake here is low marsh country, but the north side and the islands are Canadian shield."

July 4. "The dock is at the end of the little point marked by an anchor on the Fort Chipewyan map, and the town extends in a thin line around the bay on both sides. Much of the town is built on bare rock, but the most densely settled part is on lower ground back from the dock, with a soil covering.

"According to Jimmy Fraser, an old-timer here, the Peace River is high now and water is flowing up the Slave River into the lake, so the lake is rising. He says there are remains of chimneys of an old fort on English Island, just west of here, and a small prairie representing where a fort was on Potato Island, to the south. He does not know whether anything is on Old Fort Point. Apparently at highest water it may be five feet higher than now. He says that the flats along the shore here used to be open water, and that the delta country at the west end of the lake has changed greatly—filled in.

"When the load was off we left the dock, picked up the other barges and left at 1:30 P.M., headed for the Peace River. Most of the area shown on the map as mud flats along the northwest end of the lake is covered by willows, and when we rounded Dog Head I thought we were about to enter the Rivière des Rochers. Actually we still had several miles to go in what is officially lake. This area consists of a hundred-yard channel through extensive area of willows. The willows are dense, very skinny (not more than one inch in diameter), up to perhaps ten feet tall. At the present high water their bases are submerged. Scattered about are rock islands, rising perhaps twenty-five feet above the water, rounded by glaciers, the sides usually sloping into the water, the tops and cracks with conifers. After we entered the river proper the rocks almost disappeared and the banks—perhaps five to ten feet above water, were covered with thick bushes. Farther back were larger deciduous trees—mostly aspen—and a few conifers. This area probably has been logged. It looks rather a mess. At Mile 223 we passed Little Rapids, which are now completely submerged. At low water the boats sometimes go up the Chenal des Quatre Fourches (Mackenzie's Pine River, between the western end of Lake Athabasca and the lower Peace River) to bypass these rapids.

"At the mouth of the Peace the water is wide, with complicated eddies and boils. There were several tree trunks in the middle, caught in the eddies. We entered the Peace, to deliver freight to lumber camps on its banks. The river in the lower ten miles is maybe two hundred yards wide or more now [actually, much wider], but there are wide sand bars when the water is low. Small boils and eddies are scattered around. This river is much more impressive than others seen so far. There is more timber along its banks, including spruce or fir saw timber. The banks are mostly low but steep, of loose sediments. Goodlad says that one point has been shortened one hundred fifty yards since he was first here. In places the river has been cutting the bank and the trees falling into the water. As a result there are tall thin conifers right on the water edge, without low vegetation, looking like the center of a stand. We passed the mouth of the Chenal des Quatre Fourches. It is narrow but usable by the boats at all times. Mackenzie no doubt took the west side of the island at its head, if the island existed then. Mosquitoes terrible—worst I have seen—thousands in sight at once."

July 5. "The river is high and muddy and has quite a bit of trash and foam. Goodlad says it is always muddy except perhaps at low water late in the season. The Peace may rise or fall fifteen feet, while the Athabasca does so only a few feet. Now the Peace is muddier than the Athabasca."

We followed Mackenzie about twenty-five miles up the Peace River, then went back downstream to the mouth, where the Peace and the 323

Rochers rivers join to form the Slave River. We went down the Slave to the end of the run, at Fitzgerald, where the freight is unloaded to be trucked around the Rapids of the Drowned to boats waiting at Bell Rock below. The next day, after unloading, the *Peace* started back up the Slave, bound for Waterways. I left the boat at Fort Chipewyan, hoping to get a boat to take me to Old Fort Point.

In Chipewyan I stayed at the Anglican rectory with young Wilfred Wagner, a divinity student who is in charge of the parish for the summer. I was unable to get to the old fort, but I did have a chance to see more of Fort Chipewyan, a very beautiful and colorful and repellent place. The population is about five hundred Indians—Crees and Chipewyans—and twenty whites, but the Indian population is very mobile, many of them spending part of the year in the bush and part living in tents in town. There is a cairn commemorating Mackenzie's expedition, and two abandoned buildings painted white and very old, that are all that remains of the Hudson's Bay Company's fort here. The Company's store now is in a modern building, entirely unfortified.

On July 10 I flew from Chipewyan in a light plane, with a half-breed pilot and the local Chinese restaurateur and a sister and three Indian students from the Catholic mission school as fellow passengers. "Around Chipewyan and the Athabasca delta everything was very flat, except the places where rocks protrude—large areas at Chipewyan, but small islands of rock in a sea of muskeg on the delta. The delta was flat, wet, with winding channels. Vegetation very low. As we got toward the head of the delta the land became higher, drier, with larger and larger trees.

"Above the delta most of the country is quite flat, maybe fifty feet above river level. There is a sharp drop toward the river, sometimes forming the actual bank, more often some distance from the river. Up to a mile of low land may separate plateau from river. In places, especially near Mackay, small rivers have cut deep narrow gorges in the plateau." We changed planes at Waterways and flew to Edmonton.

From Edmonton I drove north to the bleak country along the south shore of Lesser Slave Lake and west to the flourishing farming area along the Peace River in western Alberta. On July 12, at the town of Peace River, I picked up Mackenzie's trail again.

"We crossed the river at the combination highway-railway bridge and took the old Shaftesbury Trail along the left bank of the river, upstream.

This is a dirt road in fair shape. We had gone several miles when I saw the forks of the Peace River and the Smoky River. At the mouth of the Smoky are several islands. At the end of the peninsula between the rivers is a neck of flat land. The islands are forested, but at low water much more land is exposed. The forks are roughly four miles above town. I went on to the Mackenzie cairn, ten miles above town. It claims to be opposite the site of Fort Fork, and must be approximately so. It is about the right distance, and the land opposite is one of the few flat places on that side of the river. Just downstream is a sizable farm owned by Joe Neff. The fort site now is in poplars and brush. We drove to a small truck farm just above the cairn, and a fellow there named several people in the area who have boats and could carry me across. He had been to the fort himself, but says it is hidden in brush now, and that I should come back in the fall. Three men crossed over on the ice last winter. They used to find things like old skillets and arrowheads there.

"The Shaftesbury Trail that we went out runs near the left bank of the river, on land gently sloping toward the river. Farther back the land rises more steeply to form hills. On the right bank there is an abrupt rise from the river. Both banks are steep, rising almost vertically in many places for perhaps twenty-five feet. For several miles there is a wide stretch of land on the right bank, where the Neff farm and Fort Fork are, but I saw no other farms or extensive low areas on that side.

"After supper we drove up a steep road in back of town to the grave of Twelve Foot Davis. The site is on the rim of the valley and has a fine view of the country. The country is a high plateau (elevation at airport eighteen hundred feet) deeply incised by streams, which have carved fairly steep-sided canyons for themselves. The edge of the plateau is fairly abrupt and is indicated on the map by a row of small wedges. The country is mostly in grass, with scattered patches of black poplar. The junction of the Peace and the Smoky, and the islands just downstream, are clearly visible."

July 13. "A local boat owner, Arnold Dixon, agreed to take me from Peace River town to the site of Fort Fork. We made it in half an hour to the cairn and landed on the opposite bank. Dixon had never been there and did not know just where the fort was or what to look for. Just opposite the cairn is a division—upstream is a steep bank perhaps ten feet high descending straight to the river. Downstream the total height is the same 325 but there is a terrace halfway down, curving out into the river and covered with driftwood. The land is flat, with large black poplars and thick underbrush. It was the downstream part that had been pointed out to me as the site of the fort. No doubt the bank has changed much since Mackenzie's time. We crashed through the brush looking for things, but found nothing that was definitely part of the fort. I found a small earth mound with a few rocks on it. The rocks meant little to me at the time, but now I realize that there are none naturally on that silt bottomland. The mound was a foot or so high and several feet across. In addition I saw perhaps ten or twelve scattered around, maybe three feet deep and four feet wide. By the bank were two larger holes, their outer ends open at the bank. Very roughly four feet deep, eight feet in from the bank and five feet wide. They had been roofed with small logs covered with earth. The logs had collapsed but were not badly decayed. At the time I thought these might have been part of the fort, but it seems impossible that logs would be in such good condition. We explored a couple of hundred feet downstream from the cairn and a hundred feet inland, but failed to find any of the ridges or stone piles that are supposed to be present. This was very disappointing. We were in too much of a hurry to stay any longer."

From Peace River town I drove through to Dunvegan, farther up the river. Fort Dunvegan was built by the North West Company in 1805 and at one time was the most important post on the Peace, but now the site is abandoned. "I drove up to the rim to get photos, and on a cutbank noticed the 'white scum' that Mackenzie saw on the river bank about here. It was leached from the soil and formed surface deposits over dozens of square yards, but only on a small portion of the cutbanks."

A Roman Catholic mission built in 1885 is maintained as a museum. "A sign in the mission quotes Mackenzie's 'most beautiful scenery I ever saw' passage and says it was written about this section. I doubt it because (1) there was an island where Mackenzie was camped, and the river here has none and is too straight and narrow for them; (2) he says the banks rose in a succession of terraces, while here that is not so. On the south side the banks rise at a steep grade to a great height; on the north side there is a broad terrace perhaps twenty-five feet above the river, behind which the hill rises steeply."

On July 14 I crossed into British Columbia and drove up the Alaska Highway as far as Fort St. John. The highway runs through rolling wooded country, and intersects Mackenzie's route where it crosses the Peace River. The next day I drove "out past Charlie Lake two miles to Hudson Hope Road, and west on that. The road rises and falls for some miles, then takes a long sharp drop with hairpin turns down to Bear Flat, almost at river level. From the plateau rim is a good view of the flat and up the valley. The river has a considerable amount of flat or sloping land, but in places the land rises fairly steeply from river to plateau. The plateau is deeply dissected by gorges which extend far back from the river. On the south side of the river the land is mostly steeper. In the steepest places are high dirt banks, in other places the land is forested to the river. The forests are mostly small poplar, but also some spruce and lodgepole. Much the largest stream on the north side is the Halfway River (formerly the Middle River). Characteristic of the streams here near their mouths is a very high steep bank on the outside of curves and a low wide bank on the inside.

"At the Halfway River I got out and walked to the mouth. Farther back, before leaving the plateau, I had a good view of the Rocky Mountains—more impressive than I had expected—and of a small mountain much closer called Bullhead Mountain. These were not visible from the valley. Near the Halfway River I saw both from the road, and I walked to the mouth to see whether either was visible from the Peace. Both were, the Rockies to the left of an island, Bullhead to the right. One authority says that the 'Rocky Mountains' that Mackenzie first sighted was actually Bullhead (May 15), but I doubt it. Both seem to come in sight at about the same time—perhaps one or both could be seen from farther downstream, but not from the immediate downstream area—hidden by the high banks. Mackenzie says that their summits were covered with snow —the Rockies seen from here had several summits, while Bullhead is a single low cone. There is extensive snow still in sheltered places on the Rockies, none on Bullhead, but of course I am two months later than he was."

Hudson Hope is a small town just below the Peace River Canyon. Looking for the canyon, "I drove out the continuation of the main street, to the west. Stopping two and one-half miles west of Hudson Hope, I walked a few yards down to the river and got my first view of the canyon region, though the canyon proper has not begun here. Several small, steep-sided islands are in the river here, though apparently only one fits 327

Mackenzie's description of being wider at top than bottom—locally called Flowerpot Island, appropriate because of plants on top. Mackenzie implies there were more—some may have fallen. There are several lines of rapids in the river, but the river is wide here and none go all the way across, which is why Mackenzie could continue up by making traverses. The scenery is beautiful.

"I returned to the main river road and drove west for maybe two miles. The road is poor, but I had no trouble. It climbs to a terrace high above the river and runs near the rim, giving a good view in places. The spot I had just seen could be seen in better perspective from up here. Now the river is straighter, narrower, with steep banks. Pine, spruce, and cotton-wood. The road ends at a cabin. I followed a trail for a mile along the terrace, then it dipped sharply to near river level. The river here narrows, makes a short turn south, then west again. This is the beginning of the Peace River Canyon proper. I returned to the car and to Hudson Hope, then took the portage road. It turns north off the main road just east of town, and climbs sharply out of the valley. This road follows old Rocky Mountain Portage approximately, except at the ends. It runs between Portage Mountain on the south and Bullhead Mountain on the north.

"I drove across the portage, and fifteen miles from Hudson Hope I turned off onto a road leading south, and followed it a mile or so to the river. This was above the canyon, and the water was placid but swift; banks gentle. There were some river boats here, and some old shacks. Back to the portage, and started down the next road to the river. It soon became steep and had mud puddles, and I parked and walked to the river. Here was a cabin, two barns, and another building. They were in fairly good shape. I learned later that they were built to provide transport and accommodations for prospectors and others, when there were big plans for the country years ago. Looking east from here I saw Portage Mountain and its north and south slopes, and the river cutting to the south.

"A mile down river I found the camp of some engineers who were studying a dam site. This camp is just above the head of the canyon and I walked down there. Though the lower end of the canyon peters out, the upper end is quite definite—the river flows quietly east, makes a sharp turn to the south for a few yards, then turning east again it flows between steep rock walls with a roar. I watched from a distance as a sizable spruce floated into the rapids and was swept away.

"I was told about an old trail—perhaps the original portage—that comes down the hill in back of camp. I followed it for a way—quite distinct, a foot wide, several inches deep, unvegetated. They say it goes up to the road, but they don't know where from there. There is an old cabin in the camp, now used as a generator shed.

"The geologist at the camp, Dr. Bruce Woodsworth, says that most of the rocks in the canyon are Upper Cretaceous; all are sedimentary—mostly sandstones and shales. The canyon is a new channel cut when the former channel was blocked by a glacier—the former channel was on the north side of Portage Mountain, where the road is now. During the present drilling they have found very thick glacial deposits there, without reaching bottom. The vertical walls average hundred and fifty feet high, but the hills behind rise much higher."

July 16. "I spent last night at the engineers' camp, and this morning went back to the portage road and took the next side road to the east, which led to the abandoned Peace River Coal Mine. Mackenzie saw coal burning when he came through the area and they say it still is in places; not here though. The mine is on the north rim of the canyon, probably two hundred feet above the river. The river bank just above last night's camp can be seen, but the camp is hidden by a cliff. Just below the mine the river bends south then east and enters the worst series of rapids. It has been cut through deep strata sloping slightly downstream and there is a continuous series of rapids as far as can be seen, giving off a loud roar.

"On the way out I saw a small pond and bog, maybe a hundred feet across. This is unusual here, for there is very little surface water. This land between river and hills is of smoothly varied topography, but irregular. In parts there are steep high banks of soil, and in a few places are sizable flats by the river. Farther back may be relatively flat terraces or continuous slopes. The camp office had maps made especially for this project. These show the river at the head of the canyon as 1,690 feet, just above the big rapids (high dam site) 1,670 feet, bottom of canyon not shown; Portage Mountain 4,675 feet, the highest point on portage road 2,430 feet. There is a great deal of cottonwood here, some of it merchantable, and lots of spruce. The steepest slopes are in bushes and forbs, and parts of steep riverbank are bare."

Returning to Hudson Hope, I called on Mrs. Wesley Gething. The Gethings are the oldest family in the Hope, and Mrs. Wesley was able to   329 tell me a great deal about the history of the area. "Cust's House was at the head of the canyon, and the old fireplace is still there, just in back of camp. It was the west end of portage, and boats started from there up-river. Hudson Hope was originally at Halfway River (then Middle River), later moved to opposite the present site, and early in this century to the present site. Mackenzie is thought to have left the river twelve miles above Hudson Hope, at the west end of Grant's Flat, and climbed over the south shoulder of Portage Mountain. The first coal mine in the area was at this point. I could see the place by walking in from King's Mine."

Leaving Mrs. Gething, I drove part of the way back over the portage and, following her instructions, found a road and trail that led to a view of Grant's Flat. This is a flat area of several acres, just above the river level on the north side of the river. It is bounded by steep hills, and if Mackenzie climbed up from there he had quite a haul. Later I returned to Fort St. John, stopping on the way seven miles east of Hudson Hope to see the so-called "gates of the canyon"—two islands with high vertical rock sides. Most of the many islands in the river are low and alluvial.

From Fort St. John I drove down the Alaska Highway and the Hart Highway toward Prince George. The Hart Highway crosses the middle portion of the Parsnip River. When I saw it, the river was swift and fairly high, but much lower than it was when Mackenzie made his way up it. The banks are low and densely wooded. There are a few small islands.

At Prince George I reached the Fraser River. I crossed to the left bank of the Fraser and found roads leading to the river in several places between the mouth of the McGregor River, where Mackenzie reached the Fraser, and Prince George. At all of these places the banks were low and wooded, and at one there was a large island in the river.

July 20. "Just across the Fraser River bridge from Prince George I stopped to see the junction with the Nechako River. The mouth of the Nechako is partly plugged by small islands, but it is obvious that a river comes in there. The islands are not long and narrow like those in the river, but rather are small and rounded. The narrow channels between them obviously lead back to something. Besides, the north bank of the Nechako is high, with a plainly visible cut bank, while the islands and the south bank are low. If Mackenzie had seen this spot he surely would have realized that a river came in there. It seems strange that he failed to see the Nechako—he passed it twice.

330

Appendixes

"I followed directions to Fort George Canyon (locally called Red Rock Canyon), about sixteen miles south of Prince George. This is not much of a canyon, but it is rough for boats. The banks are rock, maybe twenty-five feet high on the east side, less on the other. The river is broken by high rock islands. It should not be difficult to portage on the west side, but I did not see all of the canyon. (Mackenzie portaged on the east side.) I have read that some of the rocks were blasted out so that steamboats could get through, but I don't see how they could get through here."

The place where Mackenzie left the Fraser to travel overland is not visible from the highway. At Quesnel I crossed to the west side of the river and took a dirt road northwest to the town of Blackwater.

"This country is all high rolling plateau, densely wooded with poplar, lodgepole pine, and some spruce and Douglas fir. The highway map shows a town called Blackwater on the north side of the West Road River, but there is nothing here except two abandoned cabins. There are two others on the south side. The West Road is called the Blackwater locally—the water is dark because of organic acids from all the muskeg. Where the road crosses, it flows through a small canyon cut through rock. The banks are maybe twenty feet high here, and there are large logs strewn over them to that height—the river must flood badly.

"I drove north to Punchaw Lake, where Mackenzie is supposed to have spent his first night on the trail. It seems to be a couple of miles long on the map, but doesn't look it to me. There is some flat dry land by the lake at the northwest end, where the Indian camp probably was. Otherwise, the north end is too wet, the west side too high. At this end anyway the lake is shallow, with lily pads.

"By road it is about ten miles from the lake to the rim of the West Road valley, and the road supposedly follows Mackenzie's trail. At first there are a couple of fairly steep ups and downs, but after that the land is flat. He says it is open country, sprinkled with 'cypruss,' that is, lodgepole pine. Now the country is well forested, but lodgepole is still dominant. Near the valley are also numbers of large (fifteen-inch in diameter) Douglas fir. The trail must have run along the rim of the plateau, because he saw the river from it. I could not see it where the road crosses the rim, but several hundred yards west I saw short stretches of it. He says that the descent was too long and steep for them to go down for water. It is long and steep, and I was very thirsty while I waited for sunlight on the valley. 331

Finally I gave up and took a picture of the valley in shadow. There is a good view of the valley to the west, eventually curving south in the distance. The plateau seems to be of uniform elevation, but farther back to the south and southwest is a low row of hills rising above the plateau. The valley is densely wooded, more with conifers than with poplar."

July 21. "I drove most of the way back to Quesnel, then turned off on a side road, hoping to find Cottonwood Canyon. About seven miles out there is a good view of the river and valley. Just south of here the Fraser River makes a great **S** bend, and just north the Cottonwood River comes in from the east, its valley plugged with sand or something. Several miles farther on I walked up a short road for another look—river fairly straight, nothing special. Eleven miles out the road ends. Just above here the river makes a bend to the right (going up), just below seems to be the head of the canyon (out of sight around the bend). On this side there is a sharp drop of at least fifty feet, and on the other side is a sheer rock wall much higher. There was some rough water and some roaring, but not as much as I had expected."

July 22. From Quesnel I drove south down the Cariboo Highway.

"In various places the river can be seen and is similar here to elsewhere —deep steep valley, in places with high yellow banks rising from the river. I was looking for old Fort Alexandria, where Mackenzie turned back. Between Alexandria town and Marguerite is a cairn, saying this is the site of Fort Alexandria. This surprised me because I thought it was on the west side of the river. I went to Marguerite and took the ferry across there. The ferryman said that the fort was on the west side as I had thought, and told me how to get there. I followed his directions to a ranch on the west bank of the river. The rancher, Irving Twan, told me that there was a Hudson's Bay store from the old fort standing where his chicken house was, when he was a boy. Twenty or thirty years ago it was torn down for firewood. He knew nothing of Mackenzie, but said that there had been Indian villages on both sides of the river. On this side of the river is a long flat area, and a gently sloping bank, now with many boulders, and logs. On the east side is a high steep sand bank above here, and a low area below, where there might have been a village. I went back to the house, and Twan showed me an old photo of the late HBC building. It was square, of squared logs, maybe twenty-five feet on a side, with a pyramidal roof."

332

Appendixes

Mackenzie's overland route from the Fraser to the coast is almost entirely inaccessible today. The Indian trail that he followed is long since overgrown, but there are trails following the same general course that are still used by the Indians and perhaps a few ranchers. I had no time to take these, and had to get across to Bella Coola by the new road that goes west from Williams Lake, far south of Mackenzie's route. At Klenna Kleene the road turns north toward Anahim Lake, approaching Mackenzie's route. The country here is similar to the country that he came through. On the western part of the plateau are small scattered mountain ranges, including the Rainbow Range that Mackenzie crossed, and farther west is the continuous mass of the British Columbia Coast Range. From the edge of the plateau the road drops sharply into the Bella Coola valley, where it meets Mackenzie's trail.

July 23. "Beginning east of Tatla Lake various mountain ranges are often in view. They seem to be scattered about, at first mostly to the west, later in all directions. It is not first-rate mountain scenery, but it is impressive. They are rugged and with quite a bit of snow and ice. The plateau becomes increasingly wooded, largely with lodgepole pine, but ranching continues. West of Anahim the road first cuts across rolling lodgepole pine country, with an occasional view across muskeg to a mountain range. It hits the edge of the plateau at Young Creek and begins to drop down this valley, to the south. The hill is twelve miles long. I think it replaces the hill up from the Fraser yesterday as the worst I have ever driven."

At the bottom of the hill the road crosses the Atnarko River and turns west toward Bella Coola, fifty miles away. I turned east to visit Bert Robson, who lives near here. Bert has lived in this region for many years and has a great store of reliable information about it. "He showed me several magazine articles on Mackenzie and this area. A piece on the Bella Coola road in *The Beaver,* 1957, shows Mackenzie coming down the east side of Burnt Bridge Creek, but the present trail is on the west side. Bert does not know where the Great Village was. The original Indian village (at Bella Coola—Rascal's Village) was on the south side of the river, but the site has washed away."

July 24. Bert and I drove to Bella Coola today, stopping along the way to talk to people. At a government survey camp we "met George New, in charge, and talked with him a while. Atnarko is 1,140 feet, Firvale about

333

385 feet (near the mouth of Burnt Bridge Creek), top of Burnt Bridge Trail about 4,000 feet, Stupendous Mountain (which Mackenzie saw across the valley) 8,790 feet.

"Near Bella Coola I visited the camp of Ben Ferrier, who has canoed very extensively in the north. In the past seven summers, he has covered most of Mackenzie's route by canoe. This year he has done the Parsnip and the upper Peace. Is here to do the Bella Coola and out to the rock. They are going down the Bella Coola River tomorrow and he invited me along. He has been up the Rat River (westernmost channel of the Mackenzie River delta) and crossed over to the Porcupine River. He says Mackenzie could not have gone from the Mackenzie River down the Yukon in the time and conditions prevailing in 1789."

July 25. "At 8:00 A.M. we set off upriver for the canoe trip down. They stopped at one place to check a rapid, to see whether they could run it—decided they could. Unloaded the boats a couple of hundred yards below Canoe Crossing, where the road crosses the river. The river is high now, and fast, but later it will be maybe five feet lower and can be waded. We stood around while Ben took movies and stills of us, then took off. The water was quiet at first, but later we hit fast water in places. The river is lined with tree trunks, many of them enormous, and they form frequent partial jams. The mountains are very high on both sides, separated by deep stream valleys. The rapids were not as bad as I expected, and we usually were able to bypass the worst parts. The breakers often reached a foot or more in height, and there were tricky side currents. We shipped some water in places, which I bailed out with my handkerchief. At one place we tipped and the right gunwales were only a couple of inches from the water. Where the water was shallow it boiled up quietly, throwing sand against the bottom of the canoe, producing a fine pattering sound. This eventually wears off the paint. Around noon we landed at the mouth of Thorsen Creek, on which we are camped, for lunch. Then we continued almost to the mouth of the river. There was only a little bad water on this stretch. We did about thirty miles in about three hours, but most of the speed was supplied by the current. Ben says this was the fastest long stretch of water that Mackenzie encountered west of Grand Portage, and that because of the log jams it is a somewhat dangerous river."

July 26. "Ben and I went into Bella Coola to see Clayton Mack, an Indian fisherman and guide, to discuss plans to have him accompany Ben's canoes in his gas boat to Mackenzie's rock. Mack says that some people contend that Mackenzie went down the Dean River, but Bella Coola Indian legend says he came down the Bella Coola River. He also says that two war canoes accompanied him down the arm—they would have stayed some distance away for safety, as was the custom—one behind, the other across the channel. The Bella Coolas and Bella Bellas still are enemies.

"Later I spent some time on the marshes at the mouth of the river. The south part of the marsh is intersected by sloughs, some tiny, others large. Farther north are the two branches of the river. Of course the present channels are not the same as in Mackenzie's time. The mountains were hidden by clouds and a headwind was blowing, as when Mackenzie went down."

July 28. "Ben and his party left for the rock yesterday, but I could not make it. Today I talked for a while with one of the Indians, who told me about a cedar he had cut down recently that was perfectly round outside but that inside showed a deep cut made by an axe, in white man's style. It had grown completely over. Rings showed it was cut one hundred fifty years ago (1809) by Mackenzie, they think. This was twenty miles up the river from Bella Coola.

"After lunch I broke camp and headed east. At Burnt Bridge (Kahylskt) Creek I stopped to look for Mackenzie's Friendly Village, which is supposed to be two hundred yards above the mouth. I walked along the east side of the creek a mile or more to its mouth, but found nothing. Most of the way the country is fairly open, but along the river is a dense growth of roses. The creek is only six or eight feet wide now, but it flows across a wide boulder-strewn floodplain. Most of the land here seems to be older stabilized floodplain of this sort, now with mature timber. The river has a narrow active floodplain. Its course is now near the south side of the valley. Next I drove to the Burnt Bridge (Summer) Trail and walked up it for half a mile, trying to fit the country to Mackenzie's account. Where the road crosses the creek it flows from between steep rock walls onto the boulder strewn area. Above here the walls are very steep and high as far as can be seen. In Mackenzie's account the river twelve yards wide is Burnt Bridge Creek and the river fifty yards wide is the Bella Coola."

I returned to the car and continued east. "At Stuie the fairly clear Atnarko River and the milky (glacial-flour) Whitewater join to form the 335

Bella Coola River. The Bella Coola is milky, and even the head of north Bentinck Arm is distinctly so."

That was the end of the trip, so far as Mackenzie was concerned. I returned to Williams Lake and turned south to Vancouver. Bad weather and lack of time had kept me from getting to many of the places I had wanted to see, but I had visited some of the main places on Mackenzie's route. I had found vegetation and river courses changed somewhat from the conditions Mackenzie described, but the whole route is surprisingly unaffected by human activity. There is not a single dam on any of the streams Mackenzie traveled in 1793, and most of the country is little affected by farming or logging. Unfortunately this country is developing so fast that this will not be true for long.

Note on the Text

The *Voyages* was presented as Mackenzie's own work, but it seems that he did what many others have done before and since—hire a ghost writer (see Montgomery). The *Voyages* is written with a skill that would hardly have been possible in those days for a man who had had only a few years of irregular schooling. The journals of Lewis and Clark, both of whom were better educated than Mackenzie, are a jumble of misspellings, incorrect punctuation, and bad grammar, and this seems to have been the rule at that time with most men who did anything worth writing about.

Mackenzie was aware of his shortcomings as a writer, and his letters show that he had planned to have his cousin Roderick McKenzie revise his manuscript. There is no evidence that Roderick ever did this, but there is reason to believe that this was done by William Combe. Combe was a competent writer who made a business of preparing the journals of travelers and others for publication. Mackenzie's *Voyages* is included on a list that Combe prepared of his anonymous writings. There is no further evidence supporting this claim, or indicating how much of the writing was done by Combe and how much by Mackenzie. The British Museum and the Library of Congress accept Combe's claim and there seems to be no evidence to contradict it.

Apparently Combe compiled the *Voyages* from Mackenzie's notes, but it is not known how extensive these notes were. Mackenzie's letters show that he did some work on them during the winter of 1793-94 at Fort Chipewyan, but these notes are not known to exist. Mackenzie's papers were lost when his estate, Avoch, burned in 1832. There is a manuscript journal of the 1789 voyage in the British Museum, in someone else's handwriting, but there is no known manuscript of the 1793 voyage (see Wade, p. 257). The 1789 manuscript has not been compared with the published *Voyages*. The footnotes to his description of the Pacific coast cannot have been written before 1798, when Vancouver's *Voyage* was published.

The *Voyages* was published in London in 1801, and was immediately successful. A second edition was published the next year, with hundreds of trivial changes. Most of these are in punctuation or in spelling; most seem desirable and have been retained. The text of the original is arbitrarily broken into chapters, each chapter heading followed by an outline of the contents. These chapter headings and outlines are deleted in the present book, to make a continuous narrative. The method of indicating dates has been changed slightly, and a few datelines have been moved or inserted. The text itself is complete.

The letters are a much more difficult problem. Not one original letter by Mackenzie is known to exist, so that we do not know what he actually wrote. Instead we must rely on faulty copies by other hands. Most of the known letters are those that Mackenzie wrote to his cousin Roderick. In preparation for his history of the fur trade Roderick McKenzie copied parts of these letters, omitting large parts and undoubtedly making changes. He did not complete this history, but his papers came into the hands of his son-in-law, Louis Masson, who included parts of them in his "Bourgeois de la Compagnie du Nord-ouest." It is in this form that the letters are known today. Unfortunately Masson shared the nineteenth-century habit of revising manuscripts to his own taste, so that the published version of the letters apparently is even further from the original than Roderick McKenzie's copy.

The pertinent Masson papers are now in the Public Archives at Ottawa. There are three copies of many of the letters—two on small loosely bound sheets of very old paper and one in a bound manuscript book which contains the full text of Roderick McKenzie's account as printed in Masson. These versions do not agree with each other or with the published version, and until they have been carefully studied it will not be possible to say which of them is closest to the original. There are differences in paper, ink, and handwriting which may permit a successful analysis.

At the suggestion of Dr. W. K. Lamb, the dominion archivist, I have followed what seemed to be the oldest of the loosely bound copies. Presumably some of these are the copies made by Roderick McKenzie, but there are two or more handwritings. Some letters were not found in this form at all, and had to be copied from the bound manuscript volume. The present version is far from definitive, but I believe that it is closer to the original than that of Masson.

Appendixes

Most of the differences among the various versions are in detail only—punctuation, spelling, the addition or deletion of minor words—but there are a few substantial differences. One of these is in the letter of December 2, 1787. The sentence indicating that Mackenzie and Peter Pond "agreed very well" during their winter at Athabasca is not included in the printed version. The Masson version of the letter written in March, 1791, refers to the Mackenzie River as the River Disappointment. This has been interpreted as showing that Mackenzie considered his first exploration a failure. Unfortunately none of the extant manuscript copies of the letter uses this name. The version used here refers to the Mackenzie as "the Grand River visited by me."

The maps published with the *Voyages* were prepared by Aaron Arrowsmith, the leading mapmaker in London at that time. They were based on Arrowsmith's map of North America, which had been published in 1795 and revised since from time to time (see Wheat). The map on page 313 of the present edition is a reproduction of part of the principal map from the first edition.

Notes

NOTES TO PROLOGUE
(Pp. 4-45)

1. This section is based largely on DeVoto, 1952. See also Brebner and Burpee.

2. Mackenzie, p. viii, says that the Kaministiquia route was the main French route until the Conquest.

3. Mackenzie describes the canoe route from Montreal to Athabasca in detail in the General History of the Fur Trade that is printed with the *Voyages*. See also Burpee.

4. Crouse, p. 235.

5. See Crouse, pp. 230–233 and DeVoto, 1952, p. 215.

6. Mackenzie, p. viii.

7. *Ibid.*, p. ix, says 1775, but Hearne's journal (Tyrrel, 1934) shows that it was in 1774.

8. Henry, p. 328.

9. Mackenzie, pp. xii ff.

10. Burpee, pp. 328 f.

11. Mackenzie, pp. ix f.

12. Innis, 1956, p. 214.

13. Wallace, p. 5.

14. Basic references for the history of the North West Company are Campbell, Davidson, Innis 1956, Wallace, and Mackenzie.

15. Mackenzie, p. xxxix.

16. *Ibid.*, p. xlv.

17. Morton, 1939, p. 355.

18. Mackenzie, p. xlvi.

19. *Ibid.*, p. xc.

20. *Ibid.*, p. xxvi.

21. Innis, 1928.

22. Cook.

23. Innis, 1930; Wagner, 1955.

24. Innis, 1930; Wagner, 1955; Nute.

25. Burpee, pp. 587, 601.

26. Mackenzie, p. xviii.

27. *Ibid.,* p. xvi.

28. *Ibid.,* p. xx.

29. There is no entirely satisfactory biography of Mackenzie. Wade's is the best available, and I have drawn extensively on him for this account.

30. Mackenzie, p. xix.

31. Much of our knowledge of this period is from Roderick McKenzie's account and from Mackenzie's letters to Roderick, both published in Masson.

32. Wagner, 1955, p. 15, says Mackenzie was sent to relieve Pond so that Pond could carry on his explorations.

33. Letter from Mackenzie to Roderick McKenzie, dated October 1, 1787.

34. Letter from Mackenzie to Roderick McKenzie, dated December 2, 1787.

35. Innis, 1956, p. 200. See also Morton, 1939, p. 410.

36. After Mackenzie's visit to Patrick Small in January, Small wrote to McTavish, "I am quite surprised at the wild ideas Mr. Pond has of matters, which Mr. MacKenzie told me were incomprehensibly extravagant" (letter dated February 24, 1788, in Masson, p. 25). This is usually interpreted as referring to Pond's ideas for exploration, but the context makes it clear that Small is referring to business matters.

37. Letter from Mackenzie to the governor general, Lord Dorchester, dated November 17, 1794, in Davidson, p. 275.

38. Letter from Isaac Ogden of Quebec to a relative in London, dated November 7, 1789, in Wagner, p. 86.

39. In his letter to McTavish dated February 24, 1788, Small says, "I put it in his [Pond's] option to go with or after the packs, but represented to him that he required to be expeditious, if he intended returning after seeing the Grand Portage. He is preparing a fine map to lay before the Empress of Russia." (Masson, p. 25).

40. Letter from Mackenzie to Roderick McKenzie, date not known.

41. Mackenzie, p. iv.

42. Letter from Mackenzie to Roderick McKenzie, dated May 15, 1788.

43. Mackenzie, pp. xvi f.

44. *Ibid.,* p. xci.
45. Roderick McKenzie in Masson, pp. 26–27.
46. It is not known when Fort Chipewyan was moved to its present site on the north side of Lake Athabasca. Dates much later than this are sometimes given, but from the literature, from records in Hudson's Bay House, Winnipeg, and from inquiry at Fort Chipewyan I believe that the move was made within a few years of 1800.
47. This account is based entirely on Mackenzie, pp. 1–119.
48. Pond knew approximately where the head of the Mackenzie River was, and he or one of his men may have found it. However, there is no evidence for this, and the difficulty that Mackenzie had in finding it suggests that the exact location was unknown.
49. Mackenzie, p. 34.
50. *Ibid.,* p. 41.
51. *Ibid.,* p. 54.
52. *Ibid.,* p. 55.
53. *Ibid.,* p. 61.
54. *Ibid.,* p. 77.
55. *Ibid.,* pp. 106 f.
56. Tyrrell, 1934, p. 317.
57. Letter from Mackenzie to Roderick McKenzie, dated July 1, 1790.
58. Letter from Mackenzie to Roderick McKenzie, dated July 16, 1790. Campbell, p. 69, says that as a tribute to his discovery Mackenzie was given a share bonus and was granted a furlough for the following year.
59. Innis, 1956, p. 201.
60. Letter from Mackenzie to Roderick McKenzie, dated March 2, 1791.
61. Manning.
62. Nasatir, pp. 75 ff.
63. DeVoto, 1952, p. 345.
64. This is the usual interpretation of Turnor's aims (see Tyrrel, 1934). Brebner, p. 448, says that Turnor was going to try to cross the continent to the Pacific, but there seems to be no evidence of this.
65. Letter from Mackenzie to Roderick McKenzie, dated June 1, 1791.
66. Letter from Mackenzie to Roderick McKenzie, dated August 10, 1791.
67. Plaskett; Swannell, 1959.
68. Davidson, p. 63.

NOTES TO JOURNAL
(*Pp. 49–277*)

1. Mackenzie, pp. v–viii.

2. I have used a variety of sources in identifying places, Indian tribes, plants, and animals, and indicated them in the preface.

3. There are many lakes in the marshy country at the western end of Lake Athabasca, and it is not certain which ones Mackenzie was referring to. "The lake Clear Water" should be Lake Claire, which is now the largest of these lakes.

4. Morton, 1939, p. 470 n.

5. *Ibid.*

6. *Ibid.*

7. Howay.

8. Letter from Mackenzie to Roderick McKenzie, dated January 10, 1793.

9. Dr. E. H. Moss of the University of Alberta believes that this change from tundra to the present prairie-like vegetation took place over a period of centuries and that the Indian was recounting a tribal story rather than his own experience (personal communication). The high lands are the Whitemud Hills.

10. Letter from Mackenzie to Roderick McKenzie, dated May 8, 1793. There must have been at least one express between Fort Fork and Fort Chipewyan during the winter, because in January Mackenzie wrote for McKay to come up and in May he was there.

11. Swannell (1959) gives a detailed description of Mackenzie's probable outfit.

12. Woollacott, p. 120.

13. *Ibid.*, p. 124.

14. For a different interpretation of where Mackenzie left the river, see Sage, 1950.

15. Jenness.

16. *Ibid.*

17. Mackenzie, p. 37.

18. These lakes were named by T. H. Taylor, who followed this part of Mackenzie's route in 1910. See his description of the country in Wollacott.

19. According to Morice, the interpreter, a Beaver, could hardly have understood a Carrier unless he knew the Carrier dialect. Probably they spoke a mixture of both languages.

20. Dawson, 1878, p. 25.

21. Personal communication from Mr. Wilson Duff, curator of anthropology at the Provincial Museum, Victoria, B. C.

22. McIlwraith, p. 10.

23. McIlwraith, p. 9; Smith.

24. Bishop.

25. In his journal for June 2 Vancouver records the following encounter with Indians, presumably Bella Bellas, on Dean Channel: "Three Indians appeared on the opposite side of the brook. I endeavoured by signs and offers of trinkets to prevail on their crossing over to us, but without success; at length they gave us to understand by signs, that if we would go back to our party who were at no great distance, they would follow in their canoe. They paddled after us a few yards, but again returned to the shore, on which one of them landed, and the other two again came forward. The man who had landed hastened back along the banks of the brook, with visible marks of fear, as we conjectured towards their habitations. His apprehensions operated on the other two, who also retired up the brook in their canoe. As we were preparing to depart about three o'clock, this canoe, attended by another containing six or seven Indians, came down the rivulet; but notwithstanding every means was used to invite them, they would not venture nearer us than their companions had done before" (II, 266–267).

26. Bishop.

27. McIlwraith, p. 56.

28. Cowan and Guiguet. The buffalo shot near the western end of the Peace River Canyon may be the one to which Roe refers when he says (p. 309) that Mackenzie recorded the species on the upper Parsnip River.

1. Letter from Mackenzie to Roderick McKenzie, dated January 13, 1794.

2. Letter from Mackenzie to Roderick McKenzie, dated March 5, 1794.

3. Campbell, p. 87.

4. Quoted in Fleming, 1928.

5. Roderick McKenzie, in Masson, p. 45.

6. Fleming, 1928, says that Mackenzie joined this firm before going to London in 1794.

7. Fleming, 1929.

8. Wallace, pp. 19–25; Campbell, chap. 5.

9. Fleming, 1928, covers this period. Campbell, p. 117, gives a different picture, based on evidence that presumably is better but is not specified. She believes that Mackenzie had been a friend of McTavish and McGillivray (he had been made a partner in their firm) and that Mackenzie's increasing hostility resulted from McTavish's intention of replacing the retiring Frobisher with McTavish's nephew, McGillivray.

10. Roderick McKenzie, in Masson, p. 48.

11. Alexander Henry, the younger, quoted in Innis, 1956, p. 265.

12. Roderick McKenzie, in Masson, p. 46. Campbell, p. 160, says that it was originally called Fort Kaministiquia, but later renamed Fort William in honor of William McGillivray.

13. Fleming, 1928.

14. Mackenzie, pp. iii–iv.

15. Reprinted in Wade, p. 314.

16. Morton, 1936.

17. Letter from Mackenzie to John Sullivan, under-secretary for the Colonies, dated October 25, 1802. In Wade, p. 311.

18. Letter from Mackenzie to Roderick McKenzie, dated January 24, 1805.

19. Wallace, p. 20.

20. Fleming, 1928.

21. O'Neil.

22. Morton, 1939, p. 470. Fraser's daughter Harriet says that it was in 1805 (Lamb, p. 280).

23. For Fraser's life and journals, see Lamb.

24. This is the usual version, but in a letter written in 1887 Fraser's daughter gives a slightly different one, apparently on the authority of one of Fraser's journals that has since been lost. Fraser went "up the Peace River to the foot of the Rocky Mountain Portage, where he left two clerks . . . and twelve men in charge. He then continued his route with six men to Lake McLeod, so named by him, where he left three of his men" (Lamb, p. 280).

25. By 1821 the North West Company had twelve posts west of the Rockies. In New Caledonia were the posts at McLeod Lake, Stuart Lake, and Fraser Lake, and Forts George and Alexandria. In the Columbia district were Fort George (Astoria) and posts at Walla Walla, Okanagan, Kamloops, Spokane, Flathead, and Kootenay. The two regions were connected by the Alexandria-Kamloops-Okanagan route, and beginning in 1814 many of the furs began to be taken out by this route (Morton, 1939, p. 710).

26. Innis, 1956, p. 261.

27. *Ibid.*, pp. 150–165.

28. Selkirk's motives are not clear. He usually is credited with philanthropic intentions, but he may have been concerned more with land speculation or with providing a convenient food supply for the Hudson's Bay Company's inland traders (Morton, 1939, p. 530; and Campbell, chap. 9).

29. Wallace, pp. 25–30.

30. Letter from Mackenzie to Roderick McKenzie, dated November 3, 1805.

31. Letter from Mackenzie to Roderick McKenzie, dated November 7, 1806.

32. Letter from Mackenzie to Roderick McKenzie, dated January 14, 1819.

33. DeVoto, 1953, p. xxxii. The announced purpose of the expedition was scientific exploration, but most authorities believe that Jefferson's motives were at least as much political as scientific. Bowers, for instance,

says that Jefferson sent Lewis and Clark "to blaze a path for the spreading of American trade, civilization, and institutions from Boston to the Pacific" (p. 426).

34. Coues, p. 705 (Beauchamp) and p. 777 (McKay).
35. Bryce, p. 67.

Bibliography

BIBLIOGRAPHY

Angus, H. F., ed. *British Columbia and the United States. The North Pacific Slope from Fur Trade to Aviation.* Toronto: Ryerson, 1942. 408 pp.

Biggar, Henry P. *The Early Trading Companies of New France.* Toronto: University of Toronto Press, 1901. 308 pp.

Bishop, R. P. *Mackenzie's Rock.* Ottawa: Canada Department of Interior, 1924. 31 pp.

Black, Samuel. *Black's Rocky Mountain Journal, 1824.* London: Hudson's Bay Record Society, 1955. Vol. 18, 260 pp.

Bowers, Claude G. *Jefferson in Power.* Boston: Houghton Mifflin, 1936. 538 pp.

Brebner, John Bartlet. *The Explorers of North America, 1492–1806.* New York: Macmillan, 1933. 502 pp.

Bryce, George. *Mackenzie, Selkirk, Simpson.* Toronto: Morang, 1910. 305 pp.

Burpee, Lawrence J. *The Search for the Western Sea.* 2d ed. New York: Macmillan, 1936. 2 Vols., 609 pp.

Campbell, Marjorie Wilkins. *The North West Company.* New York: St. Martin's, 1957. 295 pp.

Canadian Board of Geographical Names. *Gazeteer of Canada: British Columbia.* Ottawa, 1953. 641 pp.

Chevigny, Hector. *Lord of Alaska. Baranov and the Russian Adventure.* New York: Viking, 1942. 320 pp.

Chittenden, Hiram. *The American Fur Trade of the Far West.* 2d ed. New York: Barnes and Noble, 1935. 2 Vols., 1014 pp.

Cook, James. *A Voyage to the Pacific Ocean.* London: Nichol and Cadell, 1784. 3 Vols.

Coues, Elliot, ed. *New Light on the Early History of the Great Northwest. The Manuscript Journals of Alexander Henry and of David Thompson. 1799–1814.* New York: Harper, 1897. 3 Vols., 1027 pp.

Crouse, Nellis. *La Verendrye. Fur Trader and Explorer.* Ithaca: Cornell, 1956. 247 pp.

Davidson, Gordon Charles. *The North West Company.* Berkeley: University of California Press, 1918. 349 pp.

Dawson, George M. "Report on Explorations in British Columbia," pp. 233–265 in *Geological Survey of Canada. Report of Progress for 1875–76.* Montreal, 1877.

———. "Report on Explorations in British Columbia," pp. 17–94 in *Geological Survey of Canada Report of Progress for 1876–77.* Montreal, 1878.

DeVoto, Bernard. *The Course of Empire.* Boston: Houghton Mifflin, 1952. 647 pp.

———, ed. *The Journals of Lewis and Clark.* Boston: Houghton Mifflin, 1953. 503 pp.

Dillon, Richard H. "An Alexander Mackenzie Letter, 1793," *British Columbia Historical Quarterly,* 16 (1952), 209–210.

Fleming, R. Harvey. "The Origin of 'Sir Alexander Mackenzie and Company,'" *Canadian Historical Review,* 9 (1928), 137–155.

———. "McTavish Frobisher and Company of Montreal," *Canadian Historical Review,* 10 (1929), 136–152.

Gates, Charles, ed. *Five Fur Traders of the Northwest.* Minneapolis: University of Minnesota Press, 1933. 298 pp.

Gray, Ralph. "Across Canada by Mackenzie's Track," *National Geographic Magazine,* 108 (1955), 191–239.

Haworth, Paul L. *On the Headwaters of Peace River.* New York: Scribner, 1917. 295 pp.

Henry, Alexander (the Elder). *Travels and Adventures in Canada and the Indian Territories between the Years 1760 and 1776.* New York: I. Riley, 1908. 330 pp.

Howard, Joseph Kinsey. *Strange Empire. A Narrative of the Northwest.* New York: Morrow, 1952. 601 pp.

Howay, F. W. "An Identification of Sir Alexander Mackenzie's Fort Fork," *Transactions of the Royal Society of Canada.* Series 3, II (1928), 165–174.

Innis, Harold A. "The North West Company," *Canadian Historical Review,* 8 (1927), 308–321.

———. "Peter Pond in 1780." *Canadian Historical Review,* 9 (1928), 333.

——. *Peter Pond. Fur Trader and Adventurer.* Toronto: Irwin and Gordon, 1930. 153 pp.

——. *The Fur Trade in Canada.* Revised edition. Toronto: University of Toronto Press, 1956. 463 pp.

Jenness, Diamond. *The Sekani Indians of British Columbia.* Canada Department of Mines and Resources, Bulletin No. 84, 1937. National Museum of Canada, Anthropological Series No. 20. 82 pp.

Lamb, W. Kaye, ed. *The letters and Journals of Simon Fraser, 1806–1808.* New York: Macmillan, 1960. 292 pp.

McIlwraith, T. F. *The Bella Coola Indians.* Toronto: University of Toronto Press, 1948. 2 Vols., 743 pp.

Mackenzie, Alexander. *Voyages from Montreal, on the River St. Laurence, through the Continent of North America, to the Frozen and Pacific Oceans; in the Years 1789 and 1793. With a Preliminary Account of the Rise, Progress, and Present State of the Fur Trade of that Country.* London: Cadell and Davies, 1801. viii + cxxxii + 412 pp.

Manning, Clarence A. *Russian Influence on Early America.* New York: Library Publications, 1953. 216 pp.

Manning, W. R. "The Nootka Sound Controversy," *American Historical Association Annual Report,* 1904. Pp. 281–478.

Masson, Louis R. *Les Bourgeois de la Compagnie du Nord-ouest.* Quebec: Coté, 1889. 2 Vols.

Mirsky, Jeanette. *The Westward Crossings. Balboa. Mackenzie. Lewis and Clark.* New York: Knopf, 1946. 365 pp.

Montgomery, Franz. "Alexander Mackenzie's Literary Assistant," *Canadian Historical Review,* 18 (1937), 301–304.

Morice, Adrien G. *The History of the Northern Interior of British Columbia.* Toronto: Briggs, 1904. 349 pp.

Morton, Arthur S. "The North West Company's Columbian Enterprise and David Thompson," *Canadian Historical Review,* 17 (1936), 266–288.

——. *A History of the Canadian West to 1870–71.* London: Nelson, 1939. 987 pp.

Nute, Grace Lee. "A Peter Pond Map," *Minnesota History,* 14 (1933), 81–84.

O'Neil, Marion. "The Peace River Journal, 1799–1800," *Washington Historical Quarterly,* 19 (1928), 250–270.

Ormsby, Margaret A. *British Columbia: A History*. Toronto: Macmillan, 1951. 558 pp.

Pinckerton, Robert. *Hudson's Bay Company*. New York: Holt, 1931. 357 pp.

Plaskett, J. S. "The Astronomy of the Explorers," *British Columbia Historical Quarterly*, 4 (1940), 63–78.

Sage, Walter N. *Sir Alexander Mackenzie and His Influence on the History of the North West*. Bulletin of the Departments of Historical, Political, and Economic Science, Queens University, No. 43, 1922. 18 pp.

———. "Coal-Seekers on Peace River, 1903," *British Columbia Historical Quarterly*, 14 (1950), 83–108.

Smith, Harlan I. "The End of Alexander Mackenzie's Trip to the Pacific," *Canadian Historical Association Annual Report*, 1924. pp. 48–53.

Stefansson, Vilhjalmur. *North West to Fortune*. New York: Duell, Sloan and Pearce, 1958. 356 pp.

Swannell, F. C. "On Mackenzie's Trail," *The Beaver* (Summer, 1958), pp. 9–14.

———. "Alexander Mackenzie as Surveyor," *The Beaver* (Winter, 1959), pp. 20–25.

Swanton, John R. *The Indian Tribes of North America*. Bureau of American Ethnology Bulletin No. 145, 1953. 726 pp.

Teit, James A. "The Shuswap," *American Museum of Natural History Memoirs*, 4 (1907), 443–813.

Tyrrel, J. B., ed. *David Thompson's Narrative of His Explorations in Western America. 1784–1812*. Toronto: Champlain Society, 1916. 582 pp.

———, ed. *Journals of Samuel Hearne and Philip Turnor*. Toronto: Champlain Society, 1934. 611 pp.

Vancouver, George. *A Voyage of Discovery to the North Pacific Ocean*. London: Robinson and Edwards, 1798. 3 Vols. and atlas.

Wade, Mark S. *Mackenzie of Canada*. London: Blackwood, 1927. 332 pp.

Wagner, Henry. *The Plains and the Rockies. A Bibliography of Original Narratives of Travel and Adventure, 1800–1865*. 3d ed. rev. by Charles L. Camp. Columbus: Long's College Book Co., 1953. 601 pp.

———. *Peter Pond. Fur Trader & Explorer*. New Haven: Yale, 1955. 103 pp.

Wallace, W. Stewart, ed. *Documents Relating to the North West Company*. Toronto: Champlain Society, 1934. 527 pp.

Bibliography

Wheat, Carl I. *Mapping the Transmississippi West. 1540–1861*. Vol 1. San Francisco: Institute of Historical Cartography, 1957. 264 pp.

Woollacott, Arthur P. *Mackenzie and His Voyageurs*. London: Dent, 1927. 237 pp.

Wrong, Herbert Hume. *Sir Alexander Mackenzie, Explorer and Furtrader*. Toronto: Macmillan, 1927. 171 pp.

Index

INDEX

Index